The Writer's Crucible

Meditations on Emotion, Being, and Creativity

Susan —
I hope you write,
as write often —
Phil

the Writer's Crucible

Meditations on Emotion, Being, and Creativity

Philip Kenney

PORTLAND • OREGON
INKWATERPRESS.COM

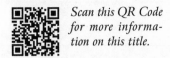

*Scan this QR Code
for more informa-
tion on this title.*

Publisher: Inkwater Press | www.inkwaterpress.com

ISBN-13 978-1-62901-524-8 | ISBN-10 1-62901-524-5

1 3 5 7 9 10 8 6 4 2

For my dear pals Gary, Larry, and John

Contents

THE MATERIALS

NOVEL IDEAS

CHARACTERS

Acknowledgments

THIS BOOK IS DEDICATED TO MY DEAR BUDS GARY, JOHN, and Larry. All are artists and familiar with the crucible. They have brought so much laughter and love to my world. Conversations with each of them have helped inspire and shape this book.

Many thanks to Ali Shaw and Jennifer Zaczek for editing and advising me along the way and to Suzy Vitello for her encouragement. And a big thank-you to Erin Littlewood, who gave me the initial nudge in this direction.

My utmost appreciation goes to the many good people I have had the privilege to know and work with in psychotherapy. They have taught me most of what I value about the work, the integrity of human suffering, and the resilience of the creative impulse. Sketches of some of these individuals are included to illustrate important ideas. These portraits have been disguised to protect their identity and confidentiality.

As always, I am indebted to my family—Lori, Joey, and Geo. You bring out the best in me. Everything I write is made possible by your love, and I hope you feel my gratitude every day of your lives.

Crucible:

A situation of severe trial, or in which different elements
interact, leading to the creation of something new.

Oxford Living Dictionary

Writing a novel is a terrible experience,
during which the hair often falls out
and the teeth decay.

Flannery O'Connor *Mystery and Manners*

When I write, I feel like an armless, legless
man with a crayon in his mouth.

Kurt Vonnegut: In His Own Words

Prologue: A Short Story

SHOULD YOU EXPLORE THE MYSTICAL TRADITION OF THIR-teenth-century Persia, you would find great poets like Rumi, Hafiz, and many other masters of word and space. If you enter those circles, you will soon hear of a character named Nasrudin, who is dear to the hearts of all who know him. Nasrudin is the adorable fool on the hill. You might think of him as the Yogi Berra of Sufi storytelling. His mind-altering stories and aphorisms are legendary in revealing the folly of human striving and in opening the mind to understand the nature of its own waywardness.

My favorite Nasrudin story as it relates to the writer's path is the following, which some call "Nasrudin's Bull's-Eye." It goes something like this: Nasrudin walks into town one morning and notices an archer practicing at the far corner of the green. He approaches the targets and is astounded to see that every single shot has hit the center of the circle! Bull's-eye! Amazed by such skill, Nasrudin approaches the archer and asks, "Good sir, how is it that you are able to make every arrow a perfect bull's-eye?" The archer turns to Nasrudin and shares his secret, "Well, you see, my friend, I take aim, pull the string, release, and draw a circle around the spot the arrow lands!"

Nothing to it. Take aim, writers, release, and circle what shows up on the page. Perfecto! You have to love it, right? Isn't this the foolproof protection against writer's block you've always wanted? And what is worse than the dreaded block? Why, self-reproach, of course. How many times have you read over an hour's worth of work and proclaimed, "Well, that sucks." Never again. Cured! Just follow the wisdom of Nasrudin's bull's-eye and all will be well. Good? Done.

Ah, were it so. Artists suffer, and writers could be at the head of the pack when it comes to agonizing in solitude, dealing with helpless spells of infertility and hopelessness. Really, why write? Why face the emotional challenges lurking with the turn of every page? Why feel so vulnerable, exposed, and subject to repeated rejections? Why? Because it is amazing. Because to dare to write is to venture into the territory Toni Morrison calls "the non-secular."

❧

What is this territory Morrison is talking about? I hope to hit the bull's-eye on that question, because connecting to the non-secular is central to what this book offers as a means to help writers through the tough times. For now, let me say that the nonsecular is that magical place that never sleeps. That mysterious impulse that wakes me at 3:00 a.m. with the answer to yesterday's writing problem. It is the home of the unbidden that beckons ever so quietly, but forcefully, with ideas, words, and sentences before birds begin to sing. Often it speaks when I am dashing off to work and must hastily grab a scrap of paper to scribble down the whisperings before they disappear. I think of these words as sacred, coming from a place that I know but can never touch. A place I feel is beloved and is more myself than am I. The nonsecular.

Finding this place, or being found, is so important because having a relationship with the nonsecular, or what I think of as the creative source of being, is the ground that makes it possible to remember and connect with our basic goodness. The vulnerability that writers and artists face is far more complicated and tricky to relate to than most of us have recognized. Every writer knows the experience and from time to time faces the emotional quagmire of feeling not good enough. This may come in an assortment of ugly translations such as "Who am I kidding? I can't write" or "I'm not worthy. I don't deserve to be published," but they all end up in the same emotional box canyon whose reality can be summed up as "I'm not enough." And it is this emotional quagmire, not a lack of talent or discipline, that is the bane of writers, artists, and all those who ask of themselves to partake in creative endeavors.

I've been practicing psychotherapy for thirty years, and you would be shocked at the number of people I have seen in that time who are struggling with the not-good-enough state of mind. I see neurologists, teachers, writers, artists, filmmakers, lawyers, and the best and brightest from big corporations, and I can tell you that these painful inner feelings are surprisingly common. Truly. What I am referring to is a salient experience, one that is often overwhelming and at times debilitating. The conventional advice offered by books on writing is well intentioned but sadly falls short.

Typically, we find either well-reasoned perspectives on the creative process, which amend our wayward expectations, or cognitive strategies to counter self-defeating thinking. When blunders and dead ends turn up, we are told to forgive ourselves. Would that we could. All such approaches are helpful to a degree. They can serve as useful reminders that our experiences of difficulty and disappointment are normal. The humanity of our feelings and failings is validated in important ways. However important the reframing of our experience may be, though, it remains limited in getting at the underlying psychological patterns that repeatedly compound our struggles. That is one of the major ambitions of this book.

I intend to make it clear that I am speaking not only from clinical experience but also from the guts of my own painful feelings as an author. These emotions have been my companions since—well, it's hard to remember a time when they weren't buzzing around my head or invading my belly and chest, leaving me weak in the knees. They still do when I think of giving a public reading.

By third grade I was sure I would be an artist. I painted murals on the huge bulletin board outside our classroom. Later that year my future turned to rock and roll, and I bet my brother five dollars I would have a hit recording on *American Bandstand* by the time I turned thirteen. By fourteen I had lost the bet and was shut down—lost in a psychological coma. Gone.

Years later, I journeyed into New York City to visit an exhibit of paintings by Matisse. That show turned on a light. Yes, the gallery walls were lined with breathtaking masterpieces, but what resonated like a Chinese gong were the pieces mounted beside each finished work of art: the original sketch and a first go at the painting. I was dumbstruck. For some reason, I had been under the absurd notion that art was created by rare geniuses who sat down and produced masterpieces in one sitting the way an assembly line makes a car. When my mind cleared, it was the early crude markings and the toddler-like brushstrokes that captured my imagination and broke the spell.

It's difficult to do justice to that moment. Everything began to crack; all the rigid, perfectionistic notions, all the impossible demands, they all began to break up—involuntarily, like arctic ice blocks in a summer thaw. And as Leonard Cohen promised, the light came through. Mistakes are openings. The original drawing, in particular, captivated me. It was so free, so unself-conscious, so terrible and so beautiful. So compelling. I felt a drop of freedom on my tongue. I could do this—I could play and make something slowly, over time. Mistakes are openings. I don't have to feel bad and inadequate for stumbling and falling.

Shortly thereafter, in one of those blessed twists of fate, I discovered the work of the great poet William Stafford. He put the final kibosh on the perfectionistic mandate. His practice and advice was to write a poem first thing every morning. And so I did. For ten years. A good 75 percent were just terrible. But oh, those moments, when a phrase comes, when the right metaphor arises, those moments are sublime, richly enlivened moments that compare to other unrivaled experiences like connecting with my boys, or falling in love again with my dear wife, Lori. Magic. Magic moments. Moments dwelling in the nonsecular. By showing up every morning, I learned that I was good enough. Not Stafford or Shakespeare, but good enough to participate in the big wave of creation's calling. Good enough to feel that pulse in my own being and plenty good enough to be touched by that faceless presence again and again.

※

This book is for you. I am writing as one of you, for all of us. Remember when John Lennon sang, "I am you, and you are me, and we are all together." It's true. And I would go further to say we are many beings sprung from one. More on that later. Suffice to say, we are more alike than not, and when we forget that, we feel separate and our problems grow as a result of being isolated from one another. What feeds the disconnect and the emotional conviction that we are not enough is shame. This is the psychological and spiritual plague of our time. Dealing with shame and the accompanying conclusion that you are not good enough is the heart and soul of this book.

Nothing isolates like shame. Shame and the cluster of emotions in that family—embarrassment, shame, humiliation—are the body of our feelings of deficiency. They cause vulnerability to collapse into the story of inadequacy, and they allow anxiety to fill our bellies when we fear exposure.

We are vulnerable. We are permeable. This is our condition, for better and for worse. There is no getting around that, despite the heroic attempts we might make and the solutions espoused by some authorities in the worlds of art and psychology. Many of the answers they provide are akin to painting the house before you scrape and sand. They look good for a while, but they don't stick. We have to go deep into the heartland of shame to find the ground of being that is the real homeland.

Mind, body, and *spirit* are three distinct words describing one dynamic and multidimensional energy, moving and grooving, in and in-between, all of us and all of this. The way through the field of shame is to fall in love with the presence of being that holds us, just like we have fallen in love with making art. It is to know that we never have been, and never could be, anything other than exquisitely and intimately of that creative spirit. I will give you practices to help take that in and some outrageous ideas to understand how all of this can go so far astray. Psychology and spirituality are not two. I would add creativity to that as well. These are not separate phenomena but different modulations of one exquisite, vibrating, and interactive field— the nonsecular field.

❧

You should know from the start that I hold three things dear to my heart. Like you, writing and making art are precious to me. But I also believe in and treasure meditation and psychotherapy. Meditation has brought me back to the deepest source of being and a connection to something much bigger than myself. Without it I would likely never have written a word. The same could be said for psychotherapy. Unlike Rilke, I have found that therapy does not eliminate the angels along with the demons; it allows them to soar freely. Often for the first time.

Therapy removes or alters the obstacles of false identifications and overwhelming emotions that bind the creative impulse, allowing an opening to connect deeply to the source of inspiration. Meditation brings us into contact with the inner presence that is fresh and fertile, and making art is the means of serving that creative spirit and expressing its wishes. I'll be talking at length about the relationship between creative work, therapy, and meditation in the pages that follow, and I'll suggest ways that these three dynamic practices can enhance one another for the benefit of your artistic pursuits.

It is my deepest experience that light is present even in the darkest of mental and emotional states, when self-doubt and self-reproach make one feel small and incapable. Though these moments are often excruciating, it is tremendously empowering to find that they have a limited life span. If entered into, even these difficult emotions can lead to profound contact with an intrinsic goodness that inspires and holds our lives dear. This book will help you face these emotions, stand in them, and work through limiting states of consciousness to find the openings that allow your expansive creative impulse the freedom to thrive.

※

In the tradition of Sufi mystical practice, there are three ways considered most effective in getting to this inner self. The first is prayer, the second is meditation, and the third and most effective is called Sohbet, which is a form of conversation. A mystical conversation that is transformative to all involved. We have all experienced this power. We experience it with a child, a dog, a lover, or a poem. We feel it in the woods or at the banks of a singing river. In its midst, we are made fresh. My greatest hope is that this work will be that kind of conversation. One that allows us to get to know each other within these pages. I invite you to converse with me in these pages — bring your questions and critiques, your affirmations and disagreements. In short, bring your full self and you will make this a better book.

With that in mind, let me end this short story with another. Nasrudin rides his donkey through town in the wee hours of the morning. He wanders around aimlessly from one side of town to another. A night watchman sees Nasrudin and asks him, "Nasrudin, what are you doing out here wandering the streets at night?" Nasrudin smiles and says, "My good man, I have no idea what I'm doing. If I did, I'd be home by now."

PART I

The Project

1
Lost and Found

WHERE AM I GOING? WHAT AM I UP TO? YOU MAY OFTEN ask yourself the same questions the night watchman asks Nasrudin: What are you doing? As is the case with most human behavior, the answer to this seemingly obvious question is, more often than not, a complicated one. Motivation is multilayered and can be dumbfounding when it turns out our actions do not reflect our intentions. Sometimes the answer is the same as Nasrudin's, "I have no idea." There are days when you might feel limitless as more ideas are streaming through your psyche than you can put down on paper. Occasionally, you and I will be glaringly grandiose.

The wheel turns like this. Round and round. But it invariably passes through days and weeks, if not years, when we must admit to being lost. Lost. You can chuckle at Nasrudin's plight, but sooner or later it becomes obvious that you cannot answer the simple question, what are you doing? You are lost. Your mind is muddled, the well is dry, and you stare at a blank page that slowly fills with idle doodling. Nothing is fresh. Body and mind feel heavy, and nearly everything you write feels contrived.

No one likes being lost. No one likes floundering, unable to get traction to begin that essay. No one likes having a good idea but no sense as to how to bring it to life. It is distressing, frightening too. Prolonged periods can leave one feeling utterly helpless, as the poet Louise Gluck reminds us in her essay "Education of the Poet." I suppose there are those artists whose creative energy is uninterrupted by periods of drought. John Updike must have written in his sleep! Okay. As for me, when I finished writing my first novel, I could sense the valve shutting, and it was over a year before I felt any stirring in the creative center. I doubted I'd ever write a good sentence again. This is how lost a writer can become and how anxious and reactive the mind can be.

These are tough feelings to bear. Very tough. But they need not lead to despair. Søren Kierkegaard, the Danish philosopher, wrote that admitting to being lost is the necessary beginning to a spiritual life. I think it is also the starting place for good writing. Or maybe I should say, good listening. William Stafford advocated writing a poem every morning. Recently a friend of mine said she could never do that practice—she thought it would be too much forced material. But it came to me in that moment that what Stafford was trying to impart was a practice of surrender. Surrendering to being lost, surrendering to not knowing, and best of all, surrendering to listening for what wants to come, not to your clever brain. He said, "Look for threads." He didn't say, "Look for genius."

This sounds simple enough, but is it? No. As great a writer as J. D. Salinger was, he admitted that it took him an hour of writing to be honest with himself. I love that. What land are we lost in? Who is the one not being honest? Why do so many writers resist and fear picking up the pencil every morning? When you feel lost, what do you associate it with? Inadequacy? Powerless feelings? Dying alone in a dark forest? (That one's mine.) And being lost isn't a one-and-done thing. It visits, uninvited, again and again.

With practice it may be possible to accept and live into lost feelings without too much anxiety. Living with not knowing, accepting the feeling of helplessness, being in the experience of

lost and alone, these approaches open the window to that myste-
rious realm of the nonsecular that pulses within. The unbidden
creative force waits in that dark realm. It waits in the no-man's-
land of being. It comes from the place you cannot reach, but
reaches out to you and me when we stop striving to be excep-
tional and answer to the call of the wild.

Experiment:

But don't take my word for it, find out for yourself. Let's experi-
ment. Find a good seat. Close your eyes and make yourself
comfortable with your back straight but not stiff. Breathe
slowly through your nose and down into the belly. Gently relax
your muscles and jaw as best you can. Bring your attention
into the chest area and let it sit there. The usual thoughts will,
no doubt, pass by. Pretend you are sitting at a train crossing
and your thoughts are a long line of freight cars lumbering
past. Bring your attention back to your heart area and try to sit
with yourself in a simple and direct way. Be honest when you
ask yourself: Where am I going? What am I doing? Who am I?
Do you have answers for these questions? Are those answers
prefab constructs? Try to let the easy, habitual notions slip
away. Just feel, if you can, the mystery, the uncertainty of this
moment. There… What answers there are to these questions
prove insubstantial. Preconceived. You are lost, in a sense. Try
not to fight it—give in to it. What is the experience of being
lost? Do any associations or fantasies come up? Breathe slowly
and let this experience be. Sit with it.

🌿

There is a funny Yiddish joke about a rabbi who leaves his house
one morning. His synagogue is across the street, and as he is
walking toward it, a Bolshevik soldier stops him and demands
to know where he is going. The rabbi says, "Don't know." The

soldier repeats his question, and the rabbi's answer is the same, "Don't know." After a couple of repetitions, the Bolshevik soldier becomes exasperated and yells at the rabbi, "All right, enough of this, Rabbi. You've been crossing this street every morning for the past twenty years, and now when I ask you where you are going, all you can say is, 'Don't know.' Is that it?" To which the rabbi replies, "Yep, don't know." The soldier grabs the rabbi by his collar and says, "You're coming with me to the station for insubordination." The rabbi looks up at the red-faced soldier with a twinkle in his eye and says to him, "See? Don't know!"

It is common to attach pejorative judgments to feeling lost. You might call yourself stupid or boring. These are some favorites I have heard over the years. You might feel anxious and out of control, certain your future as an artist is doomed. My personal favorite is, "Idiot!" You and I can be so harsh.

By giving yourself to the experience of being lost rather than fighting it, you have, in one way, found yourself. You have deepened the connection to your own experience and entered the realm of being that is most friendly to writers—the realm of paradox, where a dance of lost and found is happening. Yes, lost and found, where in finding your lost self, you are positioning to be found, by spirit and by muse. Where experiencing the lost self *is* the opening.

Why go on and on about being lost? Because it relates directly to these questions: Where are you going? What are you doing? What is this project you are working on? You and I sweat over the plot, over the way our characters are or are not coming to life on the page. We wonder if the memoir will reach people. If we have said too little, or too much. The poet can't find the right rhythm or image. The screenwriter struggles with the cadence of the dialogue. All of these are legitimate problems that authors encounter every day.

But this is not the only project. There is another project driving you and me, a project permeating our work, influencing decision making, and often running the whole show. This project is embedded in our conscious aspirations such that we easily mistake the emotions and stresses of our creative life as stemming from the work itself, when in actuality what pain we experience is more derivative of this other project. And what is this other project? I call it the Self Project.

2
The Self Project

WHAT IS THIS SELF PROJECT? WHAT ARE WE TALKING about, and what is its goal? The Self Project begins when the feeling that we are not good enough takes root. It grows when a persistent feeling that there is something wrong with us begins to occupy more and more psychic space. It takes over when we are surrounded with a feeling that we are bad and unworthy. We'll look into why these sad developments happen to people, but for now just remember that all too many artists suffer from a terrible feeling of lack, a certainty that they are not enough, and are driven to overcome those feelings and convictions at nearly any cost. That is the core of the Self Project.

What is the Self Project up to? What purpose does it serve? Come with me, back to the beginning of time, I mean, to the birth of rock and roll. For me, it is 1958, and I have discovered *American Bandstand*, rock and roll, and an energy previously outlawed in postwar Ohio. I am in love. Overcome by the music that will change the world, I vow to become a rock star. I bet my brother five dollars I will have a hit single by the time I turn thirteen. Stevie Wonder did it, and so can I.

But a strange thing happened on the way to stardom; rather than going to work practicing my guitar every night, I went to my room and sang along with Elvis, fantasizing my ascent to the top of the charts. Fantasizing adoring crowds cheering for me. Sad but true. I never put in the practice to realize my dream.

What was I up to? What the Self Project is always up to: finding a way to overcome feelings of deficiency. Like the line from George Harrison's famous song, "All through the day, I me mine, I me mine"—something within is busy trying to build up, sustain, or shore up a weakened, not-good-enough sense of self. Trying to find the love that will fill the hole within. This was my compulsion because I was disconnected from my core self. Had that connection been strong, it would have provided the necessary strength and resiliency to suffer the frustrations of learning a new instrument. Instead, I spent my evenings in dreamland, living a fantasy that helped me escape myself and create a feeling of aliveness. "All through the day," the Self Project is doing what it can to alleviate the suffering of a self separated from its source and carrying the stamp of inadequacy. In other words, we feel deep shame, and the Self Project is trying to hide and compensate for those feelings.

I have a friend who is a brilliant thinker. She has written several books analyzing the politics of our time. Her stuff could make a difference in the understanding of our current political and cultural stalemate. Yet these books sit on her desk in a perpetual state of revision. She writes and rewrites constantly. She adds new, ever more elaborate and convincing arguments. Her work never reaches the desk of a good editor or publisher because it is never good enough. My friend holds on to her work because she lives in terror, convinced of the humiliating rejections that will meet her should she attempt to get this work out in the world. Privately, she imagines her theories being called simplistic or naïve. She is trapped in a never-ending task of protecting her beleaguered self from further injury by pursuing a quest for the perfect, unassailable manuscript. How many people do you know who aspire to be an artist and never get out of the gate, or who give up when the action heats up? Debilitating shame is the reason more often than not. That shame is the motivation for the Self Project, which is less about crafting the text than it is about securing emotional safety and self-worth.

We have all seen works of art or read material by authors whose purpose is to show off. Their work screams, "Look at me!" Everything is designed to show how clever they are and to garner validation for their creative powers. It's easy to judge the self-aggrandizing efforts of these artists, but stop for a moment and consider the inner world of someone who uses creativity for the purpose of self-inflation. It's easy to tag these people as narcissists, but if you really get to know them, you'll find frightened, fragile people who have to be noticed to feel real and important. There are geniuses who can be both demanding of our attention and incredible artists, but many fall short of realizing their talents because the energy required for the work has gone into meeting the needs of the Self Project, not the art.

❧

Creativity is not the sole province of the artist. Making our way through the challenges and opportunities life presents us with requires a creative approach to living that recognizes the uniqueness of every situation no matter how repetitive. Even as the routines of the day and the necessary habits of the hour pull at familiar responses, the possibility of a fresh and spontaneous approach may emerge. We are jazz beings, called to improvise.

And yet, habits, for better and for worse, have a hold on the decision-making sector of our minds. How often do you come home from work tired and sluggish, seeking the refuge of the sofa and TV rather than going for the brisk walk that would help your energies recirculate? How often do I feel bored and reach for something to eat rather than sit down with a piece of writing that needs revision? It seems many of us are slow learners.

Few practices illuminate these phenomena more clearly than

those of an artist whose resistance to engaging the project at hand is often bewilderingly strong. It may seem as though laziness is the cause of our procrastinations, or that a weakness of sorts is the reason our manuscripts lie on the desk untouched. These interpretations amount to a character indictment, and the alleged defect takes us down a path of self-criticism that is difficult to disengage from. These derailments and the subsequent judgments reinforce the notion that "something is wrong with me" and validate the necessity of the Self Project.

I can't tell you how many times perfectly hardworking and well-meaning writers and artists have said to me, "I'm not disciplined enough." End of story. Sadly, these self-portraits pile up and contribute to a mounting pejorative caricature that generates more shameful emotions further compounding the difficulties in taking creative action. Bluntly stated, "I suck" can be heard reverberating through the brain.

People say awful things to themselves. Even when looking good on the outside, we are often plagued with terrible self-doubt, debilitating self-criticism, and an unshakable sense that says, "I'm not good enough." Variations on the theme include "Something is wrong with me," "I'm a pretender, not a real writer," and "I should get a day job." You may have heard a voice in your head say, "I'm not worthy of success, or being published, or having my own art show." And these attacks on the self are not limited to beginning or struggling writers and artists. They hound many of the most successful and respected of our creative geniuses. Insecurity abounds. Check out Virginia Woolf's suicide note for a tragic example.

What I'm describing is a condition that interferes with creative living and working. This condition produces the emotional distress and negative self-talk that disrupts focused attention, deflating the needed self-cohesion and well-being necessary to complete creative work. Rather than actually engaging in writing, the mind is preoccupied with self-doubt, endless preliminary tasks, or fantasies of grandiose successes.

What happens next further complicates the problem. Sensing a state of insufficiency or lack within, the psyche sets about attempting to repair and restore a feeling of general well-being. The compensatory strategies activated to this end are what I am calling the Self Project. This isn't a crime. It deserves our compassion, but it becomes a problem when the strivings of the Self Project are mistaken for the promptings of the muse.

Much of creative work is a dynamic interplay between the motivation to make art and the urgency to rescue the self. Sometimes this tension enhances the work. Often the demands of the Self Project undermine the capacity to live creatively and make art. When inspiration is usurped by the necessity to protect or enhance a beleaguered sense of self, creative work is more often than not hampered. At their best and most satisfying, creative endeavors originate and move from a state of union; the Self Project operates from one of fragmentation.

My experience, and that of many of the writers and artists I talk with, is that the best work comes from a state of being in which the self is forgotten or absent from consciousness. Awareness of *me* is in the background, and the work is happening in a wonderful outpouring of unconscious inspiration and skill into the project at hand. It feels like *I* am not doing the work. Some might call this a no-self experience; I think of it as connecting with a core element of our existence that desires expression and is free of the encumbrances of the ego straining for recognition. It is like being hooked up to an inner generator.

❧

I begin and end each day walking the dog. Sometimes I go for weeks walking or trudging the same route. For no apparent reason, on a given morning I might turn right instead of going straight up the hill. I look up, not down, at the activity in the treetops—how the crows are moving and the branches are swaying. Soon in the creative flow, I begin to disappear and the ballet of life's awakening brings me into step with the movement of the world. For a time I vanish along with my worries.

The Self Project insists on being center stage and dreads disappearing into the background. It creates the distraction that interrupts contact with the inner and outer worlds, thereby creating a separation from our most creative instincts and life lived in the moment. Being present isn't easy. Despite what some might say, being present is challenging. It is not a personal failure to find yourself lost in other time zones. Opening to what is happening requires a capacity of the self to hold steady as the undulations of feeling, thought, and sensation pulse through the body. If that is possible, if the self knows its basic goodness, the most wonderful relationship to life is possible. One that is not only effective but also playful and artful.

When you and I are touched by the nonsecular, sparks from a fire that ceaselessly creates life on earth and inspiration within move our hearts and we are free to dance into the dark night. That is the claim of the ancient yogic texts and the whispered wisdom of the common moment. The not-good-enough self is nothing but a mirage, albeit a convincing one, caused by a separation from being, your essence, which *is* the creative source. When the Self Project is quieted, the light of the real self shines through. Maybe not all the time but enough to remind us of what truly lies within, waiting and calling for our attention.

3
The Vulnerable Self

ALL PEOPLE ARE CREATED EQUAL, BUT ALL PEOPLE ARE not the same. Thank God. Somehow each face is different; each voice and story is new. Common struggles and dreams unite us, but the number of particular scenarios for any given life astounds the imagination. That is why there can be such a multitude of stories flooding the market. The beat goes on, and one life after another comes forth to join its human family with a unique shape and expression.

One of the most dramatic ways we are alike and not alike pertains to the reality of our vulnerability. It is not a question of whether we are vulnerable—all humans share a certain degree of vulnerability. What matters is the susceptibility of an individual to being overwhelmed by stimulation or emotion. It is painfully true that whether because of cultural styles, traumatic experiences, or inherent constitutional predispositions many dear souls spend much of their lives struggling to manage exceedingly vulnerable states of being.

Over the past forty years, a tremendous amount of research has gone into the study of vulnerability. In that time our growing understanding of what it means to be human has been expanded by two tracks of investigation. One relates to the constitutional factors determining the makeup of a person. These genetic traits have been studied in detail by observation of infants and attention to their inherent temperament and resiliency. The second factor relates to a person's experience in the world, in particular the nature of trauma, and came into focus when so many young men returned home from Vietnam and were unable to adjust to regular life. And when the denial of the sexual abuse of girls was broken, an even better understanding of the long-term effects of trauma on the psyche and nervous system became possible. In chapter 17 we'll look closely at trauma and how it influences the lives of those who have suffered traumatic experiences.

The evolving picture of who we are is a fascinating one and more complicated than once believed. Infant research has documented, through extensive filming of babies with their mothers, that some little ones are more resilient than others. This was no surprise to mothers, but it helped fill out the understanding of how children develop. Not only are some infants more resilient—that is, they can cope better and recover quicker from physical distress and are more adept at tolerating frustrations—but some babies are far more sensitive to stimulation and may experience normal touch, for instance, as harsh and invasive. These little ones are especially difficult to soothe and can make a new mother feel incompetent and bad. Thinking she is hurting her baby may create lasting relational patterns between mother and child. These discoveries helped provide insight into the mystery of why similar experiences are traumatic to some and not to others.

Thanks to the work of Brené Brown, vulnerability has become an honorable trait. Her TED Talk "The Power of Vulnerability" was groundbreaking and served as a voice of redemption for the reality of personal vulnerabilities. The emotional vulnerability human beings experience was normalized in this talk and reframed as a powerful means to connect in relationships and with humanity as a whole. Another great source of validation for our condition was Elaine Aron's publication of *The Highly Sensitive Person*. I recommend you check out both these sources. They will each help you accept and appreciate what Aron aptly reframes as the "gift of sensitivity." Seen as a gift, sensitivity becomes a strength and not a flaw. Vulnerability becomes a capacity for intimate connecting in relationships. These mark the starting point for empathy and compassion and the innate resource for the connections that make creativity possible. This is good news for artists who are, generally speaking, more sensitive than their neighbors.

Unfortunately, when in the thick of feelings like anxiety and shame, the last thing that occurs to us is to see vulnerability as a gift. Our first thought is more likely to be, "How do I get the hell out of here?" We want to flee because the experience of fear and shame can become overwhelming in a flash. As in flash flood! Vulnerability arises in the blink of an eye as these two demons of the soul invade the psyche like emotional dementors. We fear losing connection with important relationships, and we quake at the prospect of feeling small before those very people whose validation we desperately need.

This shakes down to one not-so-appetizing reality: you and I are fragile. Yes, fragile. Despite the many strengths and considerable resiliency of human beings, there is that fragile fault line that runs through the human psyche that leaves us all, albeit in varying degrees, susceptible to periodic quakes. It's true, and yet it is one of the most guarded secrets of our society.

In particular, men play into the charade that they are invincible and have no needs. Strength is considered a virtue and weakness—that is, neediness, humiliation. For years and years, this drama played out with women cast in the role of hysterical and needy. At last that myth is being busted, and believe me, when the wife has had enough and calls it quits, many a husband cracks into a million pieces of neediness and anxiety—"She's leaving me. I didn't realize how much I need her." The game is over, and invincible man is revealed to be a broken mess.

Of course women are fragile also. Though more resilient than men in many ways, they break and are undone by life along similar fault lines. There is no escaping the fragility of the human psyche. This should not be a surprise, nor should it be a source of shame. You and I aren't only fragile. We stand in the center holding the contradictions of our nature: strength and fragility, tremendous resiliency and alarming instability. Confusing, isn't it? Within an hour, or a moment, you find yourself oscillating between these disparate poles of experience and wonder, "What is happening to me? Which me is real?" Sadly, you probably find yourself hating the fragile you. I hope we can change that.

Who is it that stands in the center, holding the awareness of these apparently opposite traits? We'll get into this subject soon. For now, let's face it, you and I live on tectonic plates every bit as dangerous and unpredictable as the San Andreas. But what is the nature of this fragility? What happens in those moments when it all goes south and we feel like we're no good?

Ever been in Arizona for a flash flood? It's like that. In a flash, often with no notice, the flooding is upon us and we are swept up by a raging current of emotions that threaten our equilibrium. You feel powerless. What we call fragility is this: overwhelming feelings that pull you under and won't let go. These can be good or bad experiences. Love and tenderness can be just as threatening as rejection, but for the purposes of this line of thought, we'll stay with the painful emotions. Some people actually feel like they are drowning, while others are fighting (sometimes literally) to survive the surge. Most everyone feels that all goodness has washed away, never to be retrieved. Think I'm exaggerating? Listen to what Karl Ove Knausgaard, the Norwegian novelist, wrote about his experience with the rejection of a submission in book 5 of *My Struggle*:

> I had reacted to every other rejection with composure, they were expected, all of them. But this one crushed me. I was completely demoralized for several weeks and this led to me taking the final decision to stop writing.

But what is this overwhelming emotion? What is it that

people are crushed by? It is shame. Knausgaard goes on to say, "It was simply too humiliating." Yes, anxiety and fear can also flood the banks, but anxiety is often related to the arrival of shame. For our purposes, shame is the primary emotion that overwhelms the system. And when the self is overwhelmed, we feel small and worthless. It is the feeling, and the certainty, that we are bad and pathetic. The experience of being diminished is the result of ruthless self-judgments that we are not good enough. It's not what we do that's bad, although that may be the catalyst to the downward slide, but it feels like we are what is no good. "Me, at the core of my being, my essence is bad. I am no good."

Shame exists on a continuum from bearable embarrassment, to the kind of shame that makes you want to hide, to humiliation, which makes you want to disappear. It is the emotional and psychic cancer eating at the soul of our society and spawning addictions and manic behavior. Again, this secret is well kept, but believe me, behind the busyness of our lives and the abundance of material props, self-loathing is epidemic. And from this darkness, the striving and desperate Self Project is born, setting out to overcome the persistent internal sense that one is not good enough.

Chronic shame erodes self-esteem. It is rust eating at metal. It also compels people to hide, to isolate from others and from themselves. In short, to disconnect. In disconnecting, a separation is born, what R. D. Laing, the revolutionary Scottish psychiatrist named with his book *The Divided Self.* I first read his classic study of self-fragmentation in 1972. It was during my drifter days. I was working and living in Copenhagen, drinking Elephant beer, helping to build a youth hostel, and trying to hide my broken, shameful insides. When I read *The Divided Self,* I thought, "Oh, there I am. That's me."

Once the self splits in order to escape these feelings, once shame has the upper hand and the core self goes into retreat, the Self Project swings into high gear and life becomes work oriented, not play oriented, in the pursuit of reinventing oneself. Exhausted by the constant effort to succeed or be validated, a longing develops, often unconsciously, to be reunited with the core self. To once again know a feeling of wholeness and basic goodness. The Self Project often misdirects this pursuit toward grandiose fantasies of success and manic attempts to prove oneself. Conversely, this urgency can be perverted and take the form of self-destructive addictions designed to numb the pain.

This longing to reconnect with one's essence can be another source of shame. But in actuality, it is the stirring of the wind that will bring you home. The next time you find yourself longing and agonizing for more book sales or great reviews, pause a minute. Pause and take a big breath and ask yourself what you really want. What does your heart truly long for? Is it really sales? Really? Or is this a displacement of a deeper longing for you and self-acceptance? There's nothing wrong with sales and wanting to be on the best-seller list, but how often is this wanting tied to a feeling of lack and the urgency to feel worthy and good? I'd wager this happens more often than not. And more often than not, when we look up those sales numbers on the Amazon book page, the plunge into disappointment is swift. Swift, painful, and quickly followed by a deflation that takes the whole person down.

Depressed yet? You should be. Hang with me—this is the toughest part. A lot like drilling out decay before filling the tooth. This is painful. I wish it weren't, but it is necessary to acknowledge the truth of our condition in order to begin a new way of relating to these feelings and finding the good-enough spot. And I promise you, the good-enough spot is real. Real and closer to you than your own breath. Shame is real as well, and it enters the cells of your body like blueberry stains on a white t-shirt or blouse. You can't get it completely out, but you can work with these feelings and dissipate the charge that makes them overwhelming.

Not only can you work with these feelings, but you can also remember, pay attention to, and appreciate the dimension of you that cannot be stained. The you that is beauty and an extension of the creative force. The you that lives simultaneously as the whirlwind and as the still point, that lives in the midst of perhaps the greatest paradox, in the midst of this most awe-inspiring mystery—you are both separate and united with that creative force you love. And neither shame nor flooding can alter that.

Experiment:

Try this: pick up your pencil and write whatever comes to mind in response to these questions:

- What are you feeling right now?
- What have you read about shame that resonates?
- Write down a memory from childhood when you felt shame.
- Write down a more recent experience of shame.
- Do you have dreams in which you feel shame? Write one down.
- Do you have a worst-case, nightmare scenario of being humiliated?

These are very difficult emotions to experience. They can overwhelm our systems and cause good artists to quit or go to great lengths to stop the pain. To help yourself release the feelings evoked by this exercise, try the following meditation.

Experiment:

Put your pencil down and close your eyes. Sit comfortably, with your back straight, feet on the floor. Not rigid, relaxed. Breathe in slowly, slowly, and deep into your abdomen. Notice the tensions in your chest or belly, and gently try to let them ease. Now bring your attention to the space between breaths, the pause between inhaling and exhaling. At that point in the rhythm of taking in and letting go, just say, "Ah." Just say it softly out loud. "Ah." That's all. Repeat it a few times. "Ah."

Try, without straining, to feel the still spot inside—the sense of presence residing within. Feel it? It's there. You are there. Softly say to yourself, "Hey, I'm all right." Feel the spaciousness of that presence, the empty, fertile quiet of you. There you are, everywhere. That's all it takes. That's all.

———————————————

4

In Self-Defense

WE SHOULD HAVE BEEN BORN WITH BULLETPROOF vests. Or flak jackets. Something. Instead, we have to construct armor around our tenderness. A self-defense system around our sensitivity. For some, that means an aggressive, first-strike capability in which all incoming threats to the self are shot down. For most, that means constriction of the muscles of the body, particularly the chest and belly, to ward off emotional danger. The effectiveness in restricting feelings by contracting in this way is considerable; however, the cost to the vitality of the inner self is great.

When body armor fails to protect the self from emotional flooding, the psyche must resort to more extreme measures. At the top of the list are dissociation and denial. Dissociation is the most extreme, really desperate measure we have at our disposal. It is the ultimate flight response when flight is not possible. Consciousness actually separates from the body to escape unbearable feelings. Usually it is reserved for those experiences that are overwhelming to the point of being traumatic. If the traumatic events are repeated, dissociation becomes a habitually patterned reaction. Denial is a less extreme, intra-psychic phenomenon. Unwanted memory, feelings, or perceptions are exiled from awareness, and the illusion of safety is protected until such time as neediness or emotional pain penetrate the curtain of exclusion.

Aren't we remarkable? And isn't it sad that so much energy has to go toward self-protection? We are so permeable. Even with these elaborate defenses at work, stuff gets in and stings. Ouch! Damn, it hurts. "Sticks and stones will break my bones, but names will never hurt me." Not! Who made up that lie? Rejections, criticisms, clever reviewers trying to sound like literary gods: these hurt. They penetrate, despite our best efforts, like neutrinos passing through solid objects. And who hasn't experienced a roomful of praise only to be taken down by the one negative voice coming from the back? Ugh.

Why do we take this stuff in? Are we all masochists masquerading as artists? Not really. The problem begins with the natural process of internalization. Organisms are designed to take in necessary ingredients from the environment. You breathe in air; you chew and swallow food. Simple. Likewise, the organs of perception receive tons of information every second. Eyes and ears report to the brain on the safety of the immediate situation. Your nose identifies food locations and possibilities. All of this is managed by the brain, which does a pretty fine job of limiting input and making order.

We depend on the capacity to internalize, to receive. Writers rely on a keen sense of observation to the subtleties of form. You listen for the nuances of tone and cadence in the spoken word. You take in qualities of beauty and the variance of light and shadow. The perceptual field is oxygen for the writer's mind.

For better and for worse, the brain is also a storyteller. It constantly makes narrative out of perception and experience. "Where does that herd of buffalo graze this time of year?" The campfire is fueled by the stories that surround it. Talk to many writers of fiction and they will tell you that making up stories has been a way of life since they were little. Authors and artists, maybe more than most people, internalize the world and make stories to match what they see, hear, and feel. You can probably sniff out a good story from a mile away.

As always, there is a dark side. We take in toxins too—often unconsciously. Because of sensitivities other than the physical senses, we perceive and take in what is unwanted, as in the denied emotions of our parents. In my family it was my father's profound grief having lost his mother at the age of sixteen. Day after day, I looked at his unhappy face, the way his mouth turned down in despondency. All too often, we take in the hostilities and cruel belittlements of the family or culture at large. That might be the rampant devaluing of women and girls, or the outright contempt for people of color. These disturbing energies, though denied, are circulating at all times from subtle nuanced innuendo to outright blatant expressions of hatred. What is uncanny is the ability of human beings to sense the presence of such energies and in sensing them to take in, knowingly or not, the charge behind those forces. This is the peril of our receptive nature.

Shame begins to take hold in the shadowy regions of instinctive internalizations. We can't help ourselves. Tangled together in the bewilderment of these experiences is a story, a narrative, that attempts to make sense of what is happening but sadly ends with the punch line "It's my fault. I must be bad." I saw my father's forlorn face and concluded I was a great disappointment to him. It is important for children's sanity to protect the goodness of those they are dependent on and care about. They therefore sacrifice their own worthiness for the preservation of a sense of belief in others. The combination of terrible feelings and a narrative leaning toward self-blame creates the internal environment for shame to grow like fungus.

Sadly, for many of us, a pattern of taking in the bad develops into a persistent habit. You might be surprised how difficult it is to take in the good of life and to really feel your basic goodness under the spell of the feelings and narrative that always ends the same: "I am bad. I am unworthy." You can look to the final written words of Virginia Woolf for testimony of this tragic reality. In the suicide note to her husband, she confesses to her failure as a writer and to the absence of personal goodness. Thankfully, there is treatment now for the self-loathing that stems from the kind of sex abuse that tormented this brilliant woman. But the emotions she struggled with, though far less severe in most people, continue to shadow all too many artists today, regardless of their level of skill and success.

※

Internalization should not be a one-way process. It should be the beginning of a process that metabolizes that which has been taken in and expels that which is not needed. What is damaging to self-worth is the buildup of toxic emotion that has no viable means of release. We breathe out carbon dioxide. We sweat. But what do we do with overwhelming feelings, or with the unacknowledged grief passed down for generations and absorbed by children before they understand what is in the air? What does an abuse victim do with the shame leeching the joy out of life? Shame must be externalized. Not by reactive counterattacks, but by placing responsibility where it belongs and by holding the reality of traumatic agents firmly in mind. The narrative that ends with such faulty conclusions as "It's my fault" must be revised. Rewrites are essential to releasing self-blame.

Unfortunately, children are in a bind. They are denied a healthy expression of anger, which is the instinctive response to injustice and violation. Adults demand respect, whether or not that respect has been earned. All too often parents fail to protect children from emotional and physical harm, and the children are left to their own devices to cope and carry on. More often than not, those children end up re-creating traumatic experiences in adult life. The fact of repetition defies reason, but it is real. These are terribly hard patterns to change. Over and over, the basic premise, "I am at fault," is confirmed.

What follows is an all-out campaign of self-protection. There are three basic patterns you will find in those who feel in danger: hiding the real self, shutting down feelings and sensations, and developing an ego-ideal, typically modeled after one idealized figure or another. This is the compensatory structure of the Self Project, and it requires enormous amounts of energy. The compensatory self gradually eclipses the real self, and the anxiety of exposure dominates internal life. So many times I have heard people say to me, "I fear I'll be found out. They'll discover I don't know what I'm doing. I'm a phony."

Energy that could go into creative work is usurped by the effort it takes to sustain this system. That effort, and the effort required to elaborate the ego-ideal, robs the entire system of the generative energy required to sustain creative projects. I work with people who can't find motivation to sit down every day and write because they are emotionally exhausted by the efforts to protect themselves and cannot truly inhabit their own skin. It is a good, but sad, day when they realize the guiding motivation of their lives has not been generative but about safety and getting by without further injury to the self.

Experiment:

Pick up your pencil again and write responses to these questions:

- What is your ego-ideal? Who are you trying to be?
- How do you protect yourself from shame?
- What part of you do you fear being exposed?
- What are you most vulnerable to internalizing?

✀

There is a movement in contemporary spiritual circles known as Nonduality. In the world of Nonduality and certain mindfulness groups, the personal story has become the villain. Rid yourself of "your story" and you will be free to dwell in the inner sanctum of love and bliss.

The problem is, stories are as much us as our fingerprints are. I tell my clients to make their story more complicated. Don't try to eliminate it—you can't. But you can make it more complicated, accurate, and compassionate. You can make it an ongoing inquiry that includes the story of your parents and the culture that informed you. What is obvious and hurtful is the stark simplicity of the story whose one theme is "I'm bad." What could be more black and white? More false?

A story is still a story, and we remain susceptible to narrative that is reductive and puts a negative or limited spin on what we are. The purpose of expanding and detailing your personal story is to make every effort to see yourself clearly so that when the storms hit and self-doubt begins to breach the levy, it remains possible to hold a good-enough notion in mind of your actual strengths and weaknesses. While it may not be possible to ever see yourself completely (we do still need others to serve as mirrors), growth in your capacity to see who you are builds empathy and the wherewithal to reach out a hand of friendship to this bumbling you when times are hard.

If you practice this while the iron is cold, you can build new resiliency into your psyche. Recent brain research shows that it is possible to lay down new neural fibers. You can make a fresh self-portrait! One that will be supportive on those days you receive three rejections in the mail, or when the editor returns your manuscript shredded, or when everything you write or paint seems stale—then you have an alternative story and image in your brain. Yay! One that will enable you to field the attacks and say, "Hey, wait a minute. That's not who I am!" Or you might say, "Stop!" or "No," or "F#%* off," or even laugh and say, "Wow, there you go again." The point is, you will get better and better at holding yourself, protecting yourself, and soothing yourself when the whitewater rocks your boat.

Experiment:

Try it with your story now. Whatever it may be. "I'm selfish. It's all my fault. I'm no good, defective, damaged." You name it. Now change it up a little. Be the good writer that you are. Add some detail, some complexity and ambiguity. Make all the characters real people, with real strengths and weaknesses. Take one event that comes to mind and make it three-dimensional. Breathe deep and relax into the scene. Juxtapose the habitual version with the new one. Make an effort to really see who you are in detail. Try to forgive the mistakes of others and your own, or hold people accountable if they should be. Understand that whatever negative judgment you have placed on your head is unfair to you.

Place your hand over your heart and say, "You're all right."

5
The Good-Enough Self

AT THE HEIGHT OF WORLD WAR II, DURING THE BOMBING of London, children were evacuated to the country for their safety. Not surprisingly, this caused a great deal of angst in the parents, who experienced terrible guilt and anxiety having been separated from their children. The British government recruited the pediatrician and psychoanalyst D. W. Winnicott to give a series of radio talks to the people of London in an effort to soothe the anxiety of an already frightened population. Winnicott was the perfect choice. His talks were intimate and reassuring. He spoke to mothers in a very direct way, assuring them of their children's resiliency. And he reassured them that the care provided over the years had developed a strong sense of self in their children that would support them through the ordeal of separation.

Winnicott understood babies and children. He was a bit of a mystic as well as a keen student of human psychology. The theories he developed after the war changed psychoanalysis into a more humane, relational system. He rescued mothers from the prison of blame by postulating that they had given substantial but not perfect attention to their children's needs and, by doing so, enabled their children to develop in such a way as to become the person each was capable of being.

As such, he coined the term "the good enough mother." I think this makes for a pretty good model for writers and artists. Good enough. Imagine if we could form a relationship with ourselves that provides the kind of care and support that a mother gives her little one. What if we responded to our frustrations and failures with kindness and not rebuke? With an empathic gaze and not the harsh, critical eye of self-loathing. With comfort and encouragement. What then? What would an artist's life look like and feel like?

Crucial to the development of a relationship of nurturance like that of mother to her child is the notion of adequate holding and recognition. Good-enough mothers hold and recognize their children. What does this mean? It means mothers comfort their little ones and touch them in ways that create a secure feeling inside and the ability to regulate sensations and emotions. When distressed, the children are soothed by good-enough mothers and learn that distress has a beginning and an end, and it can be eased. Eventually children internalize this capacity and are able to care for and regulate their own upsets.

But holding is also a psychological property and involves the crucial aspect of recognition. While engaging with one another post-feeding, mothers begin to see their children and the expressions that are unique to each baby. When children grow older, good-enough mothers are able to see the mind of the child at work in the form of play and desire. Being seen is crucial in the development of a secure attachment and the validation of each child's emerging personality.

The challenge of soothing ourselves and recognizing the good-enough quality in our work confronts writers and artists every day. This is not as easy as it sounds. So many of us suffer because we are unable to accept what we are feeling in a given moment. We get lost in constant demands to produce exceptional results and are blinded to the richness of a day's work by striving for perfection and success.

Wouldn't it be wonderful if we could hold ourselves more

gently and see the good in our endeavors to express that which longs to be shared? Wouldn't it be great if we could see and appreciate even the first crude marks on the drawing paper or the initial stumbling phrases on the dreaded blank page? Wouldn't it be a relief if we could slow down and feel that good enough was not a resignation into mediocrity but a loving and respectful soothing of the self?

You can offer this support to yourself by cognitively returning to an understanding that you are indeed enough. Dennis Palumbo, a prolific and accomplished novelist and screenwriter (who incidentally is also a psychotherapist), did so in his beautiful book *Writing from the Inside Out*. I highly recommend it. Listen to what he says in his introduction:

> If there is one principle that guides my work with writers, one message I fervently want to impress upon you, it's that you—everything you are, all your feelings, hopes and dreads, fears and fantasies—**you are enough.**

Yes, you are enough. Including all the things you think are wrong with you. Everything that you think needs fixing. All of it, every bit, adds up to you being good enough. Helpful as this is in easing some of the tension within, it only goes so far. Palumbo can say in a thousand ways, "You are enough," but it remains a cognitive construct that will be limited in helping you when the sirocco hits. When that happens, you need something more substantial to keep the arms of good enough holding you tight. You need a connection with something bigger and more intimate than good thoughts. You need a relationship with a more substantial part of you that you can rely on for support and soothing.

What is that? Let's go back to Winnicott. What Winnicott said next separates him from traditional psychological thought and connects psyche and spirit in a profound way. If children receive good-enough care, then development proceeds and they can continue "going on being." Wow. There you have it. The infant can continue "going on being," and the development of the real self happens without separating from the inner core. In other words, the authentic personality grows out of the safety of sufficient holding—that is, through a good-enough connection to one's own being!

We live in a society that prizes accomplishment of goals and success. In economic terms, it is the product that is revered. Not being. Nothing is wrong with achieving success and finishing your novel at long last. However, along the way, if you are separated from being, you will suffer. And your work may as well. Because at one juncture or another, you will become lost, or you will fail or lose faith, and without the support of the *experience* of knowing your basic goodness—that is, without the connection to being that holds mind and body together—you will feel shame, and the strategies of the Self Project will move into high gear.

When being is our comfort and ground, the salient urgency of the Self Project begins to dissipate. As it does, the critical judge in your head begins to quiet and recede. Not completely and not forever, but enough so that you can begin to develop some ability to notice when the Self Project system has activated and take measures to regulate the force gearing up. With a connection to your core self, an internal space opens that allows the creative impulse to move as it will. You aren't overriding the contracted state with your cognitive implants, and you aren't taking rigid defensive positions saying it doesn't matter—it does—but it is now possible to care for you and your work like a mother. Like a mother who nurtures her infant along the path to becoming a person while surviving the skinned knees and temper tantrums as well as the days when nothing works.

This is the fruit of the good-enough self. When you can go on being—that is, recognize the basic goodness within—you can hold steady even when the rejections start piling up. Go on being even when your manuscript comes back from the editor looking like she had a nosebleed. Go on being even when you are totally overwhelmed and confused about how to organize your memoir. Go on being even when reviews are less than enthusiastic. It doesn't mean you won't be disappointed or wounded; it means you will be able to hang on to your self-respect and still recognize your writing for what it is.

The single best way to connect with the being that holds you is to sit and meditate. Meditation is branded as a simple, peaceful practice, but it isn't. Not the kind that brings you to experiencing your inner self. It is not a piece of cake. It is not instant gratification. There are days you will hate it and want to quit. Days when your knees will hurt and the mind will torture you and you will want to get up and leave it all behind. Most days you might think nothing is happening and it is a waste of time. Measuring progress in this realm is like trying to watch your hair grow.

But remember, you have to write every day to become competent. You have to paint every day, draw every day, and practice the piano every day to become adept. Segovia practiced his guitar every day for five hours even when he was eighty years old and considered a master. The same goes for reconnecting with the inner being at your core. Lots of painful days will greet you, just like making art. Slow down and just do it. Just sit with yourself and the feeling of "I am." The quiet. The feeling of space and presence within. And when you experience the profound spaciousness and intimacy of that presence, nothing will ever be the same.

Experiment:

You are enough. Close your eyes and say softly to yourself, "Enough. I am enough." Repeat this to yourself when you sit down to write and see what happens. Try to move toward acceptance even when something in your anxious brain keeps saying you are not acceptable as you are. Try to receive this kind of support when friends, family, and colleagues give it to you. If you deflect it away or pooh-pooh it, pause, take a breath or two, and give it another chance. Practice receiving and taking it in. What does it feel like? What gets in the way of letting it be? Try again to relax into it. Ease in. Perhaps a part of you will scoff, perhaps a part of you will feel anxious, and perhaps a part of you will want to cry.

❧

Because the good-enough self is the centerpiece of this book's thesis, it is worth taking time to elaborate what this is and one approach to finding it. To do so, I'm going to borrow from one of my very favorite books, Toni Morrison's masterpiece *Beloved*. In particular I want to focus on the teachings and healing rituals transmitted by Baby Suggs, grandmother of the agitated spirit living in her house and the spiritual heart of the community of newly freed slaves living in Cincinnati. What better group of people to look to for help with how to recover from the wounds of trauma and return to a connection with the spirit of basic goodness?

Baby says to her family, "There was no bad luck in the world but white people. They don't know when to stop." No other phrase quite gets to the guts of the matter like this one: "They don't know when to stop." And who is better qualified to assess the nature of our condition than someone like Baby Suggs, who has seen the bare truth of our violent lust for more?

We don't have to look far to see the destruction that is the consequence of our greed. Even our great planet Earth, though big and resilient, is reeling from the impact of our appetite. And we the people now seem utterly enslaved by the relentless drive for more. This is the battle cry of the governing myth of progress that chains us to lives of perpetual striving and to the accompanying dread that not only is there never enough stuff, but also, we are not enough.

The collective dis-ease with ordinary life has invaded the

psyche of the individual and left most people feeling deficient, which translates into the self-talk of "I'm not good enough." This self-state eats away at psyche and spirit like rampaging bacteria. In my experience with patients in psychotherapy, this condition knows no professional, class, race, or gender boundaries. Every day I meet with doctors, lawyers, artists, and professors, men and women, and I can tell you they are suffering. They are "the best and the brightest," yet still they condemn themselves. Though successful in the world, each in his own way is held captive by the internal bully of self-reproach.

They look at me and say, "Something is wrong with me." The litany of shortcomings is disturbingly similar from hour to hour: not enough money; not enough accomplishments; not enough sex, time, fun, friends—the list is endless. They confess to their feelings of "I am bad, unworthy of love, a fraud." These are the realities hiding behind public personas. These people are not mentally ill. They suffer from self-attack. This is the violence that does not make it to the front page of the *New York Times* or the feature programming on CNN. This is the violence that all the antidepressants in the world won't eliminate. And this is the story no one wants to talk about.

Like capitalism without ethics, the mind separated from its spiritual source is often a destructive force. What to do and not do? For Baby Suggs, the "holy didn't approve of extra." She said, "Everything depends on knowing how much. Good is knowing when to stop." Easier said than done. For most of us, the problem is that we can't stop. We are driven to keep looking. We want more food, sex, money, and status. We desperately want good reviews, great book sales, and an adoring audience. What would our lives look like were we to give up on the lust for more? Stopping necessitates a connection with something within that holds all our talent and all our insecurities in an embrace of goodness. You are okay, after all.

And what kind of therapy did Baby Suggs propose? How did she get her people, the black men, women, and children born into slavery, to undo what the slave master had burned into their hearts and minds? How did she help them realize their true value? Here's how. She went with her people to a clearing in the woods. There she called up the children to laugh so their mothers could hear them. She called up the men to dance, "and ground life shuddered under their feet." And she called up the women to cry, "For the living and the dead, just cry." Soon it got all mixed up and everyone laughed, danced, and cried until exhaustion gave way to silence. And they sat in the silence, together.

Baby Suggs did not tell them to "clean up their lives or go to sin no more." She did not tell them they were blessed or saved. From her great big heart, she sang, "Here, in this here place, we flesh; flesh that weeps, laughs; flesh that dances on bare feet in grass. Love it. Love it hard." From there she introduced her children to the flesh. To the flesh and body that had been despised, whipped, and raped. "Love your hands! Love them. Raise them up and kiss them." She gave them back their hands, and necks, wombs, and life-bestowing genitals. And finally, she gave them "the prize," the heart, the battered heart, and told them, "Love your heart."

And then she stopped talking and danced with them. They all danced and sang, held by the love of their flesh and the gathering of hearts, which was plenty good enough.

✳

How I wish we could all walk into the woods with Baby Suggs and give ourselves over to those rituals of mourning and embodiment. Would that we could claim our pain and flesh with such profound passion. Imagine the release. Imagine the grand return of liveliness to your flesh, the blood flowing, that virgin laughter. Imagine loving hard, loving your flesh, your fingertips. Loving your battered heart. Imagine. I wonder if you can.

Perhaps every writing group should begin by following Baby

Suggs into the forest for a ritual of embodiment. Perhaps we should all cry and laugh and dance and sing the body electric. Loving it hard, loving the hand that picks up the pencil, loving every word and sentence, every mark and brushstroke that makes its way from the strange womb of creation onto the hungry paper and canvas before us.

Perhaps then we could be less worried about proving ourselves worthy artists and be more grateful servants of that magical longing to come into being that is creation's want. Maybe then we could write more dangerously and with abandon. Every sentence, broken or blessed, would be welcome and loved, every burst of color an ecstatic surprise. With the Self Project made superfluous, we might just disappear into the still waters of going on being and let that space shape us into what it most desires. Ah, what a wonderful world this could be.

꿏

As it is, we unduly suffer in the studio and at the writing desk. All too often we are dominated by anxiety and the Self Project. All too often enslaved by the demands of a society driven by profit and image. All too often broken in spirit by the labors of perfection and whippings at the hand of our very own minds, for failing to meet the demand of success.

Having lost the connection to the core self and the feeling of basic goodness, the issue of the day becomes how to compensate for this loss and the resultant feeling of dis-ease. With the persona dominating most of life as the real self is confused, lost, and fearful of shameful exposure, the Self Project takes on a primary role in the psyche.

At the same time, a mostly unconscious yearning begins to grow and influence the life of the self. That yearning is for home. Hello, Ulysses! Someone, something, please take me home. However, home is not a geographical place but an existential dimension: the homeland of the good-enough self wrapped in the arms of being.

And what a long, strange trip it is, finding our way through triumph and defeat, finding and losing the bigness that is our actual dimension. It took Ulysses ten years to get home. It may take us longer to travel by land and sea, only "to arrive where we started and know the place for the first time." Yes, Mr. Elliot, thank you. For the first time, to know the place that we have known all along, even while struggling under the spell of our inadequacies and straining to make everything right. Even then we sat on the treasure of our basic goodness, blind to our real nature and stranded on islands of anxiety and shame. Perhaps we felt we were winning the war of the Self Project; perhaps we felt victorious, even heroic. Perhaps we were. But there is always the long journey home after the war. Home to flesh, home to the heart, and home to peace. Home—what a long, strange trip it is.

6

The Odyssey

HAVE YOU HEARD DOC WATSON SING "THE RIDDLE"? Beautiful song. "How can there be a story, that has no end?" This is the question. When he sings this line, Doc Watson's voice is rich with wonder and a touch of melancholy. Don't you feel the same awe when you consider the volume of creative material pouring from the hearts and minds of artists all over the world? Do you feel a hint of sadness that you'll never quite understand the nature of creation's bounty or fully communicate what you long to?

When I was a boy growing up in Ohio, I used to lie in bed perplexed at the idea of infinity. Everything I knew as real had an end point: my bedroom, the closet, our yard. How could there be such a thing as never ending? I remember a cartoon from that time. Two astronauts are flying in a space capsule, and they come to a brick wall with a hand-painted sign that reads, "This is the end of the universe!" Ha. Turns out, we can't find a finish line, and there may even be many, many universes at play.

Why haven't all the books been written? Why haven't all the songs been sung? Because, *it* is infinite. And, *it* is us! You and me! You aren't an artist; you are a lover—Walt Whitman playing in the fields with eternity and delight. You have been touched by infinity! Imagine. That inspiration you feel at the oddest times? That is the kiss of infinity. Read Rumi—he says it as well as anyone: your beloved is calling you. Listen. Your beloved is caressing you, filling you with inspiration. Receive. You and I are more than we can ever imagine. We are smoke from an eternal flame. Truly. As Joseph Campbell said again and again, you are the radiant spark of creation.

So here you are, sounding like John Lennon, wondering if anyone will ever listen to your story. Yearning for an audience. Yearning for acceptance. This yearning burns. And you and I are sweating blood trying to make it work. Trying to validate this small self we have been told, and have come to believe, we are. Striving. Striving to be seen. Like old man Sisyphus, pushing that rock up the hill every day. Over and over, trying to be good enough. Ambition. The Ecclesiastes translation is wrong. All is not "vanity." All is striving.

The Self Project is endless. Until you surrender. Until you lay down the "I am bad" rock. This takes lots of time, and it's easier said than done. Surrender has gotten a bad rap in America. It is confused with submission. Do you hear the threat of humiliation in the confusion? Now the concept has been usurped by the mainstream culture, and we are told, "Let go." Piece of cake. "What's wrong with you that you can't let go, baby?" Do you hear the beat? Another club. Another injection of shame. Surrender takes lots of practice. Lots.

Here is one way. Let's take writer's block. You are Sisyphus, pushing that rock up the hill every morning, trying your damnedest to write that book. But every day you feel stuck. Blocked. It isn't happening. You try harder. "What's wrong with me? Who am I kidding? I suck. I can't write." You consider quitting and going back to school. "Maybe if I get that MFA, I'll be able to do something worthwhile." Surrender.

What if writer's block is a good thing? What if it is a signal that you are trying too hard? Perhaps the problem isn't that you can't write—perhaps there is so much of you tied up in trying to be somebody that you are in knots. You can't play in this condition. You can't wait and listen. In fact, constriction of body and mind is a hallmark of shame, or the anticipation of shame. You make a mistake, and rather than it being a useful opening, it is proof of your defectiveness. Exhibit A. Tensions of that nature bind the self, and the creative juices dry up. Relax. Breathe deep. You are all right. For a moment, surrender the demands on yourself.

Writing, it is now obvious to me, is not an exercise of genius. It is more of an act of devotion. It is a surrendering to deep listening. Listening with the whole self, heart and soul. Listen. Listen for the murmuring of the nonsecular. The fertile void. Call it what you will: the muse, the unknown, the mystery. You can't name it, but it can name you. And it will, if you make room. If you sit still and allow it. If you surrender self-importance for participation in the wild, enlivening flow of inspiration knocking at your window, you will have let go of your small self for the big you. For the light wanting to shine through you, as you. "We all shine on." John Lennon wrote that.

Here is a practice to do just that. It begins with the dedication of your work. Who are you dedicating your book to? Your parents? Your children? Your best friend? Whomever it is, take that seriously. Make it the first thing you write, before the title, before the outline, before the first sentence. Each day when you sit down with pen and paper, pause—pause and rededicate yourself and the day's writing to whomever it is you feel grateful to. Mix it up, if you wish, and offer the day's work to others in your life who have helped you become what you are: an artist. The point is to do what you can to put your small self and its insecurities aside for the well-being of your work and the freedom of the creative impulse. Try it. See what happens.

❧

The Odyssey is the literary archetype of the lost self trying to get home. Our modern version is different and the same, as are our sufferings. We greatly suffer the rejections of our work, and there is no getting around those feelings. We suffer greatly the frustrations of the craft, the editing and rewriting, and there is no way to circumvent those experiences. Many of our greatest artists, despite their successes, feel a terrible sense of inadequacy shadowing their lives. Though it is all too human to carry self-doubt, I hope you can see how your feelings are compounded by the overlay of the not-good-enough self-narrative. How the anxious striving of the Self Project to be something special or extraordinary *is* suffering and further separates us from the core self.

But it is certainly possible to get home. It is possible to go within and reconnect. In fact, the good news is, it happens all the time. We simply don't recognize it for what it is. The presence of our deepest self doesn't go anywhere when we become estranged. It doesn't wither on the vine. It is the vine! You just need to lay down the Self Project enough to turn your attention to the simplest, most obvious dimension of you that has been obscured by the debris of shame and mental anxiety maintaining the fiction that you are not good enough.

But first there is some housecleaning to do. Let me help you with this little exercise. Like Baby Suggs and her people, we need to face the emotions that follow us, not push them away. Soften to them, not brace against them. Feel and release the pain, feel and release the fear, feel and release the terrible shame. Go to the woods and shout and stomp your feet. Sit with friends and sob. Put on loud music and dance the night away and tell the funny stories that make your ribs ache. Climb down from your head and reconnect with your body, with flesh. Most of all, as Baby Suggs taught her people, "love hard." Love your heart, dare to love again and again—your work, failures, and successes— every paragraph, love it. And most of all, love you and your life, existence, and relationship with the creative energy of this world that has touched you and called your name.

My dog never gets lost. His nose is always to the ground and tells him where he is at all times. Our noses are congested. Not only can't we smell the roses, but we also have trouble embodying our senses and experience. Sit down to meditate for five minutes and you will quickly witness the hyperactive mind at its best. Nothing wrong with thinking and a good brain; however, today much of the chatter comes from the anxious mind struggling with insecurities. While an active mind is certainly part of human nature, we'll see in the next chapters how our culture and certain developmental traumas amplify the nature of that restlessness.

My dog never knows where we're going, and he doesn't seem to mind. Why? Because he's too curious. Too interested in discovering the latest postings left on winter grass and on the trunks of silver maples. Too involved with the whispers circulating in the morning air. This is the blessing of being lost: if you and I can surrender to it, being lost can alert us to the moment's communications. Like Ulysses, it can lead to great adventure. Writing and making art is such an adventure. Even though we don't know where we're going or what we're doing, like Mr. Nasrudin, it is possible to open and be found by that ineffable something leading the way.

Being found, we are reminded of Winnicott's phrase, "the good enough mother," which now reads as "the good-enough artist." Being held by this notion, it is possible to connect with a deep region of the self and experience the basic goodness that will comfort the anxious mind and curb the interruptions from our work brought on by the strivings of the Self Project. When connected to your core self—which is going on being—the Self Project loses its power and the work can flow. At our best, we forget ourselves altogether and are a conduit for the nonsecular to move from the music of the spheres to the song of our hearts.

PART II

You Are a Poem

7

Verse

TOWARD THE END OF HIS REMARKABLE LIFE, THE GREAT
Swiss scholar and psychoanalyst C. J. Jung was asked by an
interviewer what he had learned in all his years of study that
was most important to him. Jung said without hesitation that his
research, his prolific writing, his analytic work with patients, and
his forays into what he considered bouts with insanity, all of this
allowed him to "reach out a hand of friendship to this lump of clay."

Think of that. This bigger-than-life man, this prodigious
intellect, this psychological and spiritual genius, this sensitive
artist, at the age of eighty-eight and the end of a lifetime of
exploration into human nature, only then did he find it possible
to befriend himself. What can you say? Why is it so difficult
for us to realize what sounds so simple? So basic? Why do we
struggle so with extending a measure of kindness to ourselves?

And while we're asking questions, how about this: Who
is reaching out a hand of friendship to whom? Who, or what,
are we anyway? In his monumental tour de force, *The Denial of
Death*, Ernest Becker says, "We are Gods that shit." Not bad. C.
K. Williams, in his must-read poem "The Clause," wrote:

> this hive of restlessness
> this wedge of want my mind calls self,
> this self which doubts so much and which keeps
> reaching

Some would say we are a massively complex assortment of neurons and chemicals: in other words, a brain. Some have said for thousands of years we are *being* itself, pure awareness disguised as a body. What do you say? Who are you? What are you?

Answers are appealing, and certainty is seductive. In fact, there may be dozens of responses to these universal questions depending on the circumstances surrounding the asking. Unfortunately, when times are hard in the studio or at the writing desk and the brain starts turning out labels for who, or what, we are, they are often not the least bit flattering. More often than not, they are downright nasty, oversimplified verdicts that in one way or another cast us as a problem—something broken that needs fixing.

I hear this all the time when I am asked what I do for a living. When I say that I am a psychotherapist, what I hear back is usually, "Oh, that must be so rewarding." What I see in my questioner is nearly imperceptible but real: it isn't quite a flinch, but close. Something in the other recoils and freezes, sorry they asked. I try to reassure people that I am not on duty. If that works and the conversation continues, it typically proceeds with the following question: "Isn't it hard listening to people's problems all day?" Which translates to "How can you stand to be around fucked-up people?" This is more than a rhetorical question.

The prevailing assumption is that anyone who comes for psychotherapy is fucked up. Right? Of course. To those people, I wrote the following lines from a poem entitled "Shakespeare":

Don't worry.
I will speak with them.
This is what I will say:
I will tell them you are a fine poem.
I will tell them that sitting with you
Is to read Shakespeare:
The histories, the tragedies,
Divine comedy.
Even as they back away frightened

Claiming you are a problem,
Or worse,
I will tell them this:
Abundance—
That's what you are.
Abundance! Pages of sand.
You are all the great stories
From your own pen;
The tale of all, the blood of all,
Infinite laughter, the catching of breath.
You are the endless characters
Lined up around the block for the matinee.

It goes on like that. It ends like this:

Bring your nightmares and secret lusts,
The killing rage, the humiliations—
Your dark mental life.
Bring it all, your magnificent abundance.
You were never a problem.
Never.

Are you a problem? Is something wrong with you? Do you have to reinvent yourself, fix yourself, or make yourself into something grand before you can get on with life, or writing? *No!* Not true! False! As they say in the Vedas, "Neti, Neti." Not this, not this. If your brain says to you, "Man, what a loser you are," say, "Neti, Neti." Say, "Stop." Say, "Wow, there you go again." Say something to protest this announcement, this proclamation, this false yet crushing judgment.

¥

Okay, if we are not what the big brain says, then what are we? What is this thing we call self? Or is it a thing? I think you are more verb than thing. More movement than object: dynamic, shape-shifting movement, like weather. Actually, I think of you and me as a poem—as verse—rambling, undulating, confounding, illuminating, free verse. That's what we are: Ginsburg howling, an epic poem ranging over the fluid topography of an ever-changing, thousands-of-years-in-the-making, full-of-surprises, wondrous you! You are a poem. You are to be read out loud, with a tender, ferocious, and mischievous voice. A playful voice, breaking with wisdom and compassion. You are a poem, your life a haiku in the span of starlight, your reach "to infinity and beyond!"

※

We are such vulnerable beings. Our exquisite neurological makeup is capable of extraordinary scientific, artistic, and philosophical thought. It seems we are not bound by the limitations of our neurological network, remarkable as it may be, and are endowed with the capacity to connect with even more astounding domains of consciousness available to human beings. Sadly, when the real self is not adequately mirrored and celebrated, or when individuals suffer traumatic injury, something happens to the sense of inherent goodness and the connection to creative forces streaming through the psyche.

Though we may be resilient in many ways, we remain somewhat fragile and will, when subjected to various forms of affronts to the tender needs of young life, begin to contract. Over time, if those disturbances persist, the organism will become more and more rigid in that contraction and cut off from the resources of living that feed a sense of vitality, creativity, and well-being. On that sad day, we stand alone feeling separate, lost, anxious, and just not good enough. Worst of all, that is what we come to believe we really are: broken figures destined to either give up on life and simply survive or make the arduous climb of the Self Project back to the promised land of a feeling of aliveness and self-worth.

Lost is the freedom and joy of living we see in children and those fortunate enough to come through the developmental years still connected to their vital core. For those who came through childhood hardened and guarded, or sought refuge in the invulnerable fortress of the mind, what I am saying sounds like outlandish romantic nonsense. To say they are a poem seems either intellectually lightweight or completely unrelated to their experience. And truly, there are many days when I am flooded with doubt or disconnected from within when I think the same thing: "What is this craziness, this you-are-a-poem crap? Life sucks and then you die." There are dark days and dark nights of the soul.

But I have found that there is a force stronger than my bleakest hours. Something that keeps persisting and calling my name. A few years ago, I dug up some ground in the backyard in preparation for making a foundation for a new deck. I dug down four inches and was surprised to find a layer of black plastic buried there. When I pulled up the plastic, I discovered a cluster of crocuses in full bloom looking up at me! It was one of those unforgettable moments when not only is the sight so unexpectedly beautiful, but the mind is so taken aback that it stops in its tracks for an instant and the presence of life flashes with a brilliance typically lost to the senses.

I will always remember that moment as an epiphany of sorts—the flash of insight at the realization of a Zen koan—a revelation available to an ordinary person in an ordinary time and place. It gave me real confidence in a power much greater than our defenses. A power that just keeps coming, that won't be deterred or defeated. One that has been streaming for millions upon millions of years. That same creative insistence that compels you to pick up your pencil or paintbrush and join in the audacious gamble of creativity.

Those tender baby crocuses lay on their sides under dirt and plastic, their stems anemic, a pale, ghostly white. Those same stems were too long, distorted by the long stretch of yearning for air and light. But the petals—the dear, happy petals that greeted my eyes—were somehow, impossibly, of the fresh lavender, buttery yellow, and royal purple that we find each year popping their heads up above the surface of a late snowfall. Improbable life, blossoming despite all the odds.

And though I lose myself as regularly as the next person, I have confidence and find repeatedly that the force returns. That it can't be entirely shut down. That even in concentration camps, Jewish prisoners were making art. That even in cold, damp caves fifty thousand years ago, Neanderthals were making art. That even in today's penitentiaries, prisoners are making art. I believe the mystery of that impulse, the headwaters of that unfathomable streaming that is creative life, reaches out for us from the untouchable depth of existence and will not be denied.

And isn't that stream, that flow of experience and that quiet center of knowing, like good free verse trembling with all kinds of unexpected arrivals and departures? Doesn't it thrive within a field of spaciousness that says yes, yes, and yes again? Doesn't it move like a great lyrical poem from the known to the unknown and back? I know you have experienced this inner self. It can't be entirely shut down.

Think back to times in your life, probably when you were a child, when you weren't so self-conscious and thinking of yourself as an object. Perhaps it was as ordinary as a daydream, or what we came to call spacing out—a time when the boundaries of that which we call *me* melted away and an expanded, unrestricted sense of presence opened. Maybe it was during sexual experience as a teenager that you felt that transformation. Maybe you feel it when you are writing—you forget about yourself and are taken over and refreshed by the creative force.

My earliest memory of being really awake is of running home in the dark and marveling as my body slowly disappeared and I became one with breathing. Soon, even breathing fell away, and there I was, an aware being residing within the activity of the world and my body. I didn't find the lightness of being unbearable; I found it delicious.

Have you experienced this same state as an adult when overcome by a particularly arresting piece of art, or during the precious intimacy of lovemaking, or when encountering something staggeringly beautiful in the natural world? It sometimes happens looking into the eyes of an infant. I think it happens more often than we recognize. In any event, it is much of the same phenomenon whether it's that first bite of ice cream or the first sip of beer on a hot summer day. What happens? The mind stops. And when it stops, even for an instant, the spacious well of being is revealed. Your deepest, most intimate you opens, in all its fullness.

This lasts but a second, so either it isn't recognized or people attribute the experience to the ice cream. Give me one more scoop so I can feel that again! But the ice cream or beer doesn't deliver. So people take to meditation to still the mind and find that sweet spot. Meditation is just a word for sitting with yourself and being honest, paying attention. Without straining, you sit and let the anxious mind calm down. This usually takes a fair amount of time, but when it does—there you are.

It's a lot like unplugging a fan and watching the blades slowly come to a halt. You sit and let the obstacles fall away, the veil drop, the stories and the emotions dissolve; the layers and layers of ideas, the geological strata of self-definition—I am this, I am that—you see them for what they are: calcified remnants of the past and attempts to make sense of confounding emotional experience. In meditation practice you can learn to see them for what they are and not as the final word, not the gospel on who you are, not the essence, and certainly not your soul.

※

In the summer of 2014 Robin Williams took his life. The news of his suicide rocked the world. So many of us loved him and were deeply, deeply shaken when word reached us that he was gone. Zany, manic, crazy funny as he was, heartwarming and touching as he was, I always felt there was something about him, something in his eyes and that grin, something more fundamental than a brilliant mind and bouts with drug addiction and depression. To me, he was the raw nerve of heated vulnerability that is you and me. His sensitivity was ours. His yearning resonated through the cells of our bodies. His heart broke just like yours and mine. He fell hard, as have we. When I heard of his death, I cried, "*No.*" But it was too late.

On the day the news arrived, my writing canoe was in the backwaters of writer's sloth. I don't know what Robin Williams suffered, but I knew immediately that I wanted to get moving on this book and do what I can to help artists struggling with depression and anxiety no matter what the magnitude. I knew I wanted to hold nothing back, as it seems he gave every ounce of himself in expressing what he felt. I wanted to cry out to Robin Williams and every soul within shouting distance, as he did to Matt Damon in *Good Will Hunting*, "It's not your fault, it's not your fault."

Because, as I see it, that is the problem eating away at our hearts and minds, eroding relationships and creative work. That is the voice of condemnation speaking with absolute certainty and bullying us into accepting the verdict that decries, "You are bad. You are not lovable." I wish I were exaggerating. This is the worm at the core of our minds that believes something is wrong with who we are. That believes we are somehow not right and not deserving of life's bounty. That believes we must prove ourselves endlessly, improve ourselves endlessly, and earn our way into acceptability. Like the rock that Sisyphus pushes to the top of the hill each day, the Self Project strives for redemption, fails, and we fall to the bottom.

I'm afraid this element of the human psyche is like the mafia: its crime is in the extortion of our energy and resources. Existing to some degree within most, if not all, of us, this godfather proclaims with absolute authority that you are a failure, or hopeless, or pathetic and without value. Unlovable. Nothing more. Of course this internal tyrant can be projected onto others with grave consequences. We'll explore this in a later chapter, but it is enough now to recognize its presence and intent to demonize the core of you. It is enough to recognize the utter falseness of this dictatorial branding. Though the accusations are hidden, they have become perhaps the most common form of psychological suffering in today's society, crossing all class, gender, and racial boundaries.

What is lost in this tragedy is the mystery and beauty of our lives. The unimaginable outpouring of life and personality that is the poem you are. You are free verse cascading down the page, the unexpected turns and twists, the unintended meanings, the play and grand Whitman metaphors singing about the life of you, the poem of your self, building and transforming, becoming and becoming, dying and being born—the dashes that stop the mind, the exclamation points that excite, the rhyme and the lack of, the rhythm and blues, and the grand thunderstorm and rainbow of human emotion, of love and hate and a thousand others that shall remain nameless. How can a poem be reduced to a thing? How can verse be put in a box and labeled?

This should not be written off as a first-world dilemma. It is not the self-absorbed suffering of a white, privileged class. This is modern suffering. It is what Mother Theresa referred to as the spiritual poverty of the West that to her was a worse form of pain than the material poverty of India. The great James Baldwin suffered terrible, at times debilitating, depression largely because the leftovers of his stepfather's abusive attacks made him feel ugly and unwanted. This is the climate change of the inner world.

If the problems writers face were to be boiled down to a single matter, it would likely shake out as the challenge of getting out of our own way. Clearing out the attempts to control the work and letting the muse or the creative instinct be free to scribble on the page and splash paint on the canvas. Talent is often interrupted by anxiety, which attempts to bend the work to its will. These obstacles are the result of faulty, usually old and rigid, identifications with deficient portraits of oneself that prompt overzealous attempts at making art that will validate the self rather than serve the medium.

The question is whether you are inherently good. Whether your nature is basic goodness. This is not a question for most parents whose love for their children is free and unquestioned, and the next time you look into the eyes of an infant, see if this question of worthiness or goodness even occurs to you.

If that doesn't convince you, sit down in a quiet place and get to know yourself. Meditate on the inner presence of your life. I think you will find that your basic goodness is real. The truth of this is not dependent on belief or behavior or scripture. It is not a conclusion or something earned or developed. I think you will find it to be an existential reality: a direct experience of the nature of being, which is…well, you will discover for yourself what cannot be put into words, what is bigger than words but is the source of all expression. The mystics have called it many things—joy, peace, love, and bliss—but most often they name it that which resides within you, as you.

8
Rhythm and Rhyme

IT'S TRUE WHAT THEY SAY, "IT DON'T MEAN A THING, IF IT ain't got that swing." You've experienced it a hundred times, within yourself and others, at a play or a reading, with friends and loved ones: words alone cannot carry the day; without the juice it all falls flat. Flat as a pancake.

I'm a lucky guy. I was a teenager in the sixties and experienced the great cultural upheaval and transformation that was the movement from the not-so-juicy decade of the fifties to the explosion of Eros that was the revolution of the sixties. To be fair, it was heating up before the British Invasion. Long before John, Paul, George, and Ringo made it to the stage of *The Ed Sullivan Show* and my father pronounced the end of civilization, he declared the rocking pelvis of Elvis Presley a disgusting degeneration of music and culture. Poor man, he couldn't believe it would amount to much. He couldn't believe people, especially his children, would be drawn to such vulgarity. The man in the gray flannel suit was wrong. Bless his heart, he never knew the swing.

But that's the whole point, isn't it? We are drawn to the juice. We want to feel the swing, the aliveness that art brings us to. While Elvis was reminding the country of the continent of the pelvis and the mysterious life of sexuality, there was another guy "rockin' and rollin' till the break of dawn" in St. Louis. His name was Chuck Berry, and he signaled a resurgence of African bioenergy that had been oppressed for so long. Soon Detroit was the new mecca, and a tidal wave of soul music swept over a people waking from a long winter's nap.

Motown. Soul. Suddenly there was so much swing, we barely knew what to do with it all. And as Elvis reinvented the pelvic region of our new world, The Temptations, Aretha, and company brought soul and spirituality out of the gospel churches and onto the dance floor. White kids fled Catholic and Protestant cells where the gospel didn't mean a thing because it had lost all its swing, and joined their black brothers and sisters dancing in the streets.

I'm an unlucky guy. I was a teenager in the sixties and experienced the assassinations of the Kennedys and Martin Luther King Jr. as well as the terrible tearing apart of society over the battle for civil rights and the protest against the war in Vietnam. The pain of that time lives on in my heart and in the nasty polarization of our citizens and government. As Mr. Dickens said, "it was the best of times, it was the worst of times": free love and costly death. It ignited a rekindling of our nation's civil war on college campuses, in the ghettos, and within the hearts of your soul and mine.

James Brown didn't sing—he wailed. Part song, part scream, proclaiming at the top of his lungs for the whole world to hear, "I'm a Soul Man!" And the world heard him. The people heard the centuries of pain and yearning, the rage and freedom, and the insistence of his declaration. And we were moved. And nothing was ever the same, as the full power of human life was released in all its creative and destructive force.

Yes, creative and destructive. The sixties and the hippies weren't all love and peace. It all broke loose with the power of a tornado, and there was love and there was hate. But that's the way it is with life—you get it all, the good and the bad. "Full catastrophe living," as Zorba said. Full, as in the whole dynamic pulsation of form that doesn't take kindly to our versions of control and manipulation. Within that pulse moves the beat of creation and being that has not stopped for four billion years. It is that same rhythm of existence that moves through you. (How can we be depressed?) It is the soaring voice of Walt Whitman arcing over the battlefield and singing the praises of the living and the dead, the victorious and the defeated. It is the poem of you, the mysterious juice of you, the particular swing of you, that decorates this space in time like no other.

And so it goes. Expanding and contracting, expanding and contracting. The basic heartbeat of existence going on and on expressing the timeless rhythm of becoming and disolving. Ancient Hindu philosophy maintains the entire universe operates in the same manner: expanding outward from nothing into something, and contracting back from something into nothing. Each universal cycle is known as one complete breath of God. Our thirteen-billion-year history is but one exhalation in the eternal becoming of God's play.

True or not, I love this. I love considering us as being made in the image of God and subject to the rhythms of creation: the in and out of the breath, the expansion and contraction of the muscular system, and the opening and closing of the heart. Isn't it great?

For writers and artists, this should be liberating. So often we think we are stuck and nothing is happening. Impossible! We may be caught in the web of a certain trancelike state, it may feel like an LA traffic jam, hopelessly stuck, no exit. But the pulse is there just waiting to break through. This is good news and points toward the recognition of a power far stronger and more dependable than our individual will. The possibilities of movement are closer than we think if we can only connect with our deeper self.

Experiment:

Take a minute now to experience this for yourself. Find a quiet spot and either lie down on the floor or sit in a comfortable chair with your back straight. Breathe in slowly through your nose and let yourself relax into the carpet or chair. Feel yourself being held. Isn't it good to be held? Let yourself soften, if you are able. Take one wrist with the other hand and find your pulse. Put your finger on the pulse of your own biorhythm and feel that primal life force. Feel the quality of the beat, the steady state of on and off. Is it fast or slow, strong or weak? Either way let it comfort and reassure you of its devotion to your well-being. Do the same with your breathing. Feel the rhythm of inhaling and exhaling. Is it soft or tight? Are your breaths full and easy or restricted? Many of us don't breathe in all the way. We don't easily take in the good. Your breath is a good measurement of your relationship to the good of life. Many don't exhale completely. You may have trouble letting go. You may feel that you have to make everything happen by yourself. Can you really trust the availability of other resources? Feel the muscles in your body. What do they tell you about your state of being? Are you relaxed and open to experience, or are you guarded and braced against presumed trouble? Try to accept whatever you find, but try also to allow yourself access to your body. Writers spend so much time in the mind. Soften. Take a break from thinking.

Now try to apply what you found to your writing practice. Are you overthinking it? Trying too hard? Are you holding in your creative breath until the perfect sentence comes out? Come on, make a mess, let it rip. I really think it is very difficult to sustain creative work from a place of contraction. At some point you have to be able to let go and let the work take over. Take a walk and listen to wind and birdsong. Listen to the groans of the city. Look into the sky and the shadows of the day. Open the doors of perception so your mind can rest. Of course the brain plays a big part in crafting and shaping, but when you feel stuck, that is not the time to plow through with brilliance.

Take your writer's pulse often. Get to know its rhythms.

What does it tell you? Is it getting enough oxygen? What is feeding you? Is it hurried or lethargic? Maybe you need more support and stimulation from the community. Is it straining? Maybe you need to let go of what you thought would work and try something different. Wasn't it Jeffrey Eugenides, author of *Middlesex*, who said he worked for two years only to discover the voice was wrong and he needed to go back and change it? What courage! You have to listen to the rhythm of your work, to the wisdom of your own pulse.

Maybe you are writing a memoir and the material is triggering big emotions. You probably need a big pause to feel, maybe cry, maybe scream, to clear the passages. You aren't stuck or off track or a lousy writer. You are emotionally constricted and need release and support to carry on. All of this is to say there is a profound rhythm in creative work between expression and listening. Between the exhilaration of pounding out pages and the disheartening hours and days when it appears nothing is happening. It is easy to overvalue the productive times when sentences are flowing and devalue the times of emptiness. But if you think of them as being one inseparable rhythm, it is possible to enjoy the active times and be thankful for the passive times. Learn to wait and replenish. Trust the rhythm.

❧

What about rhyme? What about the music—it's not just about the percussion, right? Right on. I think I may have told you of my not-so-secret wish to be a songwriter. Have I? There are days I walk around wishing I was John Lennon or John Prine. I love their songs. I admire the hell out of all the great songwriters: Lennon, Prine, Joni Mitchell, the greats from my parents' generation, Rogers and Hammerstein, Neil Simon. What could be better than to bring word and music together and lift up the hearts of your listeners?

But my lyrics always sound contrived. I can't quite get it right, the rhyme, the rhythm. It just doesn't come together like this classic written by Ray Noble and immortalized by Nat King Cole, "The very thought of you, and I forget to do, the little ordinary things that everyone ought to do. I'm living in a kind of daydream..." Ah, ain't it lovely? Never mind, I can love these songs and have my own gifts that I find joy in. The point is to find the sweetness in your writing. The same sweet delight you feel when you hear Wordsworth spin meter and rhyme and they just flow together so effortlessly.

I'm well aware that writing isn't all fun and games, but it needn't be a trial either. You don't have to tie yourself up in all sorts of rigid iambic pentameter straitjackets. You don't have to try quite so hard. As my boys say to me on a regular basis, "Chill." Have some fun. Step back and lower your sights a bit. Delight in a sentence that comes out just right. Enjoy the movement of thought through a paragraph. Marvel at the images that come spontaneously from your blessed unconscious and elsewhere. Say thank you for the gift of the unbidden connection that makes a simile smile. Write something different now and then, like haiku or a romantic couplet. Play a little. Who says writing has to be a white-knuckle ordeal?

Rhyme leads the listener toward joy. It connects one line to another, one sound to another like precious stones in a fine necklace. Rhyme transforms words into bells and verse into music. It provides resonance to speech that vibrates on the frequency of delight.

Just the other night, my son and I had an interesting conversation about music. He criticized rock and roll for being a bunch of guys screaming into a microphone and declared rap and hip-hop far superior. I restrained myself from arguing in defense of my musical heritage and asked him why. What he said was telling. The rhyming in hip-hop is what sets it apart in his mind. It is the dexterity of language that he loves—the acrobatics of the echoing sounds, the insistence on content that is framed by rhyme, accentuated by rhyme, and amplified by rhyme. Rhyme is surprise—an explanation point that wraps the message in unforgettable ribbons of delight. It is now, as it has been for millennia, what etches the spoken word into our memory. Rhyme is our connection with the everlasting.

What is sweet in your life? And I don't mean chocolates. Where is the music? Joy? Are you infected with the spirit of seriousness? Bound by the requirement to be a suffering artist? Listen for the rhyme and rhythm within your own being. You are a poem, every bit as wonderful as Wordsworth's from the lake country. The qualities of rhyme teach us to pause and appreciate the sweet sounds passing through our lips and to recognize and accept the discordance that is also part of our magical existence.

Experiment:

The following is my John Letterman list of ten free sweets in my life. Take a minute or two to make your own top ten.

1. Birdsong
2. The blue hour
3. Sitting by a river
4. Walking in the dark
5. Listening carefully to quiet
6. Letting wind comb my hair
7. Humming, whistling, or singing, "Row, row, row your boat..."
8. Eating one raspberry as if it were the first or the last
9. Saying thank you throughout the day
10. Talking to someone over the age of eighty at least once a week

---

❧

Rhythm helps us along this bumpy earth, especially in accepting the many contradictions in ourselves and in life that can bring on doubt and confusion. For instance, how can I feel so strong and competent in one moment and so fragile and inept in the next? How do I reconcile my days when the writing sings with those when I produce nothing but trash? Why am I a loving person in one moment and a judgmental asshole in the next?

Learning to live with these contradictions in our personalities and in those of our friends and family members is one of the big challenges of adulthood. Learning to accept the sweet and sour sets the table for the enjoyment of paradox among other things. And attuning to the existence of paradox is one of the wonderful fruits of development.

My favorite from way back is understanding that light is both particle and wave. I actually think this is a wonderful metaphor for the mystery of who you are. How it is that you are simultaneously a separate individual and united with all there is? Niels Bohr, the great Danish physicist, once said, "The opposite of one profound truth may very well be another profound truth." Well said, and it applies to human beings very nicely.

Feeling the rhyme and rhythm of your own big, big self allows for the enjoyment and welcoming of the many facets of you. It allows for movement and frees the psyche from restriction, the number one killer of creative thought. Take a minute to contemplate the vastness and mystery that is you. Follow the expansion of your soul wherever it may take you. Make up a silly rhyme and whistle a silly tune. Your life will be lighter, and your writing easier, when you can play with the muse and find that swing. *Bee bop, shoo dee da.*

9
Metaphor and Image

THERE IS A BEAUTIFUL SCENE IN THE FILM *IL POSTINO,* when Pablo Neruda is on the beach talking with the postman about writing and life. Waves are crashing on the shore, and the great poet explains to the simple man by his side that everything in our world is metaphor, everything is in flux and constantly moving and becoming something else. At that moment the young postman thinks he is motivated by his infatuation with the beautiful village girl. But in fact, he is himself changing into a man and a poet in his own right. It is a profound and heartwarming scene.

A good poem is made up of images, and the structure of poetry lends itself to metaphor as well as any art form. When you find yourself in the groove, images may arrive in clusters as John Lennon wrote, "Words are flowing out like endless rain into a paper cup..." When I wrote my novel, I was often awakened at two or three in the morning with whole sentences streaming in my head from "Across the Universe". The images came unbidden. I really couldn't think them up. It was thrilling.

Have you experienced this? I'll bet you have—you are the paper cup! A Big Gulp twenty-ounce paper cup. Once you realize you are the paper cup, once this declaration is made, all the evocative imagery of you, the world, and your life is transformed into the extraordinary mystery of metaphor. Because living and writing in metaphor is to embody the great paradox of identity and existence: we are different and the same, one and many. In metaphor, unlike simile, A is not like B; A *is* B. Metaphor exposes the illusion of separate bodies, and in the same breath, it reveals the truly radical reality of our common ground.

Let's look at a few lines from Sylvia Plath's poem, "Metaphors", written while she was pregnant with her first child.

> I'm a metaphor
> an elephant,
> a ponderous house

She doesn't mess around, does she? "I'm a metaphor." Get used to it! I am not like an elephant—I *am* an elephant! I *am* a ponderous house! I'm a metaphor. This is outrageous! This is revolutionary vision. This is *you*. It is perhaps the primal coupling that got things rolling: *I am*, and everything follows from that source.

Words and images break down unity into necessary bits of diverse meanings: I am this; you are that; he, she, or it is all this other stuff. All of it is necessary brain discriminations that allow for social interactions to function smoothly and are helpful in cultivating appreciation for life's great bounty. But binary vision is very limiting and in fact dangerous when this particular structuring of reality is seen as the one and only truth and the splitting of self and other goes unchallenged. With that division shaping our consciousness, we are inevitably subject to living in some degree of fear of the world and ourselves.

Perhaps this is what Robert Frost had in mind when he wrote the following:

> Unless you are at home with the metaphor...you are
> not safe anywhere.

Now that's a strong statement. What is the great poet saying to us? How are we made safe by metaphor? It seems to me that metaphor is vision. Vision of a mind-boggling unity that connects all of existence. The pregnant woman is the elephant, is the ponderous house, is the pregnant sister on the other side of the world. Metaphor rescues us from the egregious mistake of concluding that our perception of diversity and differentiation is the whole show. In other words it protects us from becoming lost, isolated, and alienated from the intricate network of being that spawns and embraces all of creation. Without metaphor, we are not safe from the fear of differences, which inevitably devolves into violence to others and oneself.

Robert Frost believed that metaphor and poetic thinking spoke to us in such a deep way as to make it possible "to say matter in terms of spirit and spirit in terms of matter." Opening our hearts and minds in this way allows us "to leap from sight to insight, from sense to essence, from an awareness of the physical to awareness of the metaphysical." Don't you feel safer already?

You aren't who you think you are. Most of the bad things you think about yourself are false. This doesn't mean you can't make critical assessments of your work. You can. It means the judgments you make about yourself are wrong. In some respects even the good ones are. Concluding you are anything other than your essence, the *I am* of all, sets you on the endless seesaw of good and bad identifications and subjects you to the instability of elation and deflation. You and I are so much more than we imagine. We are metaphor. We are the pregnant mother, the squirrel on the wire, the swollen river. We live within and at the center of creation: the unification of differences and opposites.

⚜

Remember Neruda on the beach with the postman? What did he say? "Everything is turning into everything." This is the great liberation, the connective tissue uniting one and all. In metaphor one thing isn't like another thing; it is that thing. Like electron particles that relate to each other from across the universe, in the creative moment, the boundaries of separate objects break down, and rather than fixed entities, we find networks of energies that are in various states of transformation and communication from one form of existence to another.

This is great news for writers if we can roll with it. It enables the novelist to identify with all her characters, the poet to be the leaves of grass. The song to myself is the song to everything. What freedom! The great shackle of a separate, personal identity is undone and the creative mind is free to roam in any field it wishes. You can still take on personal identities as you like, but you can shed them just as quickly and assume any of the multiple callings of the self. The quagmire we are all vulnerable to is that of rigid identifications. Especially, as I have talked about at length, those which paint you into a negative corner. If you are stuck in the certainty that you are not good enough, you know what I'm talking about. It feels like the gospel truth of who and what you are, case closed.

When the young postman in *Il Postino* decides he wants to be a poet, he is racked with insecurity and certain he is not good enough. He tries to emulate the great Neruda only to find himself in greater despair over his shortcomings. In the end, he finds his own voice, his unique sensibility, and is rewarded by being featured at a large political rally against the Chilean dictator Augusto Pinochet.

You are the postman who found that he was so much more than he had ever considered. You are so big and so multifaceted and so vast. Just sit down with yourself and be quiet, and you will find it's true. You are the endless ribbon from the magician's hat. And everything that springs from your center is coming from that place of essential goodness. Good enough. Go find it.

※

There is a shadow side to metaphor. It involves the psychological problem of repetition. What pain we have not sufficiently processed tends to be re-created. My profession calls these enactments. You could call them a secular form of déjà vu. Enactments are largely unconscious manifestations of your history and are uncannily precise in making what we call the past come to life in the present. That is, relational patterns, emotional responses, and even dialogue find their way from the psychic archives into the reality of the every day. It really is extraordinary. I'm certain you've experienced what I'm talking about with a family member, an intimate partner, or an authority figure.

Nowhere is this more apparent than in the lives of those who have suffered trauma of one sort or another. You've probably heard of flashbacks, but what I'm talking about is much more subtle and real. What makes it the dark side of metaphor is the fact that these enactments don't feel like the trauma: they *are* the trauma. Every trauma victim dreads, above all else, the return of the traumatic event or the perpetrator of the trauma. When a situation occurs in the present day, it is experienced as the recurrence of the original event. The same fear, pain, or rage floods the body and makes effective responses to the immediate quite impossible.

Try to be aware of this phenomenon. The next time you have a fight with your partner, reflect back on the experience and ask yourself what is familiar to you about what just took place. Ask yourself if you are experiencing emotions that are directly related to historical events. Sometimes these happenings can be quite subtle and other times blatant. It is challenging to actually get to the heart of your responsibility for creating such occurrences. Not that you are the only actor on the stage. Not at all. But you will be surprised to become aware of how strong and persuasive this phenomenon can be. I call them living metaphors.

❧

For better and for worse, we seem to be creatures that make up stories, and our stories are primarily picture books. I say "for better and for worse," because sometimes the images we turn out can get us into trouble. I'm differentiating images from vision, which is largely generative and fulfilling creative energies. I'm also referring to images in their largely unconscious forms. For instance, the not-good-enough self often has an image attached to it. For me growing up, it was a skinny kid I felt captured my sense of inadequacy and weakness. It took me years to shake this image of myself. At one point I even overate and gained weight in an attempt to counter the power of that picture in my mind.

Again, the picture, sometimes unconscious, is attached to a story line—"I am weak and inadequate"—and an emotion, usually a form of shame. This is called self-image in counseling books, but the term does not quite do justice to the entrenchment and power of its influence on self-esteem.

Experiment:

It is a useful practice to flesh out an image of the *bad me*. Give it a face and a body, or let it be as grotesque as feels true to you. Give it a name if you like. Naming it and giving form to your allegedly defective self is a good way to begin to strip it of its power. When you become conscious of its presence, label it and observe the way it works, its little tricks and not-so-subtle power plays. In meditation, try to locate this bad self that appears to be so much of you. You may be amazed to find that you cannot find it. In a very real sense, it doesn't exist other than as a split-off realm of consciousness organized around the terrible feeling of lack.

Images are captivating. They are also potentially hypnotic, aren't they? Don't we love to look and be taken by the image of our children, a glorious mountain, a lovely woman, kittens, a magical sunset? Aren't we captured by beauty and art? Can't we feel invaded and pummeled by images of violence? And what fascinates the soul more than the perplexing and mysterious images of a dream?

The importance of image is well recognized in the study of narcissism. *Narcissism* is a dirty little word thrown around by my profession, and now the public, to label those who are primarily self-absorbed and in need of using people for their own self-aggrandizement. It has become an utterly pejorative word in our cultural diction. And yet, those of us engaged in the Self Project who struggle with the feeling of lack and a persistent sense of not being good enough can be self-occupied in a way that draws this accusation from friends or loved ones. And there is truth to it—we can become altogether self-involved trying to make ourselves right. Unfortunately, there usually isn't much tenderness to the labeling.

In fact, the labeling is often condemning. More often than not, I hear from my patients that what I am advocating feels selfish, self-indulgent. These are cardinal sins if you have been shackled by chains of unworthiness so common to those trapped in this dilemma. The irony is that people with low self-worth, once freed from the Self Project, are able to give themselves more freely to the needs of others. They are finally able to sacrifice for the sake of the community as well as the writing project without feeling something vital has been taken from them.

This is the beauty of the good-enough self. Unlike the narcissistic person, supported by the direct knowledge of our basic goodness, we are able to give. In other words it is possible to see and validate in others that blessed state of goodness and to give help and compassion when needed. This is not the case with narcissism.

The narcissistic agenda is organized around an image. The clinical term is *ego-ideal*. This image is not a particular picture but more of a mural depicting wide-ranging impressions of what it is to be special. You could think of it as an unconscious collage of admired people who make up the ideal, invulnerable self. I can spot this a mile away in artists who wear their identity as a creative like a uniform. In college I smoked a pipe to look like Faulkner. I drank like him, too, for special effect. Tragically, some of these identifications cover for an empty, lost sense of self and can be quite self-destructive. I'm sure you have seen or experienced this phenomenon.

The allure of the image is strong, and convincing. It is admittedly a bit of a confusing deal because, as children and adults, we learn by imitation. Everyone needs models, heroes, and mentors to develop as an artist. This is true and necessary. And still, there is vulnerability and temptation at the heart of the injured, hurting self to cling to the image of a particular artist and build a persona around that constructed ideal. For me, after Faulkner it was Ken Kesey. After Kesey it was William Stafford. At least I was getting away from alcohol and drugs! But I was still trying to shore up my insecurity with someone else's life. Still trying to fabricate a way to feel good enough. Real mentorship leads to individuation and a unique creative arc, not copying and adopting the style of another.

ﱡ

Looking to others for a script of how one should think, write, and be in the world is what Winnicott termed the "False Self." When either trauma or environmental stress overwhelms an infant or a child, its "True Self" retreats and is replaced by a reactive-self system that is overly adaptive to others and not responsive from its own center of needs, feelings, and desires. The False Self refers to our innate capacity to conform to the expectations and rules of family and cultural life. This adaptation creates a way to connect to and feel a belonging with important people in one's life. What causes trouble is when the rules and norms of families and groups do not allow for particular aspects of the True Self to grow and develop. Then, in the words of William Stafford, "Following the wrong god home we may miss our star."

The wrong god may be a requirement for a certain respectability, a fear of sexuality, a prohibition against anger that leaves a child frightened of her or anyone else's aggression. I know a painter whose parents were so anxious about her financial security that they reacted badly to her desire to be an artist. When she tries to pursue her passion for painting, she feels as though she is betraying a sacred bond. The False Self sacrifices its authenticity for what is acceptable.

The False Self is typically either anxious and compliant to the wishes and needs of attachment figures or, conversely, quite resentful and oppositional to any perceived demand to forsake one's own interests for those of another. In either case, the reference point remains externally oriented and in conflict with the creative energies of the True Self. The True Self, as Winnicott saw it, had everything to do with creativity. He wrote a book entitled *Playing and Reality*, the essence of which is that the True Self contacts—that is, plays, dances, engages—environmental figures based on feelings, needs, and impulses whose origin is the internal makeup of the individual. When children do this, these experiences strengthen and ground them in their core inner self, which paves the way for creative living to follow.

It should be clear how problematic the artist's life becomes if access to the True Self is not free. The question of finding one's voice becomes extremely difficult when the psyche is dominated by seeking validation or establishing a secure attachment. The issue becomes "How do I get seen?" rather than "How do I express what I feel?" Instead of following one's instincts and pulling on the threads to find what wants to be expressed, those who are stuck in the False Self are torn between their own creative impulse and what they feel they should make in order to be accepted or to succeed.

Of course the True Self isn't completely accessible and free in any of us, and in some respects the False Self is a necessary social self that mediates the boundary with others and the world in general. But for some the problem of connecting to the True Self, or what we might call the creative center, is greater than for others. When this is the case, the field of creativity is dominated by intrusive thoughts concerning the reaction of the world to our work. We are prematurely drawn into arguments with reviewers, battles with publishers, and so on, and the actual work is interrupted by the anxiety of facing shameful disapproval.

Again, if the False Self becomes a dominant feature of the psyche, it will take on a guiding image or ego-ideal that shapes the identification of self with a particular quality deemed acceptable or fascinating by the psyche and others. At this point writing takes a turn toward satisfying the requirements of the Self Project versus cooperating with the wishes of art. It can mean an aversion to taking risks and writing dangerous material, or it can lead to a compulsion to be outrageous and disturbing to readers.

Experiment:

Take a minute now to write some notes about yourself. Think about the people you have admired and tried to emulate. What are their characteristics? How have you tried to incorporate those? Do they feel like you? Do you feel like you have borrowed them? What about the images you have in your head of what an artist should look like, dress like, or act like? Is that really you? Be honest with yourself. You and I have heard people talking from persona, trying so hard to sound sophisticated, intellectual, and artsy. We've done it ourselves. The False Self is an idol. In order to be at one's best with creative work, it is crucial to listen. To listen, and to receive. If the True Self, what I think of as the conduit to the source of creativity, must compete with serving a false idol, the flow of inspiration is disrupted from going on being.

Going on being. I hope you know what that is. Once you do, everything changes. When Winnicott coined the phrase, he positioned himself outside the mainstream of psychology and stood next to another giant of his time who also used the terms *True Self* and *False Self*. That man was Thomas Merton. Merton is a particularly interesting character for us to study, since he was an exceptional man of letters. His literary criticism was prolific and original. When, in his forties, he became a monk in the Trappist tradition, he took to writing about spiritual life in ways never previously found in American religious circles. His writing and his uniquely psychological/spiritual view made him known and beloved all over the world.

Like Winnicott, he conceptualized a True Self and a False Self. Similarly, he did not equate the False Self with anything bad or malevolent. In fact, the False Self is not even meant to imply phony or inauthentic traits of personality. It is simply meant to describe that which is not wholly real. That which is not of and connected with the radiant source of being that is the mother of all. Included in that description is all that we now think of as the egoic self, or the relative self—that is, notions of gender, age, body type, and personality styles. In short, all the things that change over time and are subject to the laws of birth and death. Merton believed the True Self was that which was unborn and would not die: the endless river of being and creation that brings us life in all its fullness.

The implications of his theories for writers and artists are far-reaching. I have talked with many authors, those who have spiritual inclinations and those who have none, and nearly all of them say something similar: that when they are at their best, the writing comes as if from outside themselves. It is as if it arrives from a place they cannot name, locate, or identify as *me*. This is the great adventure, mystery, and delight of creative involvement, is it not?

I must say that when I am not participating in this flow, I can feel a bit empty and depressed. Moments of writing fiction and poetry, even bad prose and verse, have been among the most enlivening of my life. When I'm not there, I yearn for it. But not surprisingly, I cannot make it happen. I cannot will it, but I can put myself in a position to receive by committing to a regular writing practice, such as the one William Stafford recommended, of writing a poem every morning. If you are there and awake, you never know.

The tricky part is showing up and knowing how to get out of the way. Knowing how to discern what is coming from the False Self's constructs and what is streaming from the True Self. Of course these are theoretical points of view, and it is never so black and white. Nevertheless, they are helpful to some in differentiating that which is colored by egoic strivings, or what I have called the Self Project, and that which comes unbidden from what Merton and Winnicott named the True Self. Meditation helps enormously in this respect, as one is able to get to know in a very intimate way the raw bones of striving and the calm waters of being.

For Merton, and others of his persuasion, we are made in the image of God. There we are back to images. I'm not a Bible guy by any means, and if the truth be told, I have been rebelling against the Big Book since two years of catechism class in the Lutheran Church did me in. But it is a remarkable statement: "You are made in the image of God." If you strip away all the layers of meaning attributed by the ruling class of the church and you put aside the terrible atrocities of history allegedly inspired by the Bible (I would argue they weren't inspired but used), then it may be possible to breathe in the awe and mystery of this statement.

In this context, image is of the sort that links imagination with the creative force we might call God and not so much the image—a perversion, if you will—of what we call the narcissistic position. Then the image of God points toward creativity, abundance, luminous consciousness, and ever-evolving transformations. Being of the likeness of God may explain why it is that we are so compelled to make art and at the same time inevitably feel like our work falls short in one way or another.

It isn't that you have to believe in God, or be a mystic or any such thing, to get excited about this stuff, because if you take the meaning of this in, your life as a writer just got a lot easier. Why? Simple, you don't have to worry, "Am I really a creative, or am I fooling myself?" You are made of the creative juice! You don't have to worry about making it happen. It is happening! It can't not happen. You just have to ride the current. Learn to wait. Get out of the way and listen. Receive what is plentiful and knocking at your door. Remember, it is a lot easier when you don't have to prove yourself good enough, when you know you are good enough and you can play with the ever-dancing particles of energy looking for you to transform them into that which we call art.

10

Space(s)

AH, SPACE. DON'T WE LOVE IT? DON'T WE LOVE TO STARE into the black depth of the cosmos and the dusty fringe of the Milky Way? How many years have humans been doing just that, enraptured by the night sky? Don't we love the movies that take us out into the beyond? *Star Trek, Close Encounters of the Third Kind, Dr. Who*? Who can ever forget the remarkable scenes from *2001: A Space Odyssey* as the spaceship went deeper and deeper into outer space accompanied by Straus's *Waltz of the Blue Danube*? And wasn't it "A long time ago in a galaxy far, far away" that inspired a generation with visions of traveling through space at warp speed?

Turns out, there's a whole lot of space going on. Bill Bryson wrote a beauty of a book called *A Short History of Nearly Everything*. This book is a gem, and not only because it contains so much knowledge about the world but also because it is a literary antidepressant. Even at my melancholy best, I can't remain down when I read this stuff. It puts me immediately into an altered state. Give it a read someday and I'm sure you will find it captivating and enlightening. And Mr. Bryson has a lot to say about space as well.

For starters, there is the cosmos. Suffice it to say, it is enormous. The average distance between stars is 20 million million miles! Our nearest neighbor is roughly 2.5 million light-years away, which would take the average spaceship some twenty-five thousand years to travel. Wow, hope they have some good movies on board. These numbers overwhelm the mind. Because we are so oriented to bits of something, it is unfathomable that there could be such vast expanses of nothing. Perfectly empty nothing.

And to make things even more astounding, we find that empty space is not only the nature of the cosmos but also of the stuff we call matter. Take your regular building block of life, the atom, the primal living metaphor, which takes shape as this or that for a while and then takes the form of something else. Did you know that millions of atoms in your body once helped make up the body of Beethoven? No kidding. Well, tough as it was to learn how to split an atom, it seems that the atom, too, is predominantly space. Bryson describes the nature of the atom like this: if an atom were magnified to the size of a huge cathedral, the nucleus, that largest part of an atom, would be equivalent to the size of a fly on the wall. The rest? You got it—empty space. Staggering, isn't it?

As a species, we love to dream. Which is another way to say our love affair with space is both externally and internally oriented. In his classic book *Magical Child*, Joseph Chilton Pierce notes a study in which children of genius IQ were researched to determine what characteristics are common to their intellect. Surprisingly, the only trait that stood out in the study was their tendency to periodically "space out." That's right, they space out—that is, they go inside to inner space where the mind can rest and connect with a source that feeds and replenishes. Some people might call this meditation. Imagine all the creative children who have been reprimanded for daydreaming and you can feel pretty sad very quickly.

Captivated as we are by space, it turns out it is often ignored. We look at objects. You could say we are spellbound by the material world. In Rupert Spira's words, we look at the letters and words and not the page itself. In fact, it is seldom that we appreciate and attend to the spaciousness of life.

A few years ago, I signed up for a drawing class at the local community college. That lasted about an hour. I walked out reminded of why I have such an aversion to school. On my way to the parking lot, I passed through the bookstore and stumbled upon the most wonderful book, *Drawing from the Right Side of the Brain*. What a treasure that book is. For the next several months, I spent as much time as I could happily drawing the faces of famous people. What a great meditation.

One thing that was key to learning to draw was the concept of negative space. If you don't know what that is, it is the process of drawing lines where the attention is on the shape of the space surrounding an object. Drawing the object itself tends to lead to drawing a concept of, let's say, an ear rather than seeing and drawing the actual ear. This is great fun and releases the artist from the pressure of drawing a perfect ear. I often wonder how writers can use negative space or spaciousness to make writing more playful and descriptive. More on this later.

Remember a few pages back when I told you about Rupert Spira, the artist-turned-Nonduality-teacher? He said something one night that resonated in me like a gong. I will never forget those first words of his talk, "You are the openness in which all things appear." What? Something in that simple sentence rang so true for me that I felt dumbstruck for the next fifteen minutes at least. What? You mean I'm not this sixty-something-year-old man? I'm not this seasoned psychotherapist and aspiring writer? I'm not this dad and husband? I am the open space in which all things come and go? Wow.

That is both terrifying and exhilarating. Beautiful and dreadful. I always know when someone is getting better in psychotherapy when they report discovering a spacious inner world. Then we know the constricted state is releasing and spaciousness is opening. Ease is arriving. You are that spaciousness, that vast sea of awareness. How could you not be good enough?

❧

And yet, we look away. Our looking is fixed on objects. Why? And why is it that you imagine yourself as an object—something solid and known versus something spacious and pulsing with dynamic mystery? Why is it that you give your attention to phones and chase manically after entertainment? The fixation on objects and the need to pursue distractions appear to be endless. Space, it seems, is not our friend.

One of my patients said it best recently. She said, "I've been afraid that I'm not really here." She can't trust her own existence. Spaciousness is threatening; silence is overwhelming. She feels she must run and keep running from what she believes to be a vacancy that will swallow her up. An emptiness that will extinguish her. Another patient fears space because it became associated with the traumatic loneliness of his childhood when space threatened to engulf him in impossible feelings of pain.

Toward the end of *2001: A Space Odyssey*, the mutinous megacomputer, Hal, jettisons one of the astronauts on board from his connection with the ship. The poor man begins an eternal fall into the dark mouth of empty space until he grows smaller and smaller and finally disappears. I've always felt this was the perfect archetype for the terror living inside. Space is symbolic of our fear of disappearing. Of death and extinction. Meditation sounds so easy, so simple, right? But it isn't. It puts us right up against these fundamental fears. Space becomes menacing. Silence something to dread. The inner self, well, I'd better stay away from that.

❧

My Shakespeare professor in college once said to me that reading Shakespeare will tell you everything you need to know about human nature, and the spaces between the words will tell you everything you can know about eternity. You are a poem, and the spaces within are your portal to that eternal moment. Just as the spaces within a great poem by Blake or Frost allow for the meter and rhyme to work, the same is true for you. Pay attention and you will find spaces between the most persistent of thoughts. Giving your attention to those spaces is one way to disempower the pestering voices in your head and see through to the unreality of their claims.

Another is to meditate on the breath. You can find this in yoga as well as Tai Chi and any number of practices that work with breath, such as dance and even running. I happen to think meditation is the most direct way to experience space, but it's such a personal choice. Most meditation teachers will tell you to follow your breathing in and out. What is really amazing is to notice the space at the end of an in breath before the out breath begins: feel into that space and you will find *that*. That which is your deepest self. That space which is ever expansive.

Remember the feeling you had on a big swing set at the park when you were a kid? That great feeling of soaring upward into the wild blue yonder? And what happens at the top of that arc? The pause. The sacred pause. It's the same inside with your breath, only more so. Try it. You will find the spaciousness that is so, so sweet. The silence that is restorative. The quiet that will inspire and speak to you. The emptiness from which all this appears. The opening that holds you tenderly. And the you that is closer than your own breath. The you that is not bound by identifications with this or that characteristic, this or that success or failure, this or that thought process. The you that is connected and one with the creative impulse of life.

※

Of course it isn't possible to be a creative person without conflicts. Resistance and self-doubt resound in each and every artist. But it is also true that constriction limits the flow of life and creativity. It isn't easy to let go of long-held restrictive patterns in the body and mind, but it is possible to make small and steady movement toward easing these patterns. It is possible to find the spaces within. You can space out and go where the fruit is waiting. You can listen deeply into the silence, as William Stafford advised, and with the help of that quietude, hear the whisperings of inspiration. He called them threads. And he gently pulled, or coaxed, them into being.

Experiment:

Try a few of these experiments. Turn the radio off in the car for ten minutes. For God's sake, turn the TV off, too, once in a while. What can I say about the cell phone? Lay it down. Take walks without headphones and listen to the interplay between silence and sound. Notice how silence is always present despite the din of the city. What do you feel without all the stimulation coming at you? Feel your body moving through space. Can you relax into it? Does the space feel alive, nourishing, threatening? Pay attention to spaces. Look at photos taken from the Hubble telescope. These do me in. Imagine yourself as the eye of the hurricane. Still.

When you are writing, pay attention to how hard you are working. Are you straining? Forcing the action? Lorrie Moore once said she was happy if she wrote nine lines a day! I know this is hard if you are trying to make a living or are forced to meet a deadline, but try to ease up a bit. Constriction is the worst enemy. Every thirty minutes or so, take a minute and breathe in ten good, slow deep breaths through the nose. Make a sound with each exhale, maybe a soft *ah*. Try to befriend the negative space of your psyche. What are you resisting? What wants to come out into the space of your story that you won't allow? Close your eyes and be still. Listen for the quiet. Listen for the small rippling of the creative murmur. Remind yourself that you don't have to make it all happen. You have help. The fertile void is on your side. Spaciousness is holding you and creation's wild imagination. Holding it all. _____

PART III

The Theater
of the Mind

11
The Theater

REALLY GOOD POETRY IS SO VERY DIFFICULT TO MAKE
because it goes beyond story and meaning to resonate with
the deeper, more mysterious realms of our existence. At
its best, it reflects back to us through our experience of sound,
movement, and space something ineffable that speaks in such
a way as to help us know ourselves more completely. We are
invited to live from that generative, musical place in relationship
with all that is.

You are a poem. Epic verse. Plenty good enough. Poetry
yearns to bring us back to that understanding. Yet somehow
we keep falling asleep. We reduce our vastness to small and
broken pieces—many of which sparkle. But all too often we are
marooned on islands of self-reproach. Our inherent expansive-
ness shrinks and contracts into hardened shapes separated from
the real luster of our lives. How can this be? What happens that
distorts luminous presence into complicated bits of suffering?

In order to come to an understanding of these big questions
and develop a true appreciation for the complexities of the mind
that make an artist's life the emotional equivalent of a marine corps
obstacle course, come with me and explore the inner worlds of our
psychological life. Let's go to Broadway! There we'll take a back-
stage tour of the strange and beautiful labyrinth the British analyst

Joyce McDougall coined "Theaters of the Mind." I love this part and hope you do too. It is full of intriguing ideas about the mind and its remarkable ways. Try to be curious with this material, remembering these are maps and approximations, not to be taken as the gospel truth but rather to enhance awareness of unconscious processes that influence our behavior and our emotions.

The reality of the mind/brain, conscious/unconscious field is far too complex and dazzling to pin down with language and theory. However, a familiarity with these ideas allows one to play with and understand the bewildering ways of relationships and personal experience so as to offer oneself and others more support and empathy. Beyond that, an understanding of the dynamics of the internal worlds is tremendously helpful in working through difficult terrain in the creative process. For instance, why do so many writers resist doing the revisions on a manuscript or suffer painful self-doubt following completion of a project? The Theater of the Mind opens the door of insight into these and other mysteries of an artist's life.

⚜

Freud referred to the unconscious as uncanny, and it is just that. Although that wasn't the most scientific or sophisticated word he might have chosen, it does capture the nature of the intrapsychic world and the strange ways in which lived experience is stored in the psyche as autonomous states of consciousness. Our most intimate experience of this wild and unpredictable world is the dream. Less familiar to our understanding is the startling process whereby unconscious material is returned to our lives as reenactments of past relationships and as powerful internal crosscurrents of emotion.

McDougall brought Freud and the workings of an uncanny unconscious to the stage and illuminated both the dramatic and the marvelous nature of our human psyche. The French comedian Raymond Devos sums up her thesis quite simply, "One always hopes to become someone only to find out in the end that one is several." There you have it. While our conventional cultural viewpoint tells us we are one person—someone—in fact we are many.

Our inner universe is populated by galaxies of what we might call characters. These characters—friends, siblings, parents, old teachers, our first love, enemies—the entire cast account for the strange variations in mood and behavior that confound us. Why did I piddle around all morning when I was so eager to work on my novel? How come I was looking forward to seeing my friend and then when I got there, I felt detached? What is going on when I feel like a competent writer one day and a loser the next? We are baffled because many of the players on the interior stage are hidden. We have never been introduced. Therapy is all about making those introductions.

Think of your psychological world as an Escher drawing that has come to life in 3-D: numbers of people are moving up and down stairways that go nowhere and everywhere, that appear and disappear from nothing, that change direction in a flash and don't really lead anywhere. It may remind you of Nasrudin's plight the night the town's watchman finds him wandering about in his village late at night. "Where are you going?" These stairways are populated by an endless array of personalities, and they are all you going in many directions at once!

In the Theater of the Mind, people move and morph in the blink of an eye. They come and they go, sometimes replaced by characters that have been absent since the first act of the play—grandmothers, teachers, a first pet, a forgotten neighbor. Many of those that appear are strangers you have never met. Aspects of yourself that have never seen the light of day or had the chance to develop. Perhaps an aggressive side of you, perhaps a performing one. Some are representations of otherness that you might fear, admire, or envy. If you are feeling some vertigo, don't worry too much—the Theater of the Mind can be dizzying.

We are populated by secret selves. Unknowingly these secret agents engage in dramatic reproductions of historic roles. Many of our unconscious templates serve as good models for living and relating. Many don't serve so well. Familiar comedies and tragedies are enacted with uncanny resemblance to the original story and often end with remarkably similar and painful outcomes. Déjà vu all over again. Marriages deteriorate into frustrating battles of sibling competitiveness. Father-son relationships take on the same rejecting tone as the previous generation. Loving relationships morph into a distanced and cold standoff reminiscent of an unfortunate mother-daughter disconnect.

Our subjective world is every bit as bustling as the center of a large city, a beehive of rehearsals, reruns, and grand stage productions. It is remarkable that we feel any cohesion of that which we call *I*. It is staggering how that *I* can get tossed around in day-to-day life. But in the end it is fascinating how the entire grand fireworks show of psychic energy works toward the restoration of integrity within the personality and the realization of creative living. And in the life of an artist, the astonishing worlds of inspiration and work merge and excite each other in a magical collaboration of energies we know to be both enlivening and maddening.

❧

This world within worlds, the Theater of the Mind, is home to every facet of you and to all the people, places, animals, and things—living and not living—that have made an impression on you in your lifetime. Yes, your lifetime. You take it all in like a guesthouse, the house of seven gables, a home to the totality of relationships with the world that have stuck and become a part of you: the old childhood friends, your first bedroom, the cat with the funny tail, that cranky teacher, your first lusting, you name it. Just ask your dream world if you think I'm exaggerating.

It is all there informing your creative mind, sometimes rocketing around like a pinball wizard, sometimes stuck for days, or weeks, in the backwaters of depression and dread, uncertainty and self-doubt, anxiety and fear, or any number of moods that interrupt your work. Moods that feel impossibly in control and permanent.

More often than not, the psyche becomes mired in one of these painful emotional ruts as the result of a triggering of what we call an autonomous self-state. An autonomous self-state is a separate state of consciousness that takes shape around a particular emotional pattern and a narrative that defines a particular identity formation. Typically these are the remnants of a hurting child who feels despondent and hopeless about being seen and understood. Because they are easily triggered and act independently, these self-states can be real stoppers. I suffer them repeatedly when imagining a public reading where every seat is taken by my older brother laughing at me and mocking my thoughts. I am frozen in humiliation—struck dumb by the psychic reality of a little brother who feels small and stupid in comparison.

We'll talk more about how to work with the experience of being swamped by such a state of mind, but for now I offer this up as illustration of the ways in which the Theater of the Mind operates. What we strive for is to open the curtain and find the competent, adult self on stage. The writer self, if you will, engaged and turning out pages of work. But the complications of life and the inner world don't always line up that way.

❧

In my profession we call this world the psychodynamic realm. And is it ever. *Dynamic* is a good word because it points to the tremendous movement and energy of the inner world(s). Recently, I've taken to referring to the self as more akin to weather than anything else. Isn't it like that, all the high- and low-pressure moods, the whirlwinds of confusion and overwhelming experience? Days in which the sky is blue and brilliant, and days in which thunder and lightning charge the atmosphere? People poke fun at meteorologists, mocking their mistaken forecasts, but I like to stand up for them and recognize the very difficult task of accurately predicting which way the wind will blow. Lately, it is obvious that I am standing up for you and me, for the unfathomable complexity of a human life, for our mistaken forecasts, and for the basic goodness of every living being.

All right, I know I'm mixing my metaphors. What do weather systems and theater have in common? Please bear with me—there is a method to this madness. The truth is, our society, and even most artists, grossly underestimate the nature of the human psyche and its complexity. Every time you brand yourself as inadequate, you do violence to yourself by overlooking the great mystery and multiplicity of you.

The history of you is staggeringly and miraculously improbable. You should marvel at your existence, not denigrate it. As I mentioned earlier, give Bill Bryson's book *A Short History of Nearly Everything* a read one day (I find it a great antidepressant) and you will be astounded to learn of the astronomical odds that trillions of anonymous atoms plus countless generations of your hairy ancestors have connected and made you. When you think you know who you are, remember that you would be nothing without the trillions of microbes working 24-7 in your stomach.

And what about the mitochondria, those amazing creatures living in every cell of your body, providing the oxidative energy necessary to mobilize into action? Without them, you could not lift your pen. Lewis Thomas, author of a classic book of essays entitled *The Lives of a Cell*, comments on the wondrous mitochondria and then remarks, "A good case can be made for our nonexistence as entities."

Okay, what's going on here? Good question. As we delve into the Theater of the Mind, it is a good idea to work the ground of our preconceptions. And the most basic, the most unquestioned, of all our psychic premises is that you and I are separate entities.

Different people. Individuals alone trying to make it in this world. In his poem "Ars Poetica," Czeslaw Milosz puts it bluntly when he writes, "The purpose of poetry is to remind us how difficult it is to remain just one person." So while the Self Project may be earnestly working to craft you into your ideal self, the Theater of the Mind goes on and on making it extremely difficult to shape yourself into the one-person mold.

It is becoming clear that our personhood is constructed by, connected to, and dependent on a vast field of relationships that makes up the big reality of subjective experience. You don't belong in a box. In other words, not only is it "difficult... to remain just one person," but it isn't possible because it is an illusion. And trying to do so, as in trying way too hard to be a successful artist, is the cause of much of our suffering and stagnation in the work.

In the West, the individual is glorified. The neoliberal economy depends on it. We must become good consumers and continuously validate our uniqueness. Moreover, from early on in childhood, we are asked, "Who is your hero?" If you grew up male in America, let's say in the mid-twentieth century, your hero might be George Washington, Abraham Lincoln, FDR, JFK, James Bond, or Michael Jordan. Until recently, there weren't many women on that list. The cultural ideal was decidedly male, strong and independent, exceedingly rational, and with an aura of invincibility. "Bond, James Bond."

This amounts to a thinly veiled attack on women, especially mothers, and the sanctity of interdependent, human need. Our culture honors self-sufficiency and promotes an idealization of the singular, separate self: the superstar, the celebrity, the talented and gifted. Obviously, in this system the masculine is privileged over the feminine and the existence of a fixed, individual identity is given the highest standing. The notion of a self that is porous and intimately interconnected with all life is considered blasphemy. That the self might be discontinuous and actually composed of multiple dimensions is considered craziness.

To suggest that it may not exist at all, as an entity separate from the larger fabric of the universe, is considered ludicrous.

❧

But is it? The Theater of the Mind is really quite extraordinary. It operates at quantum velocity. The architecture resembles an Escher drawing, and a cast of thousands waits for the curtain call. The scenarios spun within that fluid space are as numerous as the stars. It is for good reason the Greeks named psyche after the butterfly: sit down and watch your mind flutter about the garden. Is it a straight path? Not at all. In fact, it moves more like a dancing electron than a stationary neuron.

Freud divided things up like a good scientist. He gave us the tripartite structure of id, ego, and super-ego and the tidy separation of conscious and unconscious states. Sounds more like a prefab house than a grand theater. Which is odd, because that doesn't line up with the "uncanny" nature of the unconscious, nor does it fit with his enduring trust in the efficacy of free association, which is a marvelously unpredictable and flowing method of self-discovery.

His theories were developed before the quantum revolution. Once it was appreciated that light is both particle and wave, our understanding of psyche and the unconscious underwent a radical transformation. And isn't it your experience that the unconscious moves at the speed of light? Don't your dreams morph in a flash? That butterfly moves quickly.

Uncanny, fascinating, and complex as all these phenomena may be, the oddest, most mysterious and freeing of the many ways to think about mind and self is to consider the startling multiplicity of our nature. The Greeks and Hindus have it right: we are one, and many. Perhaps because we live in a monotheistic culture that shapes and defines the parameters of what we believe to be real, it is especially difficult to come to terms with the plurality of the self. From this perspective, an identity crisis is really the opening to a much broader type of existence. Light and being won't be pinned down. Neither should we.

We have a term for these varying experiences of self: *self-states*. This is a theoretical name for what we know as the varied moods that rise and fall during the course of a day. They are like beads on a necklace. Which one is the real you? The optimistic artist, the defeated writer, the enthusiastic painter, the envious member of a writing group? What makes our inner world so complicated is two things: first, each mode of consciousness has a certain amount of autonomy to its existence, and second, each can play off of another like a pinball game. This gets very exciting when you consider the possible permutations of the relationships circulating through past and present, internal and external.

⚜

My hope is that understanding the psychology of the inner theater helps put the not-good-enough self into context. The story of a fixed, individual self is the underlying closed narrative of our time and the structural edifice for the tale of a defective self. The not-good-enough self is wallpapered in shame and repeatedly given the primary position in the psyche. An ironic twist, that one. While the self is as fluid and dynamic as the world's weather systems, and while it is as multifaceted as the most auspicious diamond, the defective self is rigid and singularly structured into a fixed identity: feet in concrete. While the big self defies definitive explanations, or the identification of a certain beginning, middle, or end, the small self, the self of shame, insists on absolute knowledge of its essence and lack of worth.

The Theater of the Mind performs day and night. Where does it get the energy? Our task is to make sure that all the characters get on stage and are able to talk to each other when necessary. The big story must be told, and the shame that binds us to the loneliness of the small story must be released. It is possible, through therapy and meditation and community support, to do so. Make your story more complete, understand the spaciousness that holds it, and tell your story to those who will listen with open arms.

Experiment:

Try these on for size:

- Write down four or five self-states you inhabit that seem to be out of your control: perhaps a jealous you, a rebellious teenager, a child wanting to be taken care of.
- Give a name to the bad self, and maybe an image. When you meditate, try to locate the bad you. Notice that the bad you is the feeling of shame that coheres around the story line of defectiveness.
- Feel the shame. Breathe into it and try not to fight it or run away. Do your best to relax into it, crazy as that may sound. Soften your body and lean in. What do you experience?

Try to enjoy the multiplicity of you. Try to recognize and enjoy the many characters that are you as well as the rich, varied inner world that is your own living theater. Next time you admonish yourself and say something like, "What's wrong with me?" pause. Pause and question yourself, and the assumptions you hold about this *me* you keep referring to. Ask yourself what part of you is trying to assert itself in this behavior you don't like. Make it a practice to pause, and give some room to your inner self so that it may breathe and talk to you from its depths. Remember what the great Persian poet Rumi wrote eight hundred years ago: "I stand up and this one of me turns into a hundred of me."

12

The Script

MY FRIEND HOWARD WASKOW DIED A FEW YEARS AGO. Howard was a big, brave, and blustery fellow with a laugh that could have come from the lungs of Paul Bunyan. Howard and I grew up together in the late seventies when we were reincarnated as psychotherapists. He had left Reed College where he taught American literature, and I had left the wayward life of a hippie as described by James Michner in his book *The Drifters*. We met in Gestalt therapy training and were friends for the next thirty-five years until his untimely death in 2012.

Just before he died, Howard asked me to help with the production of his last book, *Homeward Bound*. *Homeward Bound* is a beautiful work that integrates Howard's love of literature with memoir and the art of psychotherapy: you won't find another book that includes the richness of those three disciplines. Thankfully, he got to hold a galley copy in his hands a few days before he died. He was so proud of his work. You should read it sometime—it is vintage Howard, full of wisdom and the incredible generosity of his spirit, which was devoted to helping and teaching people how to live a more satisfying life.

I learned so many things from talking with Howard. We walked around Laurelhurst Park near my home and talked sports, writing, and therapy, usually in that order. Howard wasn't a Buddhist, but he was one compassionate dude. One of the most important bits of wisdom I learned from our talks had to do with self-forgiveness. Howard saw many patients who were intent on pathologizing and blaming themselves for their problems and their inability to live happy lives. As I said earlier, it is common to have a narrow view of one's life that maintains the notion of a defective self, but Howard taught people to think of their situation with more depth and sympathy. He said we are all born into the second or third act of a long, long play. In other words, it is no surprise that we are lost and have our troubles— the script of our lives was up and running long before we arrived on stage. Of course we stumble and fall.

Actually, I think Howard, quite uncharacteristically, understated his position. You and I entered a maze of activity and psychodrama set in motion generations ago. We took our first breath of air, for better and for worse, from the collective psychic accumulation of many lifetimes. This is our psychological inheritance. If the unconscious is uncanny, then the capacity of family networks to transmit the beliefs and attitudes of past generations to the new arrivals is astounding. There is an old adage in the psychotherapy literature: trauma and psychological pain that are not processed will be unconsciously transmitted to the next generation.

Scary stuff. I think of my father's terrible grief at the loss of his mother when he was only sixteen and the accompanying bitterness toward his father, who he accused of negligence in her medical care. Prior to that, his grandfather had lost nearly everything of the family farm, which was a considerable piece of land, and the family had been forced to move into town defeated and ashamed even before the Great Depression devastated the majority of rural America's economy.

There weren't many psychoanalysts practicing in Indiana back in 1929. Painful emotions that are buried and put away tend to leak like toxic waste into the vulnerable and unsuspecting psyches of children unequipped to understand the language of the body. Why did my father always look so sad? This is not parental evil or abuse; it is an oftentimes tragic psychic law that, while advantageous in passing on cultural and familial traditions, is poisonous when infiltrating the tender psychology of young ones. Is it any wonder I have felt shadowed much of my life by a depressive weight that stubbornly attached to my psyche?

What family doesn't have a track record of something similar? Step into Eugene O'Neill's play *Long Day's Journey into Night* and you will experience the suffering of an American family resulting from generations of repressed emotion and conflict. Since our society abandoned most rituals intended to soothe the soul of its anguish, mental defenses such as the radical denial of feelings have been the only recourse for abating psychological pain. They work. Sort of. But as Gregory Bateson said, "Your slip is always showing." Forgive the gender reference, but the point is that severe repressed feelings are not entirely shielded by defenses like denial and dissociation but permeate the entire atmosphere of mental and emotional life.

What this adds up to is enormous confusion. Children are bewildered when their perceptions are not validated. Why does my dad look so unhappy? Is it because I'm such a disappointment? Why does Mom look so happy and then scream and jump a foot in the air if I so much as drop a spoon? What is she afraid of, and why is she pretending she's not? Should I be afraid? For children, these are realities that burden the psyche with the riddles of generations past living on in the emotional transactions of the present.

※

Life is confusing enough, is it not? The circulation of what is known but not felt is bewildering to a mind trying to make sense of a world permeated by invisible, unacknowledged emotional debris. In his book *The Shadow of the Object*, the analyst Christopher Bollas refers to this psychological paradox as "the unthought known." Bollas goes on to talk about the myriad of ways the family teaches and transmits what he calls "the rules of living and being." Families and cultures throughout the animal kingdom establish these rules. However, human society is a wee bit more complicated than our mammalian neighbors. The laws of living and being tend to become terribly confusing and, more often than not, contradictory. Two of the more common and detrimental of these rules tend to be "Don't feel" and "Don't need." And what is the ultimate enforcer, the all-too-efficient terminator of unwanted emotion and dependency? You guessed it. Shame. What a stopper.

R. D. Laing, the revolutionary Scottish psychoanalyst, called the phenomenon of family/cultural shackles "the politics of experience." What is acceptable and what is not are laid down early on in subtle and not-so-subtle ways. Strange as it sounds, we are not in need of a lecture; "Don't be angry. Be a good girl and take care of your mother" and similar injunctions are communicated nonverbally through modeling, the language of the body, and the absence of certain transactions. In Ohio, for instance, I never heard anyone ask for help. If you spoke proudly of something you'd accomplished, you might encounter a disapproving frown because one of the golden rules was "Don't brag."

Every regional culture has these norms, as does every family. When these customs become rigid in the service of restricting emotion or unconventional behavior, the consequence is the creation of emotional and psychological knots. These knots become embedded in the body and defy simple techniques for loosening and untangling. People often come to me underestimating what it takes to get free of their psychological distress. The cultural demand to "get over it" perpetuates the original learning, which tells us not to feel.

※

The script is living and dynamic, less audible than your heart-beat but just as influential. In psychotherapy, you develop an ear for such things. You can hear the chanting in the background. The script was written before you developed eyes to see and ears to hear, but like all scripts, it must be revised; rewrites and edits are the stuff of our lives. Without editing the script, we are prone to either repeating the original norms of family and culture or radically opposing most rules. Either way, we maintain the tie to the past. Facing our heritage brings the subtleties of our conditioning into consciousness and makes being open to change a real possibility. And, we hope, it promotes compassion along the way for the uniquely puzzling and remarkable story that is yours and not yours alone.

Experiment:

Take a minute to contemplate the drama you were born into. What preceded you? Go back two generations. What was their struggle? What did they worship and dread? Were your parents' lives an answer to that puzzle? What were the assumptions about life that shaped the norms of your world? What were the boundaries of what you could and could not be? Could feel and could not feel? What were the spoken and not spoken rules about what you could say out loud? And to whom? What were the limits on self-expression, on joy, play, laughter, or sorrow? Was anger allowed or forbidden? Where do you get stuck with your writing and art, and does it have a parallel restriction in the family or community culture? What are the conditioned blind spots you contend with? Can't bring sexuality into your writing? Can't make yourself central to the story? Talking these things over with other artists or a good therapist may help loosen up the ties to the historical patterns of living that you learned along the way.

13
Stage and Set

"**A**LL THE WORLD'S A STAGE." SHAKESPEARE SAID IT, and isn't it true? Life, the rising and falling of experience, is the full-time, greatest teacher. No let up. Another great poet, Zorba the Greek, called it "full catastrophe living." And that's about how it is, reeling and rocking till the break of dawn on this great big shifting stage of the present moment. I thought I had a pretty good idea of this wild, untamable ride until Lori and I had kids. Was I mistaken.

It all happens on the stage. Day after day, night after night: "The show must go on!" And it does. You sit down at your writing desk, take out paper and pencil, computer, and say hello to that empty, inviting page and to the particular you that shows up: confident, doubting, eager, resistant you. All that appears within your experience—and all that doesn't: Where is it now? Why doesn't inspiration happen at your command? Why does it show up at the oddest time, unbidden when you don't have a pen and paper handy?

The stage is not discriminating, is it? It allows villains, victims, heroes, and nobodies to enter and stand, to walk and play their parts. We need to do the same. Allowing in what may come: emotions, fantasies, thoughts, dreams, and memories. The wanted and the despised, the planned and the crazy intrusions:

the entirety of the Theater of the Mind, the whole chorus line. The stage says yes to all of this. The light and shadow. The props and curtain. Can you do the same? Can you say yes to your whole self? You will need it.

The stage holds the show. It is the foundation. The ground. What is your foundation, your ground? Be careful. If you are lost in the Self Project, your ground may be becoming a best-selling author. Uh-oh. Is that solid ground? Is that a stage that will hold you steady? Take a minute and contemplate this. What is your support? Other writers? The discipline of a writing practice? Meditation? A mentor's wisdom? What are you standing on? Dreams? Fantasy? Past success? Maybe it is the love you feel for writing.

Whatever it may be, ask yourself how solid it is. How broad is your stage? How deep? When I began writing, I took William Stafford's advice and wrote a poem every morning. I did this for ten years. I can tell you, this is a mighty fine stage. Thousands of poems, most not worth a damn. But the stage doesn't care if it is the first rehearsal, opening night, or the final performance. It doesn't care if the lights are out and the seats empty, if the actor is a star or a fill-in. The stage accepts what may come. Do you?

The stage gives meaning to space. What takes place within that space is the drama that makes the world turn. Who enters that space, and what do they do? What is spoken, what is felt? What is born, and what dies?

❦

From the perspective of the Theater of the Mind, the notion of psyche is expanded and the curious dynamics of experience are illuminated. We no longer consider mind a solitary entity turning out thought at the will of a separate individual. This was a formulation shaped by the metaphor of industrial productivity. It has become clear that psyche is profoundly relational, interconnected, and very, very quick on its feet. It's a little like the old Xerox typewriter with the whirling typeset ball. Remember those dinosaurs? When operated by a speedy typist, they could spin like excited electrons around an atom. Your psyche is many times that fast. Take self-talk, for instance. Isn't it incredible how quick on the draw self-criticism can be? It strikes in a flash. Some days it seems our platform resembles a trapdoor and the smallest error or slight sends us falling to the dungeon.

The multiplicity of internal characters inhabiting the stage of the self leads to different questions. Rather than focusing on the content of a given internal voice, we can ask, "Who is it that is speaking?" and "To whom?" For instance, a disapproving mother might be speaking to a vibrant little girl in subtle or not-so-subtle ways to curb her budding sexuality. The various parts of the self are in continuous communication, or at least potentially so. It is staggering to discover that some of these conversations have been going on for years, if not generations.

From this viewpoint, you are the stage. Yes, you. And the task is not to eliminate these voices and characters but to bring them fully onto the stage. Let the set change. Let it be the kitchen in today's world; let it be the garage in yesterday's; let your mantra be "Include, include..." It is a lot like playing hide-and-seek in the dark as a kid. Then, we hid and waited for the chance to dash home free before being tagged and eliminated from the game. Now we get to call, "All ye, all ye in free!" for ourselves. Every expression of you is valuable. Even the ones you are in the habit of forsaking.

> All the world's a stage,
> And all the men and women merely players;
> They have their exits and their entrances,
> And one man plays many parts,
> His acts being seven ages.

Please forgive Mr. Shakespeare his gender bias because this phenomenon is not at all gender specific. Not at all. Just the opposite—like a good Shakespearean play, the stage is full of the comings and goings of all sorts of characters, and the set is moving and changing to reflect the context of the drama.

So ask yourself: What is my foundation? What grounds me? What aspects of myself am I trying to exile? Who are my internal villains, and who am I dueling with every time I sit down to write? Is it someone from my writing group who says my stuff is too florid? Is it my dad, who says I'm wasting my time with all this writing? Who keeps coming around knocking at the door? What ancestral ghosts are hovering about, seeking my attention or casting a spell over me?

What can help keep this kaleidoscope of characters and monologues from being utterly overwhelming is meditation. For thousands of years, Vedic literature has been teaching that this wild and crazy show is really the "Play of Consciousness." "All the world's a stage" is transformed into "All the world's your Self." That is, your big self, which isn't actually yours, although you are *it*!

When you sit for meditation, you find that you, the seat of awareness, are the opening in which an infinite supply of characters, images, thoughts, feelings, memories, and conversations abide. Try to stop them. Go ahead. You cannot. But you, as awareness, as the knower of experience, can watch and marvel at the cast of characters that flows, like an epic poem, on and on and on through innumerable stage settings.

Why bother? Because in the process of sitting for meditation, two things happen that are invaluable in an artist's relationship to the not-good-enough indictments handed down by the ruling court in this psychodrama. (By the way, this "drama" is completely deserving of a compassionate touch, not the "Oh, she's such a drama queen" contemptuous slur we hear so often today.)

First of all, thanks to a meditation practice, it becomes possible not to take the internal dialogue quite so seriously. When the righteous critic in your head says you suck, a space opens up that allows for you to either laugh, be curious, or say, "F you." You get better and better at recognizing this as fabrication and not reality. You can inhabit this space. Live in it and you will not be jettisoned into the trance of self-loathing.

Second, in meditation the experience of consciousness and its attributes begin to speak to your heart. You recognize something of yourself that has always been there but you never noticed. You have been asleep. You don't have to make everything happen by yourself. You don't have to overwork your brain and figure it all out, as so many artists feel they must. It isn't all on you—you are held by the very creative force you love. This inner self, this presence that is so fundamentally you, is abundantly full of love and creative energy. This is the constant, ever-present stage, the "groundless ground of being" that holds past, present, future, and all creatures great and small in its limitless and unbounded mind.

I'm not making this up—it is my direct experience, and it can be yours. When you find this essential you—the ground of your being, which is love—at that moment the shroud of shame begins to dissipate. It is now a real possibility to pick up that pencil and write with true freedom and inspiration, unimpeded by the Self Project.

Sound too good to be true? Like a fantasy or like religious dogma creeping in? Not so. There isn't anything you have to believe or have faith in other than your direct experience.

Experiment:

Try sitting with yourself and paying attention to the *I* that is you but is not painted with ideas of gender, age, or the usual narrative labels. Try sitting with the bare *I am* of your existence, the sense of presence that is so close. Try to find the edges of that *I*. Rupert Spira has a nice way of talking about it. Think of a page of written material. We are conditioned to fix our attention on the printed letters and words, taking no notice of the white page that is the background. Consider your essential self to be analogous to the page: ever present, the space in which the story of your life happens. Try reading the poetry of the Upanishads, which elaborates on the nature of that space and describes it as unconditioned being, love. See if you can imagine this space as the universal stage of existence and this time of your life as the set piece that gives definition to creation's desire.

14
The Actors

NEEDLESS TO SAY, THERE ARE SCORES AND SCORES OF "players" on the stage. So many people, so many relationships! It takes a mighty big stage to hold all the actors, past and present—family, friends, neighbors, schoolmates, teachers, employers, fellow workers, casual friends, friends of friends. Phew. How can all those players fit inside this three-pound brain? If you wrote out a program of the players in your cast of characters, it would stretch halfway to the moon!

I exaggerate. But not by much. You see, within this marvelous, confounding, and complex psyche of ours—which, you will remember, is dynamic and many faceted—every part of you, each facet, has a unique relationship with all other aspects. Moreover, each has a relationship with the characters mentioned above, who themselves are a complex arrangement of the many people in their lives who influence their personalities. All of this is somehow neatly bundled in an elaborate network of relationships and stored in the iCloud of what we call the mind. Is it any wonder we get overwhelmed?

If you remember your high school math and the laws of permutation, you can quickly imagine that the number of relationships may indeed stretch to the moon. And you can also appreciate why we are more often than not colliding with each other like bumper cars at an amusement park—except that lots of the time, it isn't so amusing. In fact, it can be downright bewildering and painful. Unless, of course, you're Shakespeare in a prankster mood and you have all sorts of folks running around on stage confusing one person for another.

Let's consider an example most people can relate to. You arrive home for a family visit, perhaps a birthday or holiday, feeling relatively settled and okay with your life. Within an hour of walking in the front door of the old family house, you feel twelve years old, stumbling about and panting after the approval of one or both parents. Or maybe you feel invisible until a familiar game of sibling rivalry breaks out over dinner and you find yourself in an all-too-familiar, ridiculous argument with your big brother. Now you feel really lousy and baffled as to how you could have regressed so far, so fast.

The needy twelve-year-old who shows up is what I am calling a self-state. Each self-state is a singular bit of consciousness characterized by a particular emotion and a corresponding story line connected in relationship to a significant other. "I feel small" and "I am inadequate compared to my big brother." These self-states are like trances, automatic and reactive states of consciousness that can envelop us in a cloud-like stupor that is very difficult to shake. Do you recognize what I am saying? Can you write down one or two self-states that are particularly common to your experience?

Let's examine a mood common to all writers and artists: self-confidence. Don't think for a minute that great writers don't suffer moments of broken confidence. (If you do, consider that you are under the influence of a particularly blinding self-state.) Listen to what Norman Mailer said, "In one mood I thought it was terrific, and then in another I'd think, Oh you don't f*#$ing know how to write!" And you might wonder, how could as fine a writer as Alice Munro not have all the confidence in the world? But here is what she once said: "I've always had a lot of confidence mixed with a dread that this confidence is entirely misplaced."

Clearly even the most accomplished and celebrated authors are vulnerable to mood swings that contribute to insecurity. More than indicating a personal flaw, this reality reveals the power of the self-states residing in our psyche. What we know as self-talk is just the edge of this phenomenon. What is much harder to know is the full dimension of self-states that govern our feelings. We have learned that these moods are not generated by an isolated cognitive event—which is what negative self-talk appears to be, such as "That's the worst poem ever. So trite, so sentimental"—but are in actuality unconscious conversations with important figures in your life. They are relational systems embedded in the mind, living psychodramas going on behind the curtain of awareness. You might be in dialogue with an internal father telling you to get a real job. With another writer criticizing your work for lack of depth, with a sibling telling you you're dumb. Possibly with a cultural value of your native community warning you to play it safe: "Don't stand out!" "Don't blow your own horn." The list is miles long.

The result of these varying self-states is astonishing. They can be triggered by the most minute details and move at lightning speed when set in motion—"Why didn't my friend respond more enthusiastically to my book proposal?" In a flash your partner turns into a dominating control freak. Faster than the speed of light, you become the tyrannical father you vowed never to be. Where did the loving guy go? What happened to the kind parent you know yourself to be? It seems this can't be happening! You may scratch your head and say to your fuming sister, "How did you get that from what I said?" It is as though we are living in separate realities, and in a very real way, we are.

Communication is an astounding accomplishment because the psychological reality we are endowed with resembles a broken mirror reflecting multiple images of self and other. For every character that walks out on the stage, a hundred different representations may emerge. Finding what is real in yourself or another and making empathic connections is not a gimme. In fact, intimacy is such a treasured event precisely because it is so challenging. We long to be seen and known but often feel alone and misunderstood.

※

Relationships are the spice of life. The intimacy that develops between people who know and respect one another is a beautiful, beautiful feature of human existence. And yet, we all know how derailed even loving relationships can become. Close friendships rupture and end. Intimates become strangers. How can this be? Why can't we get along? Why are connections so fragile?

One reason this is so is because of the susceptibility we have to projecting our inner constellation of important figures onto the faces of loved ones or people of importance, like a boss or an editor. Similarly, we are vulnerable to experiencing the very people we love as we might have experienced family members or old friends from the past. The colleague in our writing group who is trying to make a helpful point becomes the attacking sister who used to torment you. The publisher who wants you to rewrite your book becomes the rejecting boyfriend from high school. The silent space that grows and grows while waiting for a reply from an agent becomes the abandoning father of childhood.

The external world mirrors the internal. In fact, when I am working with adults in psychotherapy and things are going badly, I consider descriptions of life experiences as a sketch of internal stagings. This doesn't mean stressful circumstances aren't real, or that bad things don't happen to people. Of course many unfortunate and hurtful things occur in our lives, but even then, those happenings are colored to a significant extent by the overlay of meaning lodged in the unconscious library of this grand theater.

No wonder Woody Allen is confused by his relationships. I am too. People come and go in our lives, and they leave a mark.

Some are good and nourishing; some aren't. Every day the curtain goes up and the show repeats. Day after day. Some shows play for a long, long time. In the Theater of the Mind, it is a cast of thousands, like one of Hollywood's epic films. Some have a particular talent at evoking the feeling of not good enough, and they show up in one form or another until we work it out. Until we accept ourselves and can extend a hand of friendship to our vastly complicated and imperfect but beautiful self.

The good news is, the stage welcomes all comers. Everyone belongs. Everyone. The villain, the supporting cast, the protagonist—everybody! Including you and each and every aspect of you. Even the ones you wish would disappear. Even the despised parts you have tried to banish, amputate, or ignore. Perhaps it is the needy you, the possessive, jealous, vengeful, or ambitious you—the unwanted. Even those. All of it belongs, despite what the foot soldiers of the Self Project might say. Better still, all of it, the whole of you, will help you be a better writer. Will help bring your characters to life, allow your poetry to sing and your storytelling to connect with universal emotion and experience. Sing along now, "All of me, why not take all of me?" Nice song.

When you read a good story or look into the heart of a fine painting, what happens? What draws you into a well-structured plot? What captures you in the painting so you can't take your eyes from it? Connection. Consider the many twists and turns and unexpected developments of an Agatha Christie mystery. Why are her stories so hard to figure out? Because she was a master at obscuring the true villain by creating a baffling collage of events and relationships that make suspects of all. The reader is then compelled to find the connection that links the unfolding story to the murderer. The Theater of the Mind makes mystery of life and relatedness. We find ourselves in a grand ecology of interconnected hearts and minds.

✳

When you come right down to it, my life is not much different from yours. Artists too often lose contact with this basic truth. They can feel so alone. So isolated. Then, rather than feel supported and connected to the great gathering of creative individuals around the globe, they set up camp in a process of comparison and evaluation. Those evaluations invariably lead to negative spiraling of self-accusation and the arrival of one of the most erosive of feeling states: the dreaded jealousies.

I wish I were a songwriter. I wish I could write like John Prine and another John, as in Lennon. Yes, I admit, I am envious of their talents: the phrasing and images, the rhyme and rhythm of their lyrics: "Sitting on a cornflake..." Don't you know that feeling? Where did Lennon come up with that stuff? "Pools of sorrow, waves of joy, possessing and caressing me." Oh yeah, I have felt possessed once or twice, and have been caressed by a love so tender I could barely allow its touch. And I have adopted a line from John Prine that I sing out loud every time I open a thin envelope from an agent or publisher. It goes something like this: "Felt about as welcome as a Walmart Super Store." You know what he means.

I can handle the envy I feel for Prine and Lennon because they are superstars and most of what I feel is awe and admiration. But when a member of my writing group or a peer gets published, look out. More than likely, that's envy shakin' and bakin' in my stomach. I guarantee you, a lot of Portland writers were green with envy when Cheryl Strayed hit the jackpot with her best-selling memoir, *Wild*. You better believe it. Envy strikes deep into the vulnerable heart even when the subject of that envy is a lovable person like Ms. Strayed.

Envy is a first cousin of shame. Behind the envy of another's talents lurks a terrible sense of personal deficiency. Remember in the movie *Amadeus* when Antonio Salieri, knowing he will never be Mozart's equal, is driven mad by the genius? Insanity proved preferable to the unbearable feeling of inferiority that plagued his ambitious mind. Shame and envy are molds that grow in the humidity of the not-good-enough environment. Shame is the passive, internalized emotion—except in relation to the self when it can be quite vicious—while envy looks outward toward others and is usually more aggressive and painfully reactive. When we are in the grip of envy, others become mirrors to our shortcomings. Comparisons abound and the inner self contracts mercilessly around the disdain for the other who has what you want. The certainty of your own inadequacy is confirmed. Envy will eat you up.

It can also turn aggressive with counter-phobic attacks to spoil what is perceived as good. An embarrassing example of this erupted in me when I was in sixth grade. A very talented boy in my class, whose name I cannot remember, was asked to make a chalk drawing on the blackboard the last day of school. Of course I had no consciousness of the feelings of inferiority growing inside me, nor of the yearning to make art, so when our class Leonardo completed his drawing, my initial awe quickly morphed into envy, and before I knew it, I found myself at the blackboard erasing what I could not erase inside.

This scene still horrifies me. If I could remember his name, I would try to track him down on Facebook and apologize profusely. The power of envy should not be underestimated, and my behavior makes it clear how envy can lead to actions that compound the sense of a *bad me* growing within. Boy, did I feel bad for ruining his drawing. Boy, did I ever feel humiliated in front of my classmates.

Why am I going on about envy, and what does that have to do with the Theater of the Mind and actors? Only because shame and envy contaminate our relationships, and relationships—internal and external—are central to our lives. For better and for worse, we are engaged with any number of relationships, past and present, actual and internal. Our minds are overpopulated: as densely crowded as a New York City sidewalk. Even if you are an introvert and shy away from contact. Even if you are isolated at your writing desk, yours is a social brain and will be pin-balling through multiple characters in your life, past and present, throughout the day. A very talented writer I know reports dreams that are packed with people, and he rarely ventures out of his house. It's Grand Central Station at rush hour in our psyche, even while we sleep!

Envy will eat you up; it operates a bit like acid, burning whatever it touches, and it erodes something of the generative connections with other writers and artists. In short, it compromises learning in the way described by Lucy Adkins and Becky Breed in their beautiful book, *Writing in Community.* In fact, community becomes dangerous when shame and envy rule the internal world. You can bet it's present when members of a writing group either shrink and disappear or become overly critical. The process of self-grading and judgment infiltrates relatedness as a continuous comparison to others and judgment of the self. Shame compares your work to an ego-ideal and fills the self with a feeling of insufficiency, while envy compares the self to the triumphs of others and always falls short. Unless, that is, one defends against this pain by projecting all shortcomings onto the world. We call these people art critics.

If you can work with envy, wrestle with it and the not-good-enough stamp, envy can be transformed into respect and admiration and an opening to the help of a mentor. If not, any need for support will evoke terrible feelings of defectiveness and the anxiety of imminent attack. Shame can be transformed into a healthy, realistic set of goals and aspirations: I will write one page a day before work. If not transformed, you won't feel worthy and shame won't let you get anything done, appreciate the value in your work, or take in the support of others.

Learning from others is a must if your art is going to grow and your life to blossom. These difficult emotions can be accepted and embraced, soothed and held with sympathy so that they are not destructive and creating more of the same. They needn't be an allergen that interferes with learning. But it can take a lot of work to get there, and the way is difficult because it passes through the pain. Sorry. You can't dodge it.

Experiment:

Take a minute to reflect on envy. Try to be curious about it. Feel the nuances and edges. Notice how it morphs in and out of shame. Who do you envy? Why? What qualities do you find in others that you desire? Notice how you compare yourself in ways that make you feel small. How you are grading yourself incessantly. Feel the contraction—lean in and try not to push it away or even overcome it. Just be in it and feel the contours and nuances of the contracted state of being. Are you breathing? Is it shallow? Now try to relax and breathe in fresh air. Slowly. Softening with each breath. Say, "Ah," out loud as you exhale. Try to settle into your body. Soften. Breathe into the contraction and soften as you exhale, giving that tension up to the surrounding space.

How is that? The great thing about meditation and practices like this is that you can do them anytime. Even if you have only a couple of minutes between appointments or you're waiting for your partner in the grocery store parking lot. Little moments of standing in the contraction and giving the tension up pay off. You don't have to go to a weeklong retreat and meditate for ten hours a day. Give it to the surrounding space with each exhale. You'll be surprised.

15
The Curtain

FOR THOUSANDS OF YEARS, SOME SAY AS MANY AS TEN thousand, Indian yogis have been studying consciousness and the nature of the mind. Think of that. With nothing but their own experience and the power of awareness, these scientists investigated the raw stuff of existence and consciousness, discovering gold as they probed the erroneous conclusions of thinking. They realized that much of what we believe about ourselves is false, and they named these mistaken identities illusions, or more broadly, the influence of Maya. But they went beyond our misconceptions to describe and map out the unfathomable terrain of consciousness.

Some five thousand years ago, this knowledge became shaped into what we now know as the Vedas. Vedantic literature, especially the Upanishads, slowly found its way to the West and pollinated the minds and imaginations of many of our greatest ancestors; Emerson was deeply influenced by the intellectual power of this work, as was Yeats, who wrote some remarkable poems illuminating the transcendental nature of his experience. Listen to this:

> While on the shop and street I gazed
> My body of a sudden blazed;

And twenty minutes more or less
It seemed, so great my happiness,
That I was blessed and could bless.

The Vedantic yogis discovered that the nature of the self is joy. Yeats is ablaze with it. So why is it that I'm not feeling it? How come I struggle with feelings of inadequacy if my real self is a great happiness? What the Vedas come back to again and again in describing our predicament is the notion of ignorance. We are asleep. We have forgotten who we are: our eyes are covered by a veil that obscures the reality of the inner self, causing suffering and confusion to dominate our experience of living.

This veil is made from a subtle fabric. Elusive as a dream. In fact, it is often compared to dreaming in the poetry of the Upanishads. "Life is but a dream," says the modern Vedic lyric. As such, there is much we do not see, or experience. The joy blazing within our bodies is obscured, and for many, the inner self feels either crowded or empty. Indeed, when the curtain lifts on the big stage, it reveals emptiness. However, that empty stage is a spaciousness that is full and fertile, and as yet undisturbed. Only then do the characters begin to enter and set the drama of human affairs into motion.

The curtain is the servant of mystery. We tremble with anticipation as it slowly rises above the stage. What drama awaits our eager senses? What twists of plot and happy endings? Even if it is something we've seen a hundred times, like *The Nutcracker*, our hearts quicken as the curtain makes way for the revelation of the grand set and the particular lighting that will invite the human story to unfold. We are witness to magic because the lifting of that curtain frees our perceptions and, in so doing, reveals the world in all its beauty, allowing for the great communication between creation and consciousness to take place.

❧

Psychologically, other curtains are drawn to keep out unwanted feelings and thoughts. You are endowed with some clever, built-in ways of limiting pain. Unfortunately, these methods create more suffering and estrangement within the inner world. Vonnegut wrote that the whole problem of human folly and destructiveness begins with this big brain of ours. This incredible three pounds of fatty tissue. He has a point. But it is also a remarkable feature of the brain that it can, without being asked, perform magic every bit as spellbinding as a David Copperfield show in Las Vegas.

If called on, it will erase history as though it never happened, hide upsetting knowledge in a corner of the basement you never knew existed, hold dangerous aspects of self at bay every bit as efficiently as the Hoover Dam. And, most startling of all, this three-pound mass of tissue can transport a fragment of the conscious self outside the body to the safety of distant space like a Star Trek beamer.

The clinical terms for these dynamic processes are as follows: denial (old faithful), encapsulation (hide and don't seek), repression, and when all else fails, dissociation. There are others, but these four horsemen of the battle attempt to maintain some equilibrium in the psyche and prevent the self from being utterly overwhelmed by sensation, emotion, or knowledge of unbearable realities. They lead the way in fortressing you against internal and external impingements. Let's take a peek at each of these one at a time.

Denial. Man's best friend. Sorry, doggies, but you are a distant second to this tried-and-true servant of amnesia. This is the window shade of defenses. The curtain that comes down and stays down. At its best, it allows one to take action in a dangerous situation without being paralyzed by fear. At its worst, it is a radical severing of the connection with what is real: a violent psychic evacuation. It is the Nazi's saying, "History is bunk." It is the collective forgetting of our country's history of slavery and the effect that had on the psychology of African Americans.

If you grew up in the Midwestern states in the years following

World War II, you lived in an atmosphere of denial. It was as though loss and suffering had been eliminated from human experience and the plentitude of middle-class successes had erased the traumas of the previous twenty years. Though fear and suspicion were everywhere, those emotions were silenced.

While the pain of the Great Depression and the horrors of the war were still fresh in the minds of ordinary people, it was as if the atrocities the world endured never happened. It was a bewildering time because the very emotions and worldview that survived those terrible years were denied at the same time that they so obviously shaped the rules governing how life was to be lived thereafter.

On a personal level, we see denial growing more and more dominant every day. Whereas individuals once wore black for up to two years when mourning the loss of a loved one, in today's world, the expectation is to "get over it." When my brother died of cancer a few years ago, I was devastated and grief stricken for a long, long time. I can't tell you how many people looked at me as if to say, "When are you going to get over this and get on with your life?" Of course this isn't really a question, is it? It is a club. I, too, was leaning on denial. Time and time again, I'd catch myself thinking I could just pick up the phone and call my brother. What do you mean, he's gone?

Of course some of the most destructive expressions of denial happen in relationships when resentment or hostility are denied but acted out. This is crazy making. So, too, tender feelings or emotional neediness can be denied for fear of being exposed and humiliated. My father's denial of his pain from growing up poor and losing his mother was so profound that he never once told a story from his past. It was as though all that had been amputated.

Denial is a detachment, a disconnect, whereas encapsulation neatly displaces the untouchables of inner life in a psychic storage vault and throws away the keys. Feelings and needs are put away, in the cloud of the unconscious, hopefully never to be seen or heard of again. Some would say they are placed for safekeeping until the coast is clear and the psyche can reclaim them back into the wholeness of self-organization. Christopher Bollas calls this "the unthought known." We know it's there, but we are not disturbed by the knowing.

Well into my twenties, it seemed like nothing could make me angry. I got along with everyone and never objected to much of anything, until I cracked up in my mid-twenties and entered therapy for the first time. Then anger and rage gushed from my soul like a thunderstorm over the Great Lakes. I was flabbergasted. Where had this amount of feeling come from? Where was it stored? Is this me?

As an encapsulated part of the self begins to emerge, it can be quite alarming to the ego-ideal. Jeez, maybe I'm not such a good guy after all. Maybe I'm selfish and greedy. More often than not, that which has been encapsulated and held hostage comes out clumsy as a toddler learning to walk. Lots can get broken. One can be embarrassed falling on one's can. But, as is true for all rejected facets of self, these abandoned feelings and qualities can be brought back into the fold and made accessible.

Repression was the favorite child of Freud's work. He built his theories around it, particularly around the Oedipal complex and what he called "the return of the repressed." Sounds like a horror movie. And indeed it is, if you are told your deepest wish is to run off and marry either your mother or your father! Who wouldn't leap up from the analysand's couch and run for the door?

The concept of an Oedipal drama has been vastly reworked as psychoanalysis has evolved into more of a relational system. But the notion of repressed material is still a vital and useful part of an understanding of the psychology of self-regulation. It involves an exile of sorts, only instead of Oedipus being sent away at birth, important aspects of our human self are banished. In this regard, the return of the repressed is seen as a movement toward wholeness and the psyche's way of bringing home lost and abandoned parts of the self. Come in from the cold, dear ones.

An obvious example of this repression, which is managed by

cultural controls as well as familial "rules for living and being," is the situation women have faced for centuries. Until the late sixties, that conditioning included the repression of nearly any form of aggression and sexuality or, for that matter, the assertion of self in the pursuit of competencies in the workplace. My mother was a perfect example of a very intelligent, capable woman restricted by the norms of postwar America. She lived under the tyranny of niceness. Always polite, seemingly gracious at all times, she wore a constant smile, which masked a very real dissatisfaction and loneliness she never could free herself from.

For so many women of her time, the capacity for personal power was, like Oedipus, sent away at birth. It too involved exile: banishment from the kingdom. From the earliest days of life, the rules of living meant being forbidden the expression of powers that only men were entitled to own. Sadly, these attributes withered on the vine and were replaced by culturally sanctioned ladylike stereotypes. Women became caricatures, estranged from their core self. Repression is a slave master, imprisoning the True Self and binding the False Self to the garment of persona.

⚜

Experiment:

Let's take a break before we head into dissociation. Psychologically, the curtain creates a blind spot, a hole in the notion you have of yourself. These defensive veils are meant to be self-protective, and they are. I sometimes say, "Denial is underrated!" Sometimes it is a very good ally. However, if overused, our defenses make us into Swiss cheese, compulsively in search of connection with our missing pieces.

Think back on these primary means of defense. Do you recognize them in yourself? What have you denied in your life? What was denied in the community you were raised in? Was it grief? Fear? What traits in yourself do you deny? Are you passive-aggressive at home? Are you ruthlessly ambitious? And what have you encapsulated? What emotion has been driven into hiding? What have you been unable to bear and therefore buried away? Hopelessness? Loneliness? Perhaps a secret joyfulness you felt the need to hide and protect so as to keep it yours? Have you repressed certain aspects of your sexuality? Have you driven neediness across the border?

Take a minute to contemplate these questions. Sit with yourself and be honest. How can your characters be real and believable if you aren't? Try to feel into these uncomfortable regions. Find a good therapist if it feels too hard to do alone. But try, try to feel, breathe into, and say yes to whatever you find. Pull on the threads when you write, as William Stafford taught, and when you examine yourself. Call yourself home. It's amnesty time. Everything is needed to be a writer and a person.

Last but not least, we have dissociation. I saved it for last because it is the big one: the uncanny ability of the brain to outfox terror. It is the power of the powerless. Here's a little story to show you what I mean. In 1975 I moved to the Pacific Northwest from New York and was hired for my first job teaching preschoolers to read. Given a week to prepare before the start of school, I set out for what was then the very beautiful Spirit Lake at the base of Mount St. Helens. Spirit Lake would be buried in ashes from the eruption of St. Helens a few years later, but at the time it was a magical, spacious lake surrounded by forest in the shadow of a great volcano.

I pulled into the campground that first day and barely took notice of the signs alerting the public to the nightly visitations of black bears looking for snacks. Besides, I was certain the only real bears lived in the Bronx Zoo. Talk about denial. After a light dinner, I started a fire and lay back on my backpack, happy with myself and enjoying the darkening sky and arriving star-light. Fellow campers walked nearby, heading to the commode and other campsites, so I thought nothing of the sound of more footsteps heading my way until I opened my eyes to see a rather large black bear heading toward me.

Remember, I was lying on the ground, head on my back-pack, watching sparks from the fire ascend and disappear like so many universes. If the truth be told, I was also swimming in the twilight zone of a certain weed that had traveled all the way from Columbia for this moment. So, I opened my eyes and saw that beautiful bear maybe five feet away ambling toward little ol' cookie-town me. And what did I do? Did I jump up, grab my rifle, and take aim? I had no rifle, not even a broom. What did I do? I closed my eyes. What did the bear do? He walked up to me, put his nose to my head, and sniffed me over real good. Thank God for Clairol Herbal Essence Shampoo. That didn't smell too appe-tizing to him, I reckon, and he soon turned and walked away.

Holy crap, you might say, what did you feel when he was sniffing your hair? The answer: nothing. That's right, nothing. That is dissociation. A moment or two later, I heard a scream from a neighboring campsite and heard the screamer cry out, "A bear! There's a bear in the campground!" This brought me out of my dissociative trance and convinced me the experience was not a marijuana-induced hallucination. I stood up and walked toward the adjacent campsite with a stupid grin on my face and told them what happened. They looked at me kind of funny, and I walked away mumbling to myself. When I got back to my fire, the reality of what had happened hit me. What did I feel then? I was, in the words of the great Ken Kesey, "shakin' like a dog shittin' peach pits!" In other words, I was, if not terrified, real scared.

It took me years to recover. Every camping trip, I was certain a grizzly was about to climb into the tent with me. I resorted to singing old Beatles tunes to diminish the anxiety. That big fear is what dissociation removes—or rather, dissociation removes the person from unbearable (sorry for the pun) experience. I felt nothing. In fact, I wasn't really there. You don't have to be taught how to dissociate. Sexual abuse victims find what is left of consciousness on the ceiling watching. War survivors tell tales of out-of-body experiences and the ensuing difficulty finding their way back home to the body.

Actually, they don't want to come home because the body is now the enemy that threatens to overwhelm the system again with the feelings that drove them into dissociation to begin with. If it is as difficult as it was for me to recover from one close encounter with a fairly satiated black bear, you can imagine how very hard it is to reenter the body following repeated traumatic episodes.

❦

Why go into this stuff? What does it have to do with writing or the vulnerability of the artist? Plenty. Writing is about connecting—with a reader, with yourself, and with the creative spark trying to get your attention. These defenses are primarily about disconnecting, from pain, fear, and overwhelming states of distress. Writer's block and other interferences with a fruitful, creative life aren't so much about being lazy, or lacking talent, but are more often than not complicated emotional constrictions that limit access to inspiration and the important inner resources it takes to complete projects.

Many artists come to me and say, "I'm not disciplined enough." I hear this as a camouflaged attack on the self. They might as well say, "What the hell is wrong with me? I'm a lazy good for nothing." A number of these writers cannot build the necessary structure into their lives that it takes to make progress on the writing project at hand. While these are common problems, a thorough analysis usually reveals difficulties with fears of all kinds, not a character flaw.

Writing is dangerous. So is being alive. There are periods of time in the writing of a novel or a memoir when the material triggers long-held encapsulated emotions: deep pain may be touched and shameful feelings uncovered. One terrific novelist I worked with oscillates between the competent author that he is and an emotional wreck of a little boy caught in a system that disregards his emotions and doubts the reality of his own perceptions, leaving him utterly alone with his chaotic inner world. He is a great craftsman and very competent writer, but when he turns to editing his work and reads through the material, he is a vulnerable child overwhelmingly impacted by the very world he has created.

What to do? Try not to poke yourself with moralizing or pathological labels. Watch out for words that tend to define you as flawed. Be empathic toward yourself when you can. Things are not what they appear to be. Most of all, please be curious and remember that this is not easy, and that those moments we derail from the process, or disconnect from ourselves, are complicated emotional clusters. Ask yourself what is up. What might be hidden from consciousness in the moment? Perhaps being stuck is better than feeling a troubling emotion from the point of view of the self-protection system. Rather than curse yourself, make a gesture toward relaxing into your body to feel what is there, what is real. What is, in Christopher Bollas's words, "the unthought known," and what I call the unfelt, but always near, emotional truth.

※

The Vedas and most sacred literature remind us again and again that the veil to our real self is the most opaque of all. A curtain of ignorance obscures the light that is within. Of all the ambitions that human beings embody—wealth, success, long life, the great American novel—all pale beside the realization of that light. What do human beings want? In the heart of darkness where the deepest of longings lives, it seems we want the curtain of our self-delusion to rise and allow our light to shine. That light moved John Lennon to sing, "And we all shine on, on and on and on and on." This is the great possibility of fine art, meditation, and human longing: to burn through all curtains and veils leaving the radiance of being to burn brightly and create in us what it wishes.

16
The Lights

NELSON MANDELA IS OFTEN CREDITED WITH HAVING written, "Our deepest fear is not that we are inadequate. Our deepest fear is that we are powerful beyond measure. It is our light, not our darkness, that most frightens us." Recently I discovered it was actually Marianne Williamson who penned those words in her poem "Our Deepest Fear." Mandela must have said something similar because anyone trying to uplift the spirits of the downtrodden will encounter an entrenched resistance to intrinsic power and light. In fact, it is my conviction that the fear of inadequacy and the fear of the light within are not separate phenomena but two expressions of a big anxiety about being fully here in the world.

Is it really our light that we are most frightened of? Really? Is it our bigness that gives us pause? You might argue that there are any number of competing fears: the fear of dying, the fear of losing a child, the fear of homelessness, the fear of poverty. The list is long. And what about the fear of not finding an agent, or of getting bad reviews? Those anxieties can ruin a night's sleep. Whether the fear of our light is truly our deepest fear doesn't matter, but I can tell you that when working with artists on the matter of self-worth, I inevitably encounter a very strong fear of embodying their big, full self. What often comes as a shock is how instrumental you and I are in limiting ourselves in the world. Blame comes to a screeching halt, and we stand face-to-face with our own bewildering compulsion to erode the competence and radiance of our True Self.

Freud said, "The truth will set you free, but first it will make you miserable." We don't want to be miserable, which is to say, we are at odds with freedom. One contemporary Oedipal interpretation has it that the fundamental human tendency is the turning of a blind eye. Reality is too much. Look away and don't see what is happening right before your very eyes. Though we are conscious beings, fear motivates us to dim the lights and hide in the shadows of unconsciousness. How often is this the case? How often do we really stop and look into the face of poverty? How often do we hold back from giving our full self to the canvas or that blank page? And how often do we shrink from the expansiveness that is the nature of being? Too often.

I have patients that are so talented, so bright and capable, and yet they are filled with self-criticism and doubt. Why is this? Why can't they see themselves clearly and move ahead toward their goals? Why choose to diminish the power and gifts that lie within? From the vantage point of the Theater of the Mind, realizing your bigness is not a simple thing. Often there are internal figures who are at odds with the fulfillment of the True Self. One of the most talented artists I have worked with feels tremendous anxiety whenever he approaches the full expression of his gift. We have tracked his fear down to an internal mother who doesn't like boys. Any success he might create is met by her disapproving view of him as "too big for his britches." This brilliant man shrinks from his work, fearful that it will result in more feelings of rejection from the mother whose love he yearns for. When you encounter this psychological reality, it becomes clear just how fruitless the common admonition to "grow up" really is. In the Theater of the Mind, past, present, and future coexist like moons orbiting Saturn. Little boys and little girls accompany us to work every day.

One solution to the problem of self-restriction involves a different kind of light, the light reflected from a mirror. We need mirrors to reflect our real self. We need readers to help recognize the strength and weakness of our writing before we send it out. We need a good editor to help shape it into the best manuscript it can be. This is especially true when we are stuck in the quagmire of self-doubt. Sometimes it is just impossible to see ourselves clearly: we are lost in the dark and yearning to be known and seen.

Children develop and feel most secure when they are seen and appreciated by parents and the community. This is a different light, the sort of light reflected from a mirror that is crucial to the cohesion of identity and a secure sense of self. We need good mirroring in childhood and adult life to reflect back who we are so as to validate the broad range of what we feel and think. The need for recognition is pivotal for grounding in the True Self. Without it, we are much more susceptible to getting lost in the dark forest.

Conversely, when the mirror is clouded and the reflection is distorted, as in the patient I just mentioned, a terribly painful confusion sets in. Light is not available to facilitate growth; bewilderment and disfiguration creep in. My dad said I was lazy. He was wrong—I was fighting him every step of the way—but I believed him. I internalized his declaration. My patient internalized his mother's depression and the sense that boys are bad and must be contained. These are disfigurements that sculpt the body of a bad me within the psyche.

Take a look at the paintings of Francis Bacon and you will get a feel for the gross disturbance in self-recognition that can take over one's psychic representation. Bacon was not exaggerating! It took me years of therapy to alter the image of myself as a skinny, weak, and pathetic kid. My clients see themselves in ways that literally give them nightmares. It is staggering to me how distorted the self-image can be in wonderfully creative and intelligent people. Often the need for mirroring and affirmation is seen as a terrible weakness, ugly and unlovable: we wake up soaked in shame.

This is one reason writing in community can be so helpful—because we are afforded the possibility of being seen and appreciated, not as superstars as the Self Project would like it, but as competent, talented writers working on our craft. Sadly, these opportunities are also fraught with the possibility of humiliating exposure. Competitions can emerge that derail the working function and stimulate defensive postures. Perhaps my Self Project wants me to look smart in the group and my feedback comes out as critical and superior. In some cases envy, fear, and the need to prove oneself can take over and dissuade members from the real risk taking that can advance the work.

However, a good-enough writing group is ripe with occasions for the group to act as a supportive mirror and for the light that comes from others to illuminate what is good about the project as well as what needs work. To be seen in a good-enough way is healing. The experience breaks down rigid, not-good-enough characterizations that have calcified over the years and allows new notions of self to form. Even more importantly, being seen leads to the internalization of that process so it may be possible to recognize yourself in a more complete and accurate way. At the least, the light of awareness can now be your ally, so when the old labels are applied, something in you will balk and say, "Hey, wait a minute, I'm not a loser. I can make mistakes."

✂

With that in mind, let's take a closer look at awareness and the light of consciousness that illuminates the stage. Isn't it thrilling when the curtain rises and slowly the set and stage are illuminated by the spreading of that precious light? This isn't a book about consciousness, exactly. Nevertheless, any study of the self is incomplete without a look at the nature of awareness. It is the radiance of awareness that illuminates the theater of your existence and holds experience just like a blank page holds all the written words. According to the Vedas, it is consciousness that reveals the world, becomes the world, and knows the world.

Psychotherapy depends on awareness to get in touch with the feelings stored in the body, to uncover basic belief systems that organize the self, and to identify the unconscious meanings that motivate repetitive behavior. Surprisingly, psychotherapy until recently has done very little with awareness itself. It was left to schools of meditation and the mindfulness movement to pollinate Western therapeutic modalities. Today these fields are definitely moving toward each other at a rapid pace and are, in many ways, overlapping and joining.

Meditation is primarily about the nature of consciousness and less about the particulars of consciousness, which do appear to be infinite. At some point it becomes a fascination of awareness to be aware of itself. Thereafter, everything changes. The Theater of the Mind, once so compelling and captivating, becomes less so, and the mind evolves toward amusement and curiosity. The stage is lit up, more and more is known, but it is now enough to marvel at the spaciousness that holds the drama and the light that illuminates it.

Characters come and go, the settings appear and disappear, but consciousness does not. The light that is open and receptive is present and unaffected by the arc of stories taking place within. Not that these stories are meaningless, not that these stories don't move us, but they no longer have quite the serious hold they once might have. Because we are more identified with awareness, they don't stick so much. They don't define who we are. We can learn to relate to story as we probably did as children, with curiosity and amusement. In other words, the story of the deficient self does not take us over. We don't grant it the authority of reality.

This is a radical change, and in my mind, the ultimate and necessary treatment of shame. Shame must, and will be, dissolved in the light of being that is radiant, creative, and loving. Let me give you an example. I recently completed my second novel and sent it off to my best friend and a professional editor. Neither was very complimentary. Crash. The free fall is on, and faster than you can say, "I told you so...," one wave after another of that yucky, slimy, smelly shame goo is covering me, tarring and feathering my insides. Nowhere to run. No escape. I am slimed.

At this point, the temptation is to fix it. To push the shame away. To make myself feel better as soon as possible. The temptation is strong, very strong, to fight off the shame or to overcome it with heroics. Sound familiar? Sure, we all engage our wounds in this manner at the same time we do our best to hide from others the stain of our imagined flaws. It is inconceivable that a remedy exists within that has the power to dissolve such a formidable force. But it does. These feelings are like vampires. They suck the blood out. And when you fight against it, the entanglement is compounded. Remember when in *Star Wars* the emperor taunts Luke Skywalker, inviting Luke to give in to hating and even killing him? He knows if Luke succumbs to those temptations, they will possess him and the emperor will have won. It is like that.

Shame is like sticky glue. Tough to undo once it is on your skin. So what is the remedy? What can free the self from shame? Psychotherapy is a great help, and the process is largely dependent on reversing the internalization of badness that has taken place over many years' time. Often this involves the activation of anger that may have been split off early in life. Anger is an innate protest against injustices such as the various forms of abuse we are familiar with.

In this case the active stance is one of "Not me!" Not me, in the sense of establishing a psychological boundary against the infiltration of culpability for offenses committed by others. Protest enables one to undo, and actively expel, the tendency to take responsibility for failures both large and small. Too often you may feel it's your fault for just about anything that goes wrong.

One of my patients cringes with guilt and shame for causing "a bad day." The feeling of badness and the certainty of ownership gets so large, it becomes the water we swim in. Deconstructing this habitual narrative not only lightens the load but also creates the beginning of a feeling of spaciousness within that may lead to freedom from the terribly painful identification with blame.

Powerful as therapy can be in resolving some of these issues and giving folks a new sense of their inherent goodness, I have found that it doesn't go far enough. This is where spirituality and psychotherapy need each other. Therapy can release feelings and clear room within for an inner life less encumbered by accumulated stress reactions, but it doesn't fully connect individuals to the absolving light of consciousness that is your essence. Even a good therapy cannot rid the mind of its vulnerability to make bad of experience. Shame and other disturbing emotions, strong as they are, simply cannot hold up when surrounded by the power of being.

Meditation helps connect you to the inner presence of being, to the inherent goodness of your nature and the generative energy of this big life. This remedy lovingly takes in the negativity of the mind and dissolves it into more fundamental particles of being, like the sun burning off morning clouds on a summer day. It is forgiveness on an experiential level, not the cognitive level. It is mercy that is not bestowed by an external superpower, but is the result of contact with and immersion in the warmth of your inner self. That shimmering reality of being that waits for you and calls for you. This isn't a nice idea, or a religious belief system—this is the direct experience of meditators for thousands of years, and it can be yours.

17
Drama

DRAMA RHYMES WITH TRAUMA. SO THE NEXT TIME YOU find yourself judging people for the drama in their lives, remember that where there is drama, there is sure as shootin' a backstory of trauma that makes sense of it all.

One could argue that the human race is suffering from post-traumatic stress disorder. It is alarming when you consider the list of symptoms that describes this condition and how closely we the people match it. We oscillate between states of hyper-vigilance (thank you, Starbucks) and passivity, between emotional flooding that leaves us overwhelmed and emotional detachment that leaves us deadened. Our lives resemble a bipolar disturbance, or what was once called manic depression. And aren't we that—running from here to there, always in a hurry, striving for this or that but looking so unhappy and depleted?

We walk around in perpetual states of fear, anticipating the arrival of doomsday. Catastrophe is just around the corner. Or we exhibit a state of mind-boggling denial as we go about our lives oblivious to the atrocities of the world, past and present. Have a good day. What's more, many are possessed by a lust for retaliation. For a payback on crimes committed, in some cases, hundreds of years earlier. Do you remember Kurt Vonnegut's sardonic words from *Slaughterhouse Five*? "Revenge is the sweetest thing in life."

Drama rhymes with trauma, and what is happening on stage, in the Theater of the Mind, is more often than not driven by what my line of work calls the trauma response. What is this trauma response? As I mentioned earlier, with trauma the nervous system gets stuck in one gear. Rather than moving fluidly between the parasympathetic and sympathetic nervous systems, depending on the situation at hand—that is, from relaxed to alert and back to relaxed—a nervous system overexposed to fear and stress resets to a chronic position of anticipation. You've seen animals, no doubt, tense at the scent of a predator: ears go up, head pops up, hair on the back rises, and this pose is maintained until the signs of danger have passed. Under chronic states of arousal, the vigilance of this survival mode becomes fixed and the organism does not revert back to rest. We call this a hyper-alert defense, or more commonly, dis-ease.

In other words, the radar is set and a chronic sense of readiness to face danger is established. Typically, those unfortunate enough to have endured traumatic experiences adapt by either becoming hyper-alert and ever ready for what they believe to be the inevitable return of the traumatic agent, or they collapse under the weight of the stress and dissociate from their feelings and perceptions altogether. These alternatives point to the two major fears that plague the person afflicted with the trauma response. The first is a certainty, bordering on panic, that the emergency event will repeat itself at any moment. Thus the need to brace the body and scan the environment for signs. The second fear is organized around the belief that feeling—that is, overwhelmingly terrible feelings—will have no end: emotional flooding is timeless. Hell is forever.

We have become familiar with various sorts of ugly traumas that are all too common for children, women, and soldiers. Abuses of all sorts, once denied and hidden by my parents' generation and even in psychologically aware communities, are today recognized as painful realities. Sexual and physical abuse, war atrocities, and natural disasters are well documented as producing PTSD in children and adults alike.

What is less understood, but perhaps just as prevalent, is the truth about traumatic states of loneliness and aloneness. Failures to engage children, attune to their emotional world, or fulfill their need for relationship lead to similar kinds of shutting down and dissociation from the core self. These children develop a chronic sense that something is wrong and, being children, they internalize that discord and attribute the fault to themselves. Because, as Winnicott said, experience becomes traumatic when the individual can no longer process or manage lived experience. In other words, when the self is overwhelmed and unable to bear the feelings engendered by given situations, the trauma response kicks in. Chronic loneliness is one of those situations that can become traumatic over time when children are either neglected or their inner worlds go unrecognized.

Trauma changes everything. It is now recognized that it can even alter DNA structure. Bad news. The good news is that every day we are learning more and more about how to intervene and help with this condition. It is difficult to recover one's natural balance, but it is not impossible. In therapy you can find a safe place and person so you can learn how to release the terror and overwhelming feelings held in the body. With yoga you can go even deeper and release chronic tensions at the core level. And in meditation you can learn to find the safe place within that has been eclipsed by terror. You can learn to find the place of inherent goodness within. You can find rest. Peace. You really can.

❧

The Greeks were pretty good at drama, and they seem to have understood trauma as well. Oedipus was a traumatized baby after all, sent away from his mother at birth by a father crazed by the oracle's words. Greek theater put the major themes of human life on stage for all to see and ponder. Implicitly, everyone was forgiven for being human. There's nothing wrong with you for having these problems, after all. Everyone suffers. It is the price we pay for having a psyche, you might say. Today's culture makes people feel strange and singular if they don't have it all together. This is our modern malady. How terribly sad it is that we are made to feel defective for struggling with what are very human dilemmas.

Trauma is such that our personal dramas become amplified and primarily organized around being safe or making ourselves look or feel okay. This presents obvious problems for writers and artists. Art that is fresh and alive requires a daring leap into the unknown, which may not feel safe. What will catch me? Averting risk and trying to constantly prove oneself don't usually make for good writing. Salinger didn't spend an hour finding himself every morning so that he could prove himself worthy. That striving comes from the place of the not-good-enough scenario. And when trauma is in the body, that scenario comes alive in spades.

Some people choose a partner who seems completely unthreatening and end up feeling bored or emotionally isolated. Others are counter-phobic and need danger to feel alive or to convince themselves they aren't afraid. Imagine if your motivation was the same with writing. The best writing is dangerous. It asks of us to give so much. If you are carrying unprocessed traumatic emotions, you may be averse to exploring the deep recesses of a character's personality for fear it will trigger your own unprocessed feelings. At every opportunity to go deeper into the heart of the story, you may veer off and opt for safer terrain. There are many variations on this theme. All of them get in the way.

Is it any wonder writers suffer from writer's block? Is it any wonder human beings build well-fortified walls when the anticipation of emergency calls for radical protection? It is hard to be original and fresh, to write with abandon when suffering from anxiety attacks brought on by the proximity to pain of this nature. It is hard to take risks when one is in the habit of distracting from core emotions and fearful of penetrating into deep feelings. Many writers back off then and stop before they go too far, leaving the work thin and shy of its potential.

Be honest with yourself. If you have suffered something akin to what I am calling trauma, if you identify dissociative tendencies in yourself, if you have big anxiety crashing in for no obvious reason, stop and get some help. Now. It's out there. Your life and writing will benefit enormously from finding a skilled therapist to work with and alter the trauma response that is controlling your emotional world. It is tough work and extremely painful for periods of time, but it works. I have worked with so many artists who sabotaged their work. Who did not lack talent but lacked the internal space and support to hold all the tensions and feelings engendered by the work.

Maybe you are one of these talented people who can't get going. Maybe you get going but can't follow through and finish, or you have a dozen projects going and never move deeply into any of them. Maybe you discredit the work so completely that it ends up on the shelf. It's okay. You aren't alone, and you aren't hopeless. You are constricted and might possibly be shackled by the trauma response. Find someone to help you undo the knots, and I think you'll find the work will flow.

✤

What may also flow is self-compassion. In coming to understand trauma, a genuine appreciation for what you have experienced develops and lays the ground for radical acceptance. All the things you have done over the years to try to manage the pain, all the strategies for avoiding the pain, all the crazy behaviors begin to make sense. Self-reproach is replaced by a benevolent, "Of course."

As the nervous system calms down, it is possible to find rest. Sometimes it has been years since the body and mind have truly slowed. Once you are able to feel without being overwhelmed, and to rest without feeling endangered, it becomes possible to experience spaciousness within. Entering spaciousness is remarkable for anyone and especially for those who have suffered traumas and known only constriction. For them, space itself is dangerous, identical to the terrible pain threatening to invade and take over the inner self. Anxiety insists on escape and on the creation of alternative realities that protect the core self from feeling overwhelmed with fear or despair. Perhaps it's hiding in a TV stupor or a cloud of marijuana that facilitates dissociation and pacifies the traumatic feelings. There are many escape routes to choose from.

What is stolen by trauma is the peaceful ground of existence. The ease we see in the bodies of our relatives in the mammalian world. The relaxed nature of children growing up in nurturing environments. Trauma survivors know no peace. They only know the angst of trying to stay ahead of the traumatic feelings chasing them down. Space is foreclosed. It must be opened and made accessible to those who have suffered the worst of our species' assaults on inherent goodness. Spaciousness is the doorway to being, and the bounty of being is what people long for. It is home, and the wellspring of what has been called compassion, forgiveness, mercy, and acceptance. Shame and its gang of bullies cannot survive there. They go running like Dracula from sunlight. In that space your inherent goodness glows.

Can trauma extinguish that light and deliver us to perpetual darkness and despair? Sometimes. I wish it weren't so. But trauma is not invincible. Many bright and dedicated people in the therapeutic community are working overtime to come up with methods of treating trauma that are effective at giving people back their body and soul. It is beautiful, heartening work. You can look into Peter Levine's bodywork for one. And the yoga community is expanding everywhere and offering help to nervous systems stuck in that mode of chronic tension. So there are many resources at hand to help you regain the natural intelligence of your body.

These are great resources, and we are fortunate to live in a time when trauma is understood and help is available. And still, the greater resource is you. You and that wild hunger to create, you of that inexhaustible desire to express what cannot fully be expressed, you and your terrible/wonderful yearning to be free—the you that cannot be named but is present and has been present all the days and nights of your life—that you wants for home. Wants for peace. Wants for love. Wants for its light to shine on and on and for the Theater of the Mind to come to a place of resounding joy where all the players on stage and all the members of the audience share in the experience of a connection that transforms self, space, and the world into vibrant delight.

PART IV

The Materials

18
The Pencil

NASRUDIN IS SITTING IN A TEMPLE WITH HIS FEET UP ON the altar. A priest enters and says, "Nasrudin, this is a holy place. Take your feet off the altar!" Nasrudin turns and says to the priest, "But where shall I put them?" Indeed, where? Where can you place your feet that isn't holy? That isn't sacred ground?

If this language turns your stomach having been tarnished by the abuses of religious systems over the past couple of thousand years or in your lifetime, I understand and sympathize. While I am still drawn to the beauty of these words, there are days I walk about with a feeling of utter nausea thinking of the cruel history of religious institutions. On those days, and many others, I might turn to America's wise elder, Wendell Berry, for his sage counsel. One such morning I read an interview with Mr. Berry in which he was asked a relevant question about living in a culture in which nothing seems sacred. After a lengthy conversation, the perplexed interviewer asked Mr. Berry, "What is a person to do?" To which he replied, "Treat everything as precious and do what needs doing." Amen. Oops, sorry.

What is precious to a writer? Is it sacred? What can we touch that isn't fully endowed with the spirit of our vision and work? Is it this skinny little pencil or this wrinkled piece of lined paper?

Is it this gnarled old writing table or the creaking chair I'm sitting on? Aren't all these things precious to our daily encounter with the agony and the ecstasy? And what is art up to if it isn't taking the ordinary stuff of life and presenting it in such a way as to reveal the radiant beauty inherent in objects? C. K. Williams, one of my very favorite poets, refers to the poet's difficult and risky task as that of "informing the ordinary with the transcendent." Love that guy!

We're not talking about pretty. Again, in the words of Mr. Williams:

> What I mean by vision, put most simply,
> is the belief in the possibility of a radiance in life,
> a radiance that, beyond all social and interpersonal
> insufficiencies, posits the ability to exist
> at least for some moments in a state of beauty.

Take a still-life painting by Van Gogh or Paul Gauguin or a more classic example by a Dutch master. What happens when you look at that common apple sitting on the tablecloth or in the fruit bowl? Wow! Is the apple moving? Doesn't its existence shine? Isn't it radiant?

If the world is precious, if it is sacred ground, Nasrudin is right—what can we touch that is not holy? If the act of writing and being visited by the creative spirit is not a sacred relationship, I don't know what is.

I grew up in Ohio in the fifties when the only thing precious was security. Okay, maybe the ranch house was pretty special, and the new black-and-white TV. I suppose I could throw in Mom and apple pie. By the mid-sixties the crack in the cosmic egg was breaking wide open, and the doors of perception followed, revealing a world of enchantment waiting to be discovered and adored. And did we ever. Suddenly, everything was precious, even the most ordinary and insignificant of the lot.

The beauty of writing for me is in the transformation of ordinary reality into what I think of as sacred. Actually, it is not a transformation but an illumination by way of holding what is common in the light of art. It is what makes the mundane reveal its radiance, and what makes the ordinary sing.

Take, for example, the pencil. The ubiquitous #2 yellow pencil. I remember coveting my pencils as a kid. I would line them up in neat little rows and sharpen them one at a time until the lead was just right: pointed but not brittle. Even the wood shavings sliding out from the tiny pencil sharpener, even these ribbons of skin seemed important and kind of beautiful. They had a pleasant scent that made them feel alive somehow.

The pencil is such a humble object. So simple and uncomplicated. And yet, think of Tolstoy writing *War and Peace*. How many pencils do you think he went through in preparing his masterpiece? Talk about writer's cramp. Imagine him making the lead point with his carving knife. Can you see that big Russian hand picking up his pencil, snuggling it between index finger and thumb, and beginning to write the first sentence of the day? What could he have done with a MacBook Pro?

In the literary world, the printing press and other advances in technology get most of the glory, but really, where would we be without the pencil? Even though you probably write with a computer, go now and pick up a pencil. Hold it in your hand gently. Feel the wood, the octagonal beveling balanced in your hand. Doesn't it feel just right? Light but solid. As faithful and obedient to your needs as a good dog. Say thank you and turn it between your fingers. Isn't it fine? Really look at it and appreciate what it is and think of all your ancestors of the written word holding a pencil just like yours and preparing to write those precious letters on the tablet.

Take a long look at the lead point. This is where the magic happens. The point touches the paper and, voilà, the page is no longer empty! Little baby marks begin to appear. Curves and slants, dots and dashes—an alphabet, letters lining up to make words, words collecting to make sentences—molecules of thought. And on it goes. With your own hand, your singular handwriting appears. When lead meets paper you show up. You make your point, and we hope what shows up is your very own authentic voice. What Mr. Winnicott called your True Self.

※

And what could be more ordinary, more specifically ordained by this world that loves diversity, than your very own voice? James Hillman, the Jungian analyst and prolific writer, described this phenomenon as the acorn theory. His notion of the True Self held that each of us is endowed with a particular innate expression of the infinite soul that is longing to be given the freedom to develop. Despite all the pressures of family life and society's demands, this acorn self is, from birth until death, seeking to find the space and nutrients to grow into its potential form. The soul knows no hierarchy. Each of us, in our ordinary splendor, has the stuff: the inner materials to make known to the world your very own view of life. You are the creative material to make art.

That's the beauty of it all. You don't have to make yourself special—you have been made special by the force of human life using you for its purposes. When you pick up that pencil and put it to the paper, what appears on the page in front of you is your very own sketchy handwriting—you in all your remarkable dexterity of thought, imagination, and intriguing twists and turns. What is more vulnerable than this personal signature? What is more revealing and lovable?

The pencil is a water wick that leads you to the discovery of creative streams that are not visible to ordinary consciousness. Your pencil has no agenda other than bringing you and paper together in service to the miracle of the written word. And it is a miracle. A sacred happening. Listen to what the Holocaust survivor and prolific author Aharon Appelfeld has to say about our craft:

> I was never capable of writing. Writing is a miracle. A meaningful sentence, a meaningful chapter is a miracle. It was when I began, and is so now.

Be as humble as your pencil, as devout as Nasrudin in the temple, as respectful as Wendell Berry walking about his farm— be a servant to the longing impulse of creativity asking for your help, and the work will happen. Show up every day, like your pencil, and it will happen. At the end of each day, lay your pencil down and say thank you. Say thank you to the artistic ancestors that have pollinated your mind. Say thank you to the common pencil and the miracle you are privileged to partake in. Try this and you will find that Nasrudin is right. Where can you place your feet that isn't holy? The flashes of brilliance, the wrong turns, the dead ends, the exhilarating surprises—the whole enchilada. All of it is sacred unfolding. And it all begins with that first tremulous mark made from the tip of your pencil.

The Self Project will tell you that in order to be successful, you need discipline and genius. Your pencil will tell you that in order to be successful, you need humility and resolve. The Self Project will tell you that success is essential. Nasrudin will tell you, if you listen, that love is essential. Love the day, love your pencil moving across the lines of paper. Love the engagement with the nonsecular and what lies between words. Love the stunning act of communication that connects your heart and mind with that which travels from the sacred land of the unbidden to the hearts and minds of others.

19

The Eraser

RICHARD ROHR IS A FRANCISCAN MONK LIVING IN ALBU-
querque, New Mexico. He has written extensively over
the past twenty years on many of the same topics I am
covering in this book. I like his work because he includes psy-
chological, cultural, and spiritual analyses in his discussion of
the issues of our times. In a recent book, *The Naked Now*, Father
Rohr talks at length about personal development as a matter of
subtraction. Nice little paradox: we grow by subtraction, that
is, by letting go. This runs contrary to the Self Project, which is
always striving to be better by adding on whatever accomplish-
ments or merit badges it can in the hope of one day arriving at
the promised land of feeling special.

If you remember, Baby Suggs, the spiritual leader of the com-
munity of recently freed slaves in Toni Morrison's *Beloved*, says
something similar. She says, "You got to lay it down, lay it down.
Lay down your massive grief, your bitter heart, you got to lay it
all down." We might add, you have to lay down your perfection-
istic drive, all the favorite distractions, you have to lay down the
strategies of the Self Project, and of course, the not-so-easy-to-
let-go-of notion that you are not good enough.

She also said, "The problem with the white man is he
don't know when to stop." This is a succinct and powerful

encapsulation of our problem, and it echoes the economic, political, and psychological analysis of writers like Richard Rohr. How can we know when to stop? What is enough? It is very, very difficult because, as Rohr and others have said, we are hypnotized, conditioned, and actually addicted to the capitalist mandate of more, more, and still more. In Washington-speak, this is known as the necessity of growth. In our day, short-term profit eclipses all else, including human rights and environmental well-being.

Richard Rohr puts it in two interesting frameworks. First of all, he identifies what has become the centerpiece of the capitalist agenda, which is the conditioning of a commodity mind. That is to say, the psychology of unlimited growth depends on the development of a way of perceiving the world, others, and oneself as objects. With this worldview, things are more important than people; rather than loving people and using things, the order is reversed so we love things and use people. As one philosopher said recently, "Transactions are now more important than relationships."

You don't have to look far to see this in action—just walk down any city street and more people will be looking at their phone screens than looking to say hello to their neighbor. The commodity brain is all about consuming, as if we could purchase happiness. Case in point is the iPhone 6. Usually a leader in interesting innovations, Apple has made this new and improved version mostly about being bigger and facilitating ways to buy more stuff. The seductions are everywhere. Surely we can acquire the peace and well-being we crave.

The second of Rohr's major points is that the culture of capitalism is, in essence, a meritocracy. That is, every bit of personal goodness and integrity must be earned. I suppose this is a derivative of original sin in that it implies that all goodness, grace, and value must be won. This is the rat race at its core. And of course it is the great catch-22 of our time: you can go home when you fly your fifty missions—that is, when you fully earn your merit, your goodness, either through achievements or by way of morale behavior—then and only then can you feel okay. As was the case for Yossarian and his comrades, that day never comes. The demand for more does not abate. Your value cannot be proven.

The logical outcome of these forces is greed. In our time, greed has become institutionalized so the major players in the economy now recognize no ethical, cultural, or environmental consequences to ever more accumulation of ungodly wealth. For the first time in history, perhaps, greed—once known as one of the three poisons to Buddhists and one of the cardinal sins to Christians—has been elevated to the status of a virtue. "Greed is good," Michael Douglas said on screen. It seems many people have come to believe this. It's as though God is a capitalist.

✻

Oh dear, this is getting depressing. Who could ever endorse a sacred psychology of subtraction? Who could ever truly believe that E. F. Schumacher's *Small Is Beautiful* might just be the answer to our predicament? Who among us isn't greedy for more experiences, more book sales, more good reviews, more words, more great ideas, and on and on? If you are honest, you will admit to this lust for more. We seem to be insatiable. "Enough" is not a common utterance.

Enter the lowly eraser. That little pink stub at the end of the #2 pencil. That wad of bubble gum stuck on the end of a yellow stick. That big-as-a-giant East African cashew hunk of rubber. The eraser has been around since 1770! It was invented by an Englishman, of course. Prior to its invention, people used their daily bread to eliminate pencil marks. I'm glad the eraser was around when Tolstoy wrote *War and Peace*; otherwise, he might have starved using up his supply of bread for the winter.

In our modern world, the eraser is an endangered species, having been made nearly extinct by that omnipotent delete key in the upper right-hand corner of your keyboard. But the eraser is proving more resilient than many expected. It endures. It does so because it is, of all our writing materials, the most ordinary. The most ego-free. It is the champion of subtraction. After reading my last novel, my editor said I should put it on a Paleo diet and shed about twenty thousand words. Subtraction is where the novel as marble slab becomes a sculpture.

The eraser is the instrument of forgiveness. "Forgive us our excesses..." It is the merciful allowance to start over. To begin anew. We don't have to be perfect right out of the gate—we can erase our mistakes and get it right. I know lots of writers who think they have to make great sentences every time they pick up the pencil. How paralyzing! An eraser is like a good dog that walks up and licks you on the cheek and makes all the bad stuff disappear. Erasers make it possible to let go. Take a bow, little eraser.

❧

I wish letting go were as easy as popular culture would have us believe. This is how it works: the dominant culture annexes the property of alternative movements and sucks the life out of them. It doesn't need to censor anymore; it just incorporates and, in that hostile takeover, squeezes what was new and fresh into submission. I learned this once and for all the first time I heard Andy Williams sing a Rolling Stones song. Help me.

Subtraction is difficult and necessary. In order to get to being and spaciousness, we are confronted with the necessity of letting go of the habitual ways we think of ourselves and the emotional weight attached to them. This is what the author of *Sophie's Choice*, William Styron, said on the subject of writing and letting go:

> It's hard because there are vast baggages and impediments of one's personality that one has dragged through life, which intervene rather than open up

one's creative strategies. They come between one's desire and one's fulfillment.

Styron knew a lot about depression and the work that artists must engage in if they are to be their best. In addition to dealing with emotional baggage, we are confronted with the necessity of laying down any number of preconceptions we have about creating art. This isn't a decision but a moment-to-moment practice. Let me give you an example from the school of "small is beautiful." A common misconception of artists of all types is that insufficient time is the reason for poor productivity. I held to this faulty notion until my wife prodded me into using small chunks of time to write. She kept insisting I could make good use of fifteen to twenty minutes of focused effort. I thought she was crazy, but damn if she wasn't right.

I have a very busy life raising two teenagers, walking the dog, and caring for a full-time psychotherapy practice. But I'm here to tell you, it worked! In writing the novel, as well as this present piece, I've rarely had as much as an hour to sit down and work. More often than not, I worked in twenty-minute blocks, sometimes thirty, but one day I found myself typing, "The End," to a ninety-three-thousand-word manuscript. On many occasions I wrote fragments of thoughts on tiny scraps of paper, sometimes on the back of business cards. A patient of mine does some of his best architectural sketches on napkins at restaurants and coffee shops. We have to erase our ideas about how it works. I'm now convinced that for many, many people, big blocks of time are more a problem than a support. A certain kind of hunger and urgency is very good for the creative tensions necessary to see a project through.

❧

So take a minute to stop reading so you can reflect on the sacred cows in your life. What are you holding on to? What are your hiding places? Your distractions? What kinds of perfectionistic notions do you carry? What needs to be subtracted from your life? What needs to be erased? Are you too wordy, too clever, too cautious, too heady? Do you think you are inadequate or superior? Most of us write too much. We live in an economy of more is better. Never enough. "I have to keep saying it so that you'll get me. If you don't understand me, I must be a lousy writer, or worse, a bad person."

Give it a go: erase some of those extra words. Try saying what you mean in five words, then three, then one. I recently discovered a publishing company to send my proposal to that wants a one-sentence statement that captures the essence of this book. Whoa, from two hundred fifty pages to one sentence! Good writing is good listening, which means it is humbling. Maybe you just don't have it today. You can't connect with the muse. That's fine. Pause, take a walk, nothing's wrong, just relax into the empty spot and take some time. Letting go really begins with learning to relax. It is the first of the three Rs: relax, release, and rest. Accumulated tension is a major cause of writer's cramp of the brain and is often the result of the Self Project's anxious striving. As my seventeen-year-old son so often says, "Chill." Soften. Rest when you can.

Mary Oliver revises a single poem up to sixty times. That's a lot of erasing. I must confess, I don't like to revise my work. Maybe it's the narcissistic feature of my personality: I fall in love with what I've written, and any suggestion of change feels wrong somehow. Perhaps it's the poet in me that feels a direct link to the experience I'm writing about as well as the moment of the writing itself. I have trouble getting back in that moment to connect with what inspired me. Subtraction doesn't come easily. I really don't like picking up that gummy eraser. I'd rather keep writing.

So for me, subtraction, letting go, is in and of itself painful. For others, subtraction is threatening for another reason. Let me give you an example. Once upon a time, when NPR still played music on the morning programs, there was a show called *The*

Piano Puzzler. The object of this game was to identify a popular tune embedded in a musical score made up of a flurry of notes. Step-by-step, a number of notes were subtracted from the score and the contestant was given a chance to identify the popular melody. Finally enough notes were eliminated from the piece that the hidden melody became obvious. How amazing it was to recognize the tune that had been there all along.

Therapy is like this. People come in with a cluster of happenings buzzing around in their psychic field. It takes time to calm the system down enough to remove the distracting elements and get to the persistent theme at the heart of the individual dilemma. In many ways this "tune" is known and not known. But in a very essential way, the clutter is there so that the tune is not recognized, which is to say, so that the emotions and memories connected to the theme remain hidden and encapsulated. Subtraction can be risky.

I once worked with a man who had a million friends all over the world. He was never alone and was constantly pursued by the many people who genuinely loved him. When his wife left him (a major subtraction), he was stunned and the underlying threatening theme song of his life, the one he'd invested so much energy in never hearing, came blasting forth like a boom box. That was, of course, the song of goodbye.

This phenomenon, which I think of as psychological hoarding, is remarkable in its effectiveness. It managed to obscure the primary dread shadowing my patient's life and motivating his collection of more and more relationships. When his wife left him, the well-choreographed arrangement fell to the floor and shattered, revealing a sad, lonely, and frightened little boy. What we suspected was true—he had successfully accumulated and held on to scores of friendships for the unconscious purpose of avoiding any possibility of experiencing loss. Brilliant. And he is not alone in that agenda. Many symptoms, painful as they may be, serve to camouflage the deep anxieties haunting the self. Subtraction—that is, awareness of and letting go of these clever camouflages—allows individuals to face the original pain and restore the self to a greater sense of unity and emotional cohesion.

❧

So you see, we all struggle with ambivalence about letting go. Do we dare face the underlying hurt, fear, or rage? Don't let anyone tell you letting go is a piece of cake or shame you into feeling like a failure because you can't just "get over it." What a weapon that has become. It is easy to subtract with an eraser (though impossible to make a pencil line completely disappear) but extremely difficult when it comes to ingrained mental and emotional patterns. Most people completely underestimate the challenge this presents. In fact, the painfully slow struggle becomes more ammunition in the battle to degrade the self.

As if the mind weren't a big enough obstacle to letting go, American capitalist culture insists on making sure we are forever adding, not subtracting, to the layers and layers of stuff we don't really need. Every day it seems more true that we are conditioned addicts making our way from one substance or thing to another. Like Pavlovian dogs, the stimulus of multiple commodities, from sex to dessert, clothes to cars—the list is endless, by definition—makes you and me wag our tails and chase after the drug of choice.

Notice the staggering increase in opiate addiction among white-collar Americans. "You can have it all" is the piano player's hypnotic tune. When everything is not enough to keep the pain away, well, hand me another Oxycodone, please. Sad but true: America is terrified of subtraction. Fuck the eraser! Full speed ahead into unfettered growth.

And so it goes. Therefore, we must be aware of our situation. Remember, less is more, small *is* beautiful, and the best things in life are still free. What better symbol of the power of subtraction than the little eraser? I hope you find the truth in the age-old wisdom of letting go. Yes, it feels like loss at first, sometimes like defeat, even dying. But laying down all the things we think we are and should be delivers us into the heart of being—into the heartland of the True Self, which is always enough and bursting with creative juice.

20
Paper

There it is, the empty page. Just look at it. Take it in.

Not so fast.   Look.

Take in the space.

What are you feeling now?

Relating to paper is making friends with nothing.

With emptiness.

With yourself.

Your ancestors have been writing for many moons. They wrote on silk and bamboo, bones and papyrus. The making of actual paper began over two thousand years ago in China. Apparently the need to write is etched into our DNA. Get yourself some old paper or homemade linen paper. Hold it in your hands. Close your eyes and feel it on your fingertips. Imagine you are blind and using the sensation of touch to get to know this material you hold. Isn't it precious, this ordinary sheet of paper?

Understand that you are connected, intimately with the thousands upon thousands of writers that came before you. Feel your affiliation with those who wrote the Dead Sea Scrolls. Feel your kinship with the venerable Chinese calligraphers, brush in hand, filling the first pages in the history of mankind with that magical script. This is your lineage. What an incredible community you belong to. Let it soak in like ink on linen. Know that the inspiration they felt, you feel. The imagination they knew, you know. Their longing to communicate is your longing. This is not about you. This is about something much bigger. Do your best to grasp this in your heart and mind. Put down that Self Project for a moment and sit with this truth. Feel the elemental energy moving within. Let yourself be taken with the spirit of service to that energy, to the desire of the muse. Be taken over and used. When you feel stuck, ask that force, that fire of yearning, what it wants of you. Let it take you by the hand and show you the way.

❧

The white page is Sleeping Beauty, and you are the prince. She waits for you, asleep, open and unguarded. She waits for your kiss. She wants to wake up and take in your words, your story, and your heartbeat. She wants to play with you and dance. She needs you to come alive, to communicate. She is the grand invitation: the grand invitation to join the cosmic song, to ride the wave of creativity across the sea. She needs you to open and multiply, to move from one to many: to transform from nothing to something.

Paper. How perfectly simple. Why would you fear it? And yet you do. And so do I. Every morning. Every morning that same anxiety, that same resistance to the empty sheet of paper, seizes my belly. I want to run. I want to hide. I fear that empty mirror. I fear the field of nothing staring back at me. Am I nothing? Do I exist? I fear disappearing into what seems to be an endless landscape. I fear the loneliness, the unanswered call, a hollow interior. Every morning is a Rorschach, and dreams are nothing compared to what I see when I look into the mirror with no reflection: into the I with no substance.

Is there anything that is not a projection? A common sheet of paper holds an entire encyclopedia of collective and individual, conscious and unconscious material. Can you see it? Yes and no. Consciousness is what looks back at you: your own consciousness and that of the world. This blank sheet of paper, is it friend or foe? Will you disappear into it and die an eternal death, or will you disappear with it and be consumed by the creative fire?

Writing and meditation are not two things. I keep a pad by my meditation chair, and I often close my eyes and meditate while writing. Meditation is a dance with nothingness that is anything but empty. In fact, it is teeming with all kinds of stuff, stuff that is yours and not yours but is an infinite array of thoughts, images, feelings, and stories. What an endless parade it is! The Sufis call it a conversation. The Hindus call it the play of consciousness. I like both. I particularly like to think of a writing practice as play. I know, I know—it is hard labor. But how much of that is because of the psychological burdens we bring to it?

I'd say quite a bit. And even if it's true and it is hard work—which of course it is on a very real level—nevertheless, in the primal spirit of creative movement, it resembles play a lot more than effort. Either way, when you are struggling it's best to try to find that spirit of play. Play with your paper, talk to it, sing to it, cuss at it, sob over it. It is not inert; it will respond. Try a few of these things:

> Get out some colored paper and crayons
> Write in a sine wave over the whole paper
> or in a sin wave—write something naughty or nasty
> Write with your left hand
> Make a paper airplane and throw it out the window
> Roll it up and shoot baskets

꽃

Play when you can. And play is not the same as being silly like some of the ideas you just read might suggest. Play, in the Winnicotian sense, is more like psychic flexibility. You might move your people around the stage, come at the action from different angles. Mix it up. Ask yourself what you are avoiding. Have you bound and gagged any of your characters? Are you forcing the plot? You might try what George Costanza came upon in the famous episode of *Seinfeld* when he stumbled upon the brilliant idea of doing the opposite of everything he thinks he should do? Next thing you know, he has a beautiful girlfriend and is working for the Yankees! Now that is play. (And it is even psychologically sound as a method of reclaiming dissociated parts of the self.)

Is it possible to be serious and playful at the same time? Yes, it is. But it requires a certain kind of intimacy with paper, a certain laying down of absolute control and a willingness to enter into the unknown. Freud gave his students and patients the freedom to free-associate. That is a good model for this version of play. It also resembles William Stafford's advice about looking for the threads. There is a gentle tension between the receptivity of awareness and the ripples of ideas from the unconscious spring.

Is that blank piece of paper friend or foe? Is entering the unknown a Magical Mystery Tour or a one-way trip into the

Twilight Zone? You never know. That's why it is so enlivening and frightening. Who is waiting for you? Do you really like surprises?

I love surprises, when they come from the great unknown as a simile that really delights. I'm not so crazy about surprises that bring me face-to-face with aspects of myself I'd rather not know about. Not to mention feelings I can't bear. Ah yes, feelings, those strange creatures of the soul that knock on the door at the strangest hours. What about those guys, and how do we play with them? And why do we fear them so much?

The primary reason for this aversion is that strong feelings of grief or shame are often experienced as overwhelming. To compound this threat to the integrity of the self, an overwhelming state of emotion can feel never ending. No wonder people dissociate. No wonder in my practice I have to teach people, and not just men, to feel again. They need a great deal of support to return to their bodies. Many of my patients live almost exclusively in the head. The life of the mind offers relative safety from the storms of emotion that can crash upon you. While the mind provides relative safety, anxiety that the emotional world will break through harasses us day and night, further reinforcing the belief in a radical retreat from embodied living.

Of course you and I are afraid. Why not? Not only are we intimidated by emotional experience, but the norms of our society have also made it so that our inner world has been unrecognized to a large degree. Living in the commodity culture means what gets noticed is things: cars, houses, clothes, and behavior. Particularly valued is behavior that points toward achievement and success. We find value through earned merit.

What is forsaken, forgotten, and to a great extent nonexistent in mainstream capitalist society is the reality of the inner world. The exception to this is the identification of internal longings, which can be manipulated toward participation in consumptive spending. The reality of emotion and sensitivities of the soul are all but exiled from family and social discourse. This has been improving since the time I grew up, but it is still a tragic blindness that does damage to people and contributes to the spiritual and moral poverty of our time.

It could be said that illuminating the inner world and subjective experience of human beings is the major task of poets and writers. The inner world does not begin and end with feelings. It is rich in imaginings, and story making. Not only that, but our interior also expands into a great vastness. A vastness that we could say holds all there is. Perhaps this is why a common sheet of paper sitting before us can be so formidable, so intimidating. Strange, isn't it? But the truth is, that little 8½ ´ 11 sheet staring up at you, though it is made from wood and not glass, is one hell of a mirror, and it reflects back to you clear as can be the nature of your internal state—that is, your relationship to yourself as well as your craft. Should you be in a state of chaos, that will show up immediately and your work will be largely fragmented. Should you be under the influence of the restless mind, striving for something impossibly elusive, your work will likely be hurried and undeveloped.

If you are fortunate enough to be in a state of peacefulness, gratitude, or tingling curiosity, then the paper might smile up at you and be a wonderful invitation to enter the mystery of creative realms. An invitation to go snorkeling in the waters of the unconscious: to lose yourself in the place called being. The place that returns you to your big self: your True Self. A place of spaciousness where, at magical times, creating is effortless. Where being rests and is in constant motion. Where you are and are not.

That little piece of paper will soon be covered with a swarm of squiggly marks. Remember how accepting it is. Remember how it holds your precious thoughts. Remember how plentiful it is and how it always allows you to turn it over and begin anew. The same is true of spaciousness. The same is true of your intimate relationship with being, which allows you a multitude of beginnings and ever-gracious access to renewal.

21
The Desk

ON THE WALL IN MY STUDY IS A FRAMED PHOTOGRAPH of an antique writing desk. It is probably an early twentieth-century composition; notebooks, pencils, and pen lay on the desktop; a bookcase stands against the adjacent wall; and of course, a wicker chair sits by the desk, pushed back a foot or so as though the occupant has just left to fetch some coffee and might return at any moment.

And that is the essence of the writing desk: faithful. Always there, like a good dog ready for a walk. Your desk is your best friend who accepts you 100 percent as you are. It doesn't complain when you inexplicably go missing for a few weeks. It doesn't judge you when you curse and slam your fist down in frustration. It just stands there on all fours, ready when you are. If it had a tail, it would wag.

So beloved an object is the writing desk that we now have a twenty-first-century novel about its meaning in the psyche of the contemporary writer. Nicole Krauss, author of that beautiful book *The History of Love*, has written another captivating novel entitled *Great House*, which begins with the story of a woman whose writing desk is taken from her by the daughter of the original owner, a Chilean poet. Without her desk, the life of the author comes unraveled in short order. What we have here is the noble writing desk elevated to the order of archetype.

My favorite modern writer is Toni Morrison. I've read and reread *Beloved* a hundred times. When I learned that Ms. Morrison came home after a hard day's work, took care of her kids, and then wrote at the dining room table, I decided right then and there to park myself in the dining room and pull out pen and pad. And that's where I wrote most of those poems over ten years. When I left for work, my three-year-old son would come to the table and edit the night's verse. He drew big circles with triangles in them and wrote next to my cursive in a language that defies translation. It was the best time I've ever had with any form of literary criticism. What a treasure those notebooks are to me, and not because of the poetry.

ﷲ

Like much of our postmodern world, the desk has shape-shifted into multiple forms. I must confess, I rarely write at my desk and am seldom there other than to make copies. Instead, like many of my brothers and sisters of the word, I write at the kitchen table, the dining room table, the local coffee shop, and on and on. My first novel was written seated on the couch in the TV room, and of course, what served as the desk was, in actuality, my lap.

"Your what?" I can hear my father's incredulous voice. That's right, Dad—I do all my writing on my laptop, which sits atop my lap. Most people I know do the same. "Well, I never heard of such a thing." Dad was not designed for the modern world. Sometimes I wonder if I was. But I must admit, I like writing on the computer. I like the warmth radiating onto my thighs and knees. I like the keypad and the attention I must give it because that seems to occupy a certain sector of my brain that frees another sector to roam where it may. I like all of that, but I wonder if I'm missing something. I think of Tolstoy and Virginia Wolfe sitting at their desks hour after hour, and I feel a nostalgia for a slower way of life where not only books were written but letters as well.

I wish I could say that my lap is as stable as a writing desk. It is not. In fact, it resembles a rolling sea more than it does the solidity of the desk. My new desk squirms and fidgets, rises and falls. It is made out of flesh and bone, inherently unstable substances. Sometimes my feet go to sleep and I can't tell if I'm connected to the floor at all! And yes, there are days when my lap rebels, when it has had enough and gets up and leaves the house for a walk to the park. A good desk would never, ever do such a thing. Is it possible that the metamorphosis of the writing desk into the lap reflects a change in the stability of the self?

The writing desk is there for you. It accepts you. You are always good enough, no matter what. To the desk, there is no such thing as a bad writing day. It is completely free of the polarities of good and bad writing, success and failure, interesting and boring. Like a good-enough mother, present to attend to the needs of her infant, the desk is at your service. All you have to do is show up. This metaphor of desk as mother harkens back to times of absolute dependency, the memory of which is stored in the cells of your body, which is the same as saying that memory is alive in the deepest layers of the unconscious you.

I hope you had a very good experience of being held and finding your needs met by your mother. It is quite possible you did not. Historically, particularly in post–World War II America, our society has made it exceptionally difficult for women to realize their full development as people, and thus to mother their babies in the most nourishing way. The results have been very hard on all involved. What this points to is this: the relationship we have to the writing desk, whatever its form may be, is telling in regard to two primary issues central to life and art. The first is dependency, and the second is routine.

What is the first thing that comes to mind when you think of dependency? What do you feel in your gut when you hear the word? Take a minute to close your eyes and listen. You might feel anxiety or an aversion rise up. "No way! Fuck that." I've heard that in myself from time to time. You might feel trapped or engulfed. "Let me out of here!" (I'm giving myself away with this one.) Maybe you feel comforted and relieved. "Ah, I don't have to do it all myself." Perhaps you feel fear. "Oh no, I'll be dropped," or worse, "No one is there." Just try to be aware and accept what speaks.

Many of us are, at the least, ambivalent about dependency. Men typically see it as weakness, and women can view it as enslavement. Each might have a hidden longing for some version of reliance: a man might secretly yearn for help, or closeness, while a woman whose needs have been exploited at the cost of her autonomy may long to be taken care of, to be held both physically and emotionally. What is your posture? Do you rigidly hold to an "I don't need anybody" stance? Do you take the opposite approach and deny your separateness and bigness by clinging to others? Whatever your conflict may be, it is going to show up in your approach/avoidance to your writing—that is, in your relationship to the desk.

Dependency. Some cringe when they hear the word. Hair stands up on the back of the neck. The stomach churns. In our time, two psychological approaches to this issue dominate the profile of those who are in conflict. That would be the narcissistic style and the schizoid style. Now, this doesn't mean that anyone resembling either of these approaches has a personality disorder or anything of the sort. It just means, in the unfortunate language of psychoanalysis, that the features and conflicts surrounding dependency can be found in most of us. They are features of personality, not disfigurements. By the way, in today's psychology we think of them as disturbances to the self or as conflicts with attachment.

Of course narcissism has become a common household word, not to mention a damning accusation. Every week I see couples and can count on hearing one or more partners saying with a fair amount of contempt, "I know, it's all about you." The tendencies to be self-referencing and self-absorbed are well-known narcissistic features. What is typically missed in the firefight of accusations is any recognition of the insecurity behind narcissistic strategies. The motivation behind the self-involved posture is to avoid at any cost the experience, or expression, of need. Need is the dreaded stalker that drives the narcissist to use others, think only of him-or herself, and organize a system that altogether avoids the reality and vulnerability of interpersonal dependency.

The same can be said of the schizoid condition. The schizoid position is also intent on avoiding need, but it is more isolated from human contact than the narcissist. The schizoid condition is marked by a retreat from relatedness, whether with the world or people, as well as from the internal world of emotion and desire. In the schizoid's presence, you sense a radical detachment from internal life and a reliance on cognitive, mental life for their bearings. In the schizoid world, ideas and concepts are more important than people and feelings.

The narcissistic agenda is to save face; the schizoid would rather not have a face. The narcissist craves being seen in a positive light; the schizoid would rather not be seen at all. One avoids shame by pursuing an idealized image; the other avoids shame by isolation, or if need be, invisibility. Each style is popular in our hyper-individualized culture. Each is present within the mind of most artists.

Experiment:

Take a moment to write down who and what you are dependent on. Your writing group? Your best friend? Maybe your partner or spouse. It could be that you reach for alcohol, or pot, more comfortably than the hand of another. How do you ask for help? Or do you? Do you feel anxious when you do? What are your expectations about leaning on another? What happened when you were a kid and you needed someone? Was there a price to pay? Do you feel weak if you ask for help, like you can't possibly have needs and be strong at the same time?

❦

Let's consider a simple need like rest. There may be those whose constitution and biorhythms are more nocturnal than most, but I'd venture to say not many. It is fashionable, I suppose, to align with the romanticized image of the beat writer laboring all night over his typewriter, cigarette in hand, maybe a whiskey bottle on the side. Fashionable, but not sustainable. Okay, maybe that is a dated example—nevertheless, I'd say there are many writers out there who don't get anywhere near the amount of rest they need to be at their best. The trainer of the German National Soccer Team, recent winners of the 2014 World Cup, said the one thing that can make people feel better quickest is sleep. There was a time I hated being dependent on sleep. You too? My buddies and I felt glorified in staying up all night doing rowdy things.

Which is the perfect lead-in to routine. What is more routine than sleep? As the sky grows dark, birds take to their nests for the night. With the possible exception of crows, who like to make raucous music well past bedtime for most birdies. It's worth asking yourself what your routines are. Does your writing practice include a regular schedule? How do you feel about having a routine? Are daily practices and spontaneity mutually exclusive?

One of my clients is a brilliant scientist and sculptor. A Harvard graduate. This man is so talented, but he can't get off the block. His aversive response to routine is so strong that he is constantly fighting against himself. Even a simple structural aid like making a list sends him into rebellious reactivity and self-defeating inaction. Uh-oh. There's another one of those words—*structure*. What about structure? Does it feel supportive or restrictive to you? How about surrender—does that get your blood percolating? Americans hate the very idea of surrender. But as regards the spirituality of subtraction, you have no greater friend. Surrender has come to be synonymous with submission. With giving up one's independence and even one's self. In other words, surrender sounds masochistic.

I feel like I'm just getting to appreciate routine in my life, and I'm sixty-five. For years I have fought against it and associated such practices with the dull, repetitive habits of my father the accountant. Now I'm beginning to appreciate how supportive it feels and what good practice it is to surrender to the everydayness of it all. Toni Morrison's practice is to rise early every morning and sit with the dark until it grows light. Only then, after the world has brightened, does she begin to write. I love that.

Let's look at the routines and rituals of some other important writers. Maya Angelou rented a hotel room in town where she went every morning to write. She had all the decor taken from the walls, and she never slept there, but from 9:00 a.m. to 2:00 p.m., she wrote and then returned home to edit her work later in the day. She said that the environment helped her to get into big mind and out of small mind. That's what I'm talking about!

Haruki Murakami, the fantastic Japanese novelist, rises at 4:00 a.m.—every day. He goes to sleep at 9:00 p.m.—every day. From four to nine, he writes, and then he runs six miles. (This is the opposite of William Stafford's routine. Each to his own.) Here's what Murakami says about his practice: "The repetition itself becomes the important thing; it's a form of mesmerizing. I mesmerize to reach a deeper state of mind." There is purpose to this madness.

Now let's turn to Stephen King and see what his thoughts are. King says, "There is a certain time I sit down...I have a glass of water, my vitamins, my papers are arranged in the same places and I sit in the same spot." Why? Because he is OCD and can't stop himself? Because he is superstitious? Listen to what he says, keeping in mind the words of Maya Angelou and Haruki Murakami:

> The cumulative purpose of doing these things the same way every day seem to be a way of saying to the mind, you're going to be dreaming soon.

Dreaming, mesmerizing, transitioning from small mind to big mind—ah...here we go. What is Toni Morrison doing sitting in the dark until the break of dawn? Fretting? No! She's finding her way to the nonsecular. Okay, I confess to stacking the deck here. You can probably find lots of writers and artists who talk about ritual without making reference to altered states of consciousness. However, I think the mystery of creativity is lost or diminished if we reduce what happens to strictly rational approaches. Routine and structure allow the mind to roam. And not only that, but they also allow the big mind to find us! It clears a space for that force to come whisper the sweet nothings of its desire in our inner ear.

Giving yourself over to routine is the practice of letting go. Of what? Of the Self Project. Of ego striving. Of habits that resist helpful routines and structure because of associations to past injuries. At the risk of sounding like a boring old man (oh, my Self Project cringes at the thought!), I have come to mostly love the repetitive tasks of the day: doing the dishes, vacuuming, even paying the bills. These activities are soothing to me. They provide a structure for resting in motion. They also provide an opportunity, an occasion to practice wakefulness—to stay awake to the presence of being.

⚜

Your book rests on your desk. You rest on being.

Your desk takes its cues from being. All the great mystics who have walked the earth say the very same thing: when awakening happens and one encounters the deep presence of being within, what is most striking, most staggering, is the recognition that it has always been there. Here. Right here. Like the beloved writing desk, being is what holds everything. It is a place to rest and a place to work from.

22
The Chair

REMEMBER MY GRANDFATHER'S BIG LEATHER CHAIR WITH A
great deal of affection. It sat in his study where I would retreat
from time to time on our visits. I thought I went to that chair
because of the jar of peppermints on the table beside it, but
looking back I realize I was searching for something else. Some-
thing besides quiet and relief from the chatter, something that
was inexplicable at the time but that I found in the comfort of
that chair.

No doubt it wasn't as large as my memory tells me, but for
a lad of eight, it felt huge and like nothing we had at home. Big
as it was, it seemed to hold me close like a good jacket. The
leather was a beautiful deep crimson with brass tacks along the
seams. Like all good leather, it was tough and it was soft, solid,
and giving. I suppose it was a lot like my grandfather, who hated
Catholics and thought Democrats were fools but had a soft spot
in his heart bigger than any chair.

Looking back on those moments, I can see the profound
meanings his big stuffed chair took on for me. Because the
leather was tough and soft, and the chair solid and giving, it
was an introduction into a realization that opposites did not
have to be in opposition. This was not taught in Ohio. More-
over, it was an initiation of sorts into something way beyond

my comprehension at the time. I could not have known at that tender age just how hungry I was for holding. And I could not fathom that holding was far more than sitting on someone's lap. That holding in its most profound sense is a psychological act involving connection with another in such a way as to feel recognized, touched, and supported in one's core emotional/spiritual life. I would not understand this need for years to come.

The chair is our symbol for the indispensable need for support, and support involves these qualities of recognition, touch, and secure connection to another. Hopefully you find something supportive about sitting down day after day at your writing desk. Taking your seat, supported by a good chair, is one of the enduring pleasures and soothing practices in the long life of a writer. Try it with conscious awareness next time. Feel your feet on the floor, your butt on the seat, and your back against the chair. Feel it all holding you: the floor, the seat, and the back. Feel the steadiness. The solid position. You are well held and ready to do your work.

Any number of supports can help a writer through good and tough times. For many, a writer's group is primary. Others look to a best friend to read their work and talk about the process of making words speak. William Stafford went for a six-mile run every morning before writing his daily poem. I personally think walking, or some form of vigorous exercise, is essential to keeping the juices flowing. Much better than antidepressants or coffee, for that matter. And don't forget sleep. Sleep is not for babies. It is the primary way our brains are soothed and refreshed.

Support is one of those words like *help*, or *dependency*. One of those words that just doesn't make sense for a lot of us. Even though John Lennon wailed for the world, "Help! I need somebody!" most of us didn't get it. Or we thought it was all about finding a boyfriend or girlfriend. If we don't feel good enough, more than likely we carry shame for these basic dependency needs. When that is the case, we just won't get it and will avoid supportive, intimate relationships that risk emotional wounding.

But then we are really missing out on something crucial to well-being because support at its best touches the heart and makes an artist feel understood as well as linked to the body of those souls brave enough to weather a life devoted to making art. In other words, the feelings you think are abnormal are not. They belong to all of us, and rather than separate you, as we dread, they connect us with the vast community of writers and artists throughout the world.

❧

Perhaps you have had a favorite chair in your background. Maybe you are sitting in it right now! It could be a rocking chair you found in an antique shop or a big stuffed chair you can cuddle up in to read a new book. A good chair can be such a comfort. An old friend who is predictable and familiar. What do we do after a hard day's work? We plop down in our good old chair, kick off the shoes, and utter a big sigh. The chair is soothing. It embraces us fully, including all the ragged edges. A good chair holds all of you and soothes the weary heart and loneliness of a writer's life.

What is soothing to you? A writer takes so many blows to his self-esteem in the course of a day, is so vulnerable to falling into a pit of self-doubt and self-deprecation when the winds begin to howl. What can we do to care for ourselves? What can we draw on? Returning to the peppermint candies beside my grandfather's chair, I can see clearly the years of attempts at self-soothing with sweets, an assortment of food and drinks that sought to provide what that leather chair offered.

Developing the capacity to self-soothe is begun in the earliest days of life, primarily within the context of the mother-infant relationship. In those days if the mother can attune herself to her baby and soothe, in a good-enough way, the distress of hunger and pain, then the little one can begin to internalize the confidence and ability to soothe her-or himself. This is a no-fault assessment. If the mother is not able to soothe her infant, it is likely because she did not receive adequate comfort herself or suffered one kind of abuse or another.

These failures in mother-infant bonding can be traced back for generations. It is also true that some babies are extremely difficult to soothe. Constitutional differences exist between infants, and there are those who are so very sensitive that the slightest touch can be overwhelming. Mothers whose babies shrink from their touch are likely to feel terrible and incompetent in the most important task of their lives. This sets up a negative spiral that leaves both mother and child feeling bad and gives birth to the earliest seeds of the Self Project.

Think about what is soothing to you. Do you rely on substances to calm your system? Do you rely on food and drink to feel full? Are you in a free fall at times and unable to ease the anxiety or self-loathing? I work with people all the time who are at the mercy of these attacks and have little to no inner resources to help themselves. It really isn't surprising that opiates are becoming so popular throughout America. They take away the pain and angst of existence in short order.

❧

Sit. Feel the stability of your chair. Enjoy it. But don't mistake it for what I refer to as the myth of balance. *Balance* is a word that is tossed around and idealized as a place we should be able to get to. This is a myth and a burdensome expectation that will become a feeling of failure if we take it too seriously. As I've said, our inner world really is more like the weather: constantly in flux. The chair holds us in the dynamic whirlwind of psychic reality. The myth of balance tells us we should not be swept away, we should not react, we should not go to extremes. But we do. That's why the Greeks named the psyche after the butterfly.

Admit it, we are all over the place. Your chair keeps you steady as you write and as the winds of emotion and self-doubt blow in.

What may be a more useful concept is the notion of equilibrium. Equilibrium is more about acceptance than control, and more about inclusion of emotional movement than about pushing feelings away in order to convince ourselves that we are living in balance. When you are in equilibrium, you *are* the chair, holding all the disparate feelings and rising thoughts and memories. There are those who have meditated enough that they are able to be the eye of the hurricane and remain undisturbed no matter the strength of the winds. This is not dissociation but a radical embodiment that allows for awareness to be connected with emotions and being, while relatively free from the entanglements of the storm.

Very few people reach this state. It requires hours of practice sitting in meditation and daring to let go of layers of personal identification. Still, you can practice a form of mindfulness called witnessing, which helps ease the experience of overwhelming emotion and distress. The problem is, for many of us, especially white men who live primarily in their minds, we have to learn to feel first. We tend to be in love with abstraction and to embrace the products of thinking over what is real and relational. This is the schizoid problem and very different from that of the highly sensitive person who is so often fighting against overpowering waves of sensation and emotion. Either way, however, the challenge becomes one of what we call affect regulation. Feeling without being swept out to sea. Because the problem for each is that of flooding. The psyche is vulnerable to being flooded and seeks desperate measures to keep from being overtaken. These realities highlight the need for adequate holding.

✖

Like a writing practice, developing the capacity to live through your emotional experience rather than pushing it away takes lots of repetitions. Every morning I sit on my meditation chair and go within. When I'm done I sit on my writing chair. Every day. I practice breathing, slowly, because breath is the key to undoing anxiety and distress. I breathe slowly through my nose, filling my abdominal area and chest. Slow and steady, as the tortoise said. I feel my feet. Always practice feeling your feet: when sitting, walking, even standing at the sink washing dishes, feel your feet. They ground you to the now and help you disengage from the grip of catastrophic thoughts. Do these practices and you will slowly develop a capacity for self-regulation. When meditating, don't try to stop thinking; you can't. Just notice and label what is passing through your mind. Label it *thinking, sensation, memory, fantasy.* Whatever. From time to time, let your curiosity turn to this strange thing we call awareness. Wow, what is this? Am I really awareness itself?

We must repeat these practices to develop the capacity to support and soothe ourselves. A writing practice depends on repetition. Life depends on repetition. How many times has your heart beat in your lifetime? How many breaths do you take in a day? You brush your teeth and take out the compost. When I coached my boys in Little League baseball, we learned that it takes about a thousand repetitions to change the muscle memory of a baseball swing. The beauty of the William Stafford method of writing a poem every morning is that in regularly taking your seat, you build muscle memory of a different sort. I remember a story of a Chinese painter who tossed out most of his work before the age of seventy, referring to it as warm-up. Segovia was still practicing five hours a day at seventy-five. Day after day we return to the chair, sit down, and do our best. We have to endure despair, emotional and psychic blisters. Hopefully we have joy.

But there is always a dark side. The chair isn't always comfortable. There are days—way too many, I'm afraid—when you sit down in the electric chair! When you find yourself strapped in as jolts of electricity hit your body. When restlessness, pain, or worse is excruciating and all you want to do is run, escape that death chair, and flee to the nearest bar or movie or anything that will distract and distance you from the feelings firebombing your mind. Days when repetition feels like enslavement and you want to throw off the shackles, give the whole damn thing up, and drive a bus for a living. Days when the self-attack is so strong, you're lucky to write five lines, and don't they suck anyway? These accusations are repeated, and repeated, ad nauseam.

We all know about the terrible suffering some of our greatest writers endured. We'll never know if Hemingway, Sylvia Plath, and other tragic giants of the literary world would have survived had they lived in this era of refined therapeutic techniques and the availability of ever more sophisticated antidepressant medications. We do know they were subject to the same demons that hound us in our pursuit of a creative life. Virginia Wolfe criticized herself in her suicide note. Even the mighty Leo Tolstoy suffered from a worsening depression as he aged and in the end condemned himself for not having the courage to take his life. Artists venture into some serious psychological territory.

Most of us will encounter those dark, depressing days and the condemnations that rain down. But there is an even tougher problem with repetition. Freud said that what we repress, we repeat. The famous line about neurosis is familiar to most people: neurotic behavior is doing the same thing again and again and expecting a different result. Sure, who doesn't? And yet, it remains truly confounding how powerful a repetition compulsion can be and what a hold it can have over the workings of our minds and decision-making ability. Truly confounding. Why do some people return to obviously bad relationships? Why do some artists spend hours in front of the TV avoiding the studio and stuck in patterns they seem powerless to influence? Why do many writers ignore or reject the valuable advice given to them by agents and editors? Advice that would surely advance their work to the next level.

Despite the best of intentions, unconscious currents pull us toward rocky shores where we run aground time after time. Again and again we re-create thought patterns and behaviors etched into our psyches from history. As Faulkner said, "There is no past." There isn't. What has not been cleared out in therapy, or in deep reflection or in meditation, is vulnerable to perpetual repetition. All too often in tragic ways. This isn't a matter of weak character or stupidity—it is a fact of psychic life that we humans are subject to.

Anyone who has experienced trauma in their lives is doubly susceptible to re-creating the very abuses you would think they would avoid like the plague. Partners become perpetrators, and emotional flooding convinces us that the trauma is once again upon us. It is nearly impossible to talk someone out of this certainty. Trauma is also repeated in an automatic, unconscious way so as to alleviate the anxiety of not knowing when it will strike. You may have friends who again and again invite the same abusive patterns into their lives. You may talk rationally and plead with them not to go down that road only to discover that they have. And these aren't stupid people, are they? What is going on?

Of course of all the reasons for the repetition of self-defeating and self-destructive behaviors, the saddest is that we circle back to doing what is not in our best interest again and again because it confirms our internal notion that we are not worthy of better. This terrible sense of unworthiness shadows the lives of many an artist. The persistence of a feeling that I am bad, or not good enough, shapes the field of possibilities and limits the creative vision needed to move in new directions. At other junctures, the Self Project demands action that has no realistic chance of succeeding and sets up conditions that reinforce feelings of failure and inadequacy. Sad but true. These powerful self-states can make the best of us buckle and feel defeated.

But we are not doomed to repeat old traumas and ineffective strategies. While these behaviors are more than troubling and are too often self-defeating, there is an upside. Now we understand that an unconscious motivation to master the experience is driving many of these reenactments. Survivors of terrible assaults to the self are trying to come to terms with what was traumatic. They are making a valiant attempt to do what they could not do at the onset of the trauma—that is, process the feelings, sensations, and meaning of what occurred. Remember, trauma is not just what happens to you; it is, as Winnicott rightly said, any experience that overloads your system and its capacity to process the events that cause overwhelming feelings and sensations in the body. People who receive enough support in managing their feelings and help with understanding what has occurred may not suffer as severe a trauma reaction as those who do not. Those who do not have enough support are not so fortunate and struggle for much of their lives to undo what was done to them.

Experience that cannot be processed is stored in the cellular memory of the body and organized cognitively around stories and expectations of future encounters with traumatic agents. What develops from this point, which works both for and against the author, is what some call dark emotion. Dark emotion, what is known in Jungian terms as shadow elements, can be frightening. That fearsomeness adds to the tendency to hide what are thought to be terrible and unacceptable parts of the self. Typically, when these long-held feelings can come out into the light, they are found, with help, to be not so damning after all.

Really, when you get to know someone in the profound way that I am privileged to know the people I work with, you quickly find what has seemed so bewildering makes a whole lot of sense. Instead of saying out loud, "I can't believe I said and did that," people find themselves looking over their lives and saying, "Of course. Of course I acted that way. Of course I feel the way I do." In other words, with the help of good-enough therapy, yoga, meditation, and friendships, the perpetual cycle of thoughts, feelings, and actions that have only added to the layers of shame slowly transform into kindness and the extension of long overdue and entirely deserved compassion.

Experiment:

Now, sit yourself down. Be comfortable. Your desk holds the work; your chair holds you. Your chair grounds you. Just sit with yourself. Rest your feet flat on the floor and hold your back straight, but not rigid, against the back of the chair. Close your eyes or leave them open—either way is fine. Breathe slowly through your nose, deep into your lungs and belly. Slowly. No hurry. There. There you are. Just sit with yourself as you are in this moment. Take your seat with the good-enough quality of this moment and you, as you are, right now.

Nothing to do. Feel your chair holding you. What is it like to be held? Just feel that. Relax into the sensation of holding if you can. Don't push, just soften to being and being held. Your chair holds all of you. It holds what Rumi calls "the glory and the indignity" of you. Everything is held and accepted. Your chair grounds you. Feel your feet on the floor. Your chair grounds you to the immanent, to what is real. Feel your butt on the seat. Your chair grounds you to what is honest and unadorned. Feel your spine against the back. Your chair grounds you to your strength, to equilibrium. It teaches you how to hold yourself kindly, in all sorts of weather.

Your chair is not a throne. It is made of wood, not gold. It is not a cushion for the royalty of the ego. Not a tool for the ambitions of the Self Project. Neither is it a shelter from the storm. There are days when it feels like an electric chair. Others when it resembles an easy chair. Regardless of the particular day, it is your chair, the spot you return to day after day, week after week. The place you sit yourself down to encounter the joys and perils of a writer's life.

As the remarkable Tibetan yogi Chogyam Trungpa Rinpoche was fond of saying, sitting for meditation is putting yourself on the spot. On the spot with yourself in all honesty. On the spot with the striving to become somebody who is okay. And on the spot with what is your inherent goodness. That goodness that is not earned or acquired but rests in the center of you that is going on being at all times. Being is the ultimate soothing and supportive presence. It is the seat of your real self out of which the creative flowering grows like a field of sunflowers.

The Tibetans refer to the spaciousness of our inner world as groundless being. Being and consciousness that have no center, no edges, and no beginning. Though groundless, being holds you. You are this grand paradox. You have experienced it many, many, many times: when writing, running, lovemaking, and a hundred other ways you have known your deepest self. It visits, guides, and uses you to enhance the creative thrust of life. Anytime you wish to find this source of groundless being, just sit yourself down and take your place on the seat of your chair.

PART V

Novel Ideas

23

Scribbling

HERE IS A NOVEL IDEA: LOVE. "ALL YOU NEED IS LOVE." Simple tune. Before you can sing it, however, you have to "learn how to feel inside." Sorry, John, it ain't easy. What do you love? Who do you love? How fully are you able to love? How guarded is your heart? When does it open and how far? When does it close and for how long? Love isn't simple, and it isn't easy. Humans may crave it, sing about it, write about it, dream about it, and still push it away. We may look for it everywhere and run like hell when we find it. We may give up everything for love and then, having found it, set about to destroy it. Love is what we never have enough of and what is too much for us. As every country-western song will tell you, love is the hero and the villain of your story. It is always the problem. It is the mother of hope and dread and sure as shootin', it will bring you pain.

Your heart and my heart are basically the same. We don't like pain. We are tenderhearted creatures, and given enough hurt, we will say no thank you to any further risk of vulnerability. There it is, the v-word. Some retreat from it, some attack. Not too many handle it well. I see a lot of couples in my practice, and I can tell you that it is terribly sad to see good people so at war over the betrayal of love and unable to risk being vulnerable together.

Many people mistake the mask of the Self Project in their partner for the real deal and are deeply disappointed when the unpolished version shows up looking for acceptance. They feel deceived. Of course the partner who has dropped the persona, believing that at last he or she will be loved unconditionally, is devastated when encountering a negative reaction to the True Self. From there, it can only get more and more tangled and usually pretty ugly.

❧

Love is dangerous. When I was a kid, Lawrence Welk and company sang, "Love is a many splendored thing," as if it were a return to Eden. But it isn't. When you dare to love, whether in a relationship or at your writing desk, you will suffer. Guaranteed. The challenge is how to go on loving when the going gets rough. What about the days when you feel empty and dull and just can't write a good sentence to save your life? What about the days you are filled with anxiety and doubt, when you feel it's hopeless and the best solution is to chuck it all? Sometimes those days stretch into weeks, months, and even years. I'm the type of creative person who has long periods of gestation. As long as two years when nothing—and I mean nothing—is germinating. I love to write. When I'm in the groove, it comes easily, but in times of drought, a feeling of helplessness comes over me that is hard to bear.

These are facts of life for most writers. The tendency is to try to grind something out. Make it happen. Will the muse back into your life. I haven't found that to make anything happen other than more frustration, anguish, and contraction. What if the approach were different? What if we try to get back to love? Loving words, sounds, and meanings. Loving writing a simple sentence. What if we were to try laying down the serious approach, the ambitious agenda, the sometimes grandiose expectations and dreams? Love brings out the best and the worst in people. At its best it is playful and unrestricted. At its very best it is free and inclusive. Spontaneous and daring. When was the last time you wrote from that place? When was the last time you wrote like a jazz musician playing his saxophone? Or like a child with a paintbrush in her hand?

꙰

My friend Winnicott worked with children, and he favored a game he called squiggle. He drew a random, doodling line on paper, and the child took it from there and continued doodling until he or she made the lines and marks into a drawing of something real. This allowed Winnicott to see into the child's inner world and to witness his or her approach to engaging with the real world and the creative instinct.

I often think of this experiment when I'm feeling stuck. Some days I'm too stuck to think of anything. It seems to me, we could do something comparable to the squiggle with letters and words. How about you turn yourself into a trumpet for a while and make up sounds? Write them down in big letters. Turn yourself into Ella Fitzgerald and make those great monosyllabic bebop notes fly off your pen for five to ten minutes. Let yourself go, write in sine waves so your sentence looks like a roller coaster ride when you're done. Write in circles, in collage, until some gestalt emerges on its own from the wild.

Remember those Matisse drawings I talked about in the prologue? Let it rip, scribble, squiggle, tickle your funny bone, be the little piggy: weeeeeeee, all the way home. The beauty of the squiggle is you cannot fail. You make something, and it is the making that counts. Because the simple, childlike making loosens you up. Not that there's anything wrong with failure. I try to think of the sage advice Samuel Beckett gave us, "Fail again, fail better." Becoming familiar, even friendly, with failure is the sign of real maturity in an artist. Trying to make it right, trying for perfection, is the psychic straitjacket that binds artists. Too much will and not enough soul. Listen to what Faulkner once said about failing:

> All of us failed to match our dream of perfection so I rate us on the basis of our splendid failure to do the impossible.

※

Of course the Self Project doesn't like failure one bit. It freezes up like a cat spotting a dog. Dylan said it well, "Ain't no success like failure, and failure ain't no success at all." All right, it sucks. It ain't easy to keep affirming yourself as a writer when day after day you turn out stuff that just isn't so hot. When I wrote all those poems day after day, like William Stafford suggested, maybe one or two out of ten were good. And I don't think the great poets have a whole lot better percentage. We might as well admit that yes, we are striving "to match our dream of perfection." Sometimes desperately. It seems we can't help ourselves.

One thing that helped me through the muddy days and lousy poems was loving the process. It became less and less about me. This was the second invaluable piece of wisdom offered by Mr. Stafford: listen. Listen, as in pay attention, feel deep into yourself for any murmurs or, as he called them, threads of inspiration. This resonated with me because as a psychotherapist, I rely on free association and subtle intuitive nudges to guide my work. I truly love the process of looking and listening for the threads, even if they don't amount to much. I think of them as flickering lights. Where they come from, who knows? What is crucial and lovely is developing the antenna and trust and then marveling at the mystery of the creative process.

What is also essential is a different relationship to the act of writing. One that is less ego bound or governed by will and determination. Will and determination are useful later on when revising and editing, but for getting out of the mud and generating momentum, a more actively passive approach is needed. Sit and listen. Be quiet and listen. Remember that obedience means to listen in a deep way. Gentle tugs on the threads that emerge facilitate movement far more than force. Of course the Self Project is in a hurry to prove itself by way of accomplishing all sorts of great things, but the Stafford approach is about waiting. And receiving. This isn't so much about you. Sorry. If you're honest, you know that the credit is not all yours. Tough on the poor ego that wants to be admired, but liberating to any writer and artist who wants to get in the river and go. Try being taken over rather than trying to take over. Stop. Listen. Receive.

❧

Ah, receiving. That should be easy, right? Doesn't everyone like presents? Not so fast. Turns out, for those who don't feel good enough, receiving presents a problem. We can take in all sorts of pollution. No doubt you have had the experience of giving a reading or a talk and have fielded many compliments, some of which you may have taken in. Maybe. But oh, that one critical question from the back row, that one gets hauled in like a rainbow trout at the end of your line. And that negative review from the East Coast blogger, well you could probably recite that one word for word. Man, we are good at taking in bad air. Internalizing, necessary as it is, does not always act as our friend. And internalizing is not the same as receiving. We should be more like two-year-olds and know when to spit something out.

Receiving has to do with accepting that which has been bestowed upon you. By definition, being endowed with a gift, your talent, an inspiration, means it didn't come from you. It was given. You didn't make it or earn it: it was bestowed unto you. Sorry if this sounds religious—I don't mean it that way, but I do intend the spiritual aspect of it. I like that word, *bestow*. And that's how it feels to me, that something that is altogether intimate, not from me and decidedly of me, has arrived. It lives in our house, as Rumi wrote, like a guest. How I welcome and treat my guest is the question.

That question is answered, in part, by the feeling of worthiness I carry within. If the bad me is dominating the landscape, I will find it very difficult to receive the full measure of this gift. There are a million ways to deflect, diminish, and defeat what is given. I'm not just talking about literary potential. I'm talking about a very fundamental problem the people of today have with relating to and taking in goodness. If you don't feel good enough, you will find a way to spoil or dismiss the good coming into your life. You will feast on negative and self-destructive food instead. You might not even recognize what is good, nourishing, and freely given. Instead, you might think the only stuff worth celebrating is the big success, the big six-figure contract with Penguin Random House, the brilliant review in the *New York Times*. That would be depriving yourself of the many satisfying and nourishing possibilities in your life.

You might feel that to receive leaves you beholden to the giver and bound to give up yourself as the price of receiving. You might feel so cheated by what you were not given as a child that you don't trust that real giving exists, or you might feel that to receive would bring up the terrible pain of past disappointments. These are very real and difficult obstacles to overcome. And they all point back to a persistent sense of unworthiness and the underlying feeling of shame that feeds a certainty that declares, "I don't deserve to be given to." Which is always longhand for "I don't deserve love."

Truly, nothing is further from the truth. Love is not something you can or need to earn. It is not about being good or successful or any of the things that you hear every day from capitalist propaganda. It is not something that you acquire through the accomplishments insisted upon by the Self Project. We have all been duped. But to find and receive the love that is yours, you have to face your pain. Sorry. You can't outrun it. Fast as you are, it is faster than you. It will always ambush or outrun you. You have to stop running, hiding, and trying to push it away.

The crazy, amazing, and counterintuitive thing is this: If you stop and face pain, if you step into it, lean into it, relax into it, something is altered. You survive. It isn't killing you like you were sure it would. And you find it doesn't last forever. Like everything, it passes if you release the constriction that binds you to it. The best person to turn to for help in understanding this is Pema Chodron. Try her book *The Places That Scare You* or any of her recordings on the practice of living into pain and suffering. Find a good therapist who can be with you as you brave these tough spaces. You may not believe me yet, but you might find through experience that it is possible with help.

You may also find, having faced the pain of your life, that when it dissipates, the sun comes out and you'll find the love you have longed for all these years waiting for you inside. That love that comes for no reason. How many love songs have been written in our time? Really, how many? Most of us are searching for love, longing for love, or trying to give up on it. The capitalist culture treats it as another commodity to acquire. And we fall victim to this massive trance, hypnotized by the promise that love can be gotten. Wrong. Not only can it not be gotten, but it is sitting inside you right now, waiting to be received. Waiting to find you. How can this be? Mystics for thousands of years have been crying out for us to hear that our inner being, the very presence within, is love. Unconditioned love. They have told us that being and love are one. You love your neighbor because we are one being, disguised as many. You "love the one you're with" because we are one being, disguised as many.

I can't prove that, and from the point of view of the separate, rational mind, it is ridiculous. But you can find out for yourself. Be courageous and face your pain. At the least it will bring you increased self-respect and very likely more peace in your life. It will hurt bad and maybe feel overwhelming at times, but hang with it and you will find release. Practice taking in good. Even in little ways like noticing colors and variation in colors. Feel the texture of the air and the quality of the sunshine. Look up at the night sky and let yourself be taken by awe.

Experiment:

And try out this little experiment, this little love meditation. Be comfortable in a chair and close your eyes. Picture something or someone you really love. A dog or a cat, a person, maybe your mother or sister or best friend. Maybe it is a tree or a river or a building. It doesn't matter as long as it fills you with love. Let that love grow in you and spread from your heart throughout your body. Let it spread like morning sunlight. Let it take you over. If you can't, that's fine—just feel what you can. Good? Getting it? Feel it, feel your love for whatever it is that you have chosen. Just soak it up. Yum. Let it bathe you. Okay, now slowly bring your attention from that object of your love to the love itself. Slowly—and this might take some practice—disengage from the object you think is causing the feeling of love and bring your attention directly to love itself. To the embodied experience of love so that it is now love, and only love, on the stage. There. Be there. Be that love. Practice this. This is your deepest self. This makes the question of whether you are good enough laughable. This makes shame dissolve into nothing.

❧

One of our really fine contemporary writers is George Saunders. If you haven't read his collection of stories entitled *Tenth of December*, please do. Besides being a very fine writer, Mr. Saunders practices meditation, I believe in the Zen tradition. I want to end this chapter with something he said in a commencement address to the students at the University of Syracuse, where he teaches. His words are very moving to me and beautifully capture what I have been trying to convey in the last few pages. I hope you love it.

> My heartfelt wish for you:
> As you get older, your self will diminish
> and you will grow in love,
> YOU will gradually be replaced by LOVE.

24
Plot

THE GREAT MYSTERY OF PSYCHOTHERAPY IS THAT IT
works. Even Consumer Reports says so! Eighty percent
of people who go into counseling of one form or another
report being helped and are glad they did so. If it works for
Tony Soprano, it should for you and me, right? Still, what makes
it work is vigorously debated among psychotherapists. The
following are samples of what some would say makes all the
difference:

- Resolution of the transference
- Greater capacity for affect regulation
- Illumination of unconscious belief systems
- Development of the capacity to reflect

How's that for a list? If you ask our patients, they would
probably say something like this: "I realized that you really
cared." You heard it from the experts. We like to complicate it,
partially because it is complicated and partly to validate our own
professional insecurity. But clearly, the not-good-enough self is
transformed over time by connecting with another who hangs in
there and is caring and accepting. Big surprise. All the psycho-
logical markers I mentioned above may be necessary and helpful,

and all the new techniques, like EDMR and DBT, may facilitate movement, but it remains amazing, and somewhat mysterious, what power a genuine, close relationship has to melt the personal defenses developed over years of coping. Therapy works, not quickly or without pain, not by insight alone, but it works.

🌿

The paradox of therapy resides in this: the more therapy is working, the less certain people are about what and who they are. In the beginning, when the bad me is most dominant, a resigned certainty rules the psyche. This branding is relatively unquestioned and unchallenged. No doubt at one time or another, you have tried to talk someone out of this state of mind. Certain that reason and perspective would prevail, you probably got increasingly frustrated with the tenacity of the grip your friend had on this conviction. Perplexing, isn't it? There are those who react in manic and defiant ways to the threat of condemnation, but if you poke beneath the surface, or if life deals them a blow to their compensatory posture, you'll find a remarkably similar bad kid cowering in the corner. Sad but true.

It is an encouraging signal to me when someone in therapy becomes confused. When the automatic self-blaming begins to be discordant. When an inner voice of protest starts to wake up and say, "Hey, wait a minute." It is surprising how uncomfortable this state of uncertainty can be. It's almost as if the suffering of the diminished self is preferable. Why is that? Well, there are many reasons why we might hold on. For one thing, that notion has probably been around for a long time and has worn some grooves in the pavement. For another, the bad me is often held in place in fantasy as preserving a tie to a significant loved one. Letting go means facing some really terrible grief about the reality of that relationship.

As it relates to the here and now, the bad me may offer a

hiding place to the all-too-vulnerable self. Coming out into one's bigness is a very threatening prospect. The feelings of expansiveness and spaciousness can be overwhelming to those who have lived in constricted states for most of their years. In other words, it's real scary.

That's why we call it cracking up or falling apart. Because it is. The calcified views of self and other are breaking down. The dependable body armor is cracking. This is not a fun time. It requires lots of support and holding from a therapist who has gone through the process and understands the breakup will be followed by new, more flexible formations. Though this experience can feel chaotic, or like plunging into a groundless world, there are usually new moments of expansive feeling and spaciousness. New moments of creativity and skill. New moments of fresh air and aliveness. A bit of hope stirs. And curiosity is freed to stick its neck out of the bunker. But it does take real courage to venture into these new parts of town. To walk in neighborhoods that have been off limits. Most of us—and the culture, for sure—underestimate the trials that one must face to let go and move out in the world from a different place. But it will happen, and it is worth it.

Because nothing kills the development of plot like the restrictions of the known world. I don't care if you have outlined your novel in great detail—without embracing uncertainty, how will you inspire curiosity in your readers? Without surprise, how will your readers find the magic of life in your pages? Of all the great joys in reading and living, exploration and discovery rank near the top. Few things are more important. These qualities are exactly what is eliminated in contracted ways of being and a plot line that nearly always ends with you being at fault. With you being unlovable. You would be startled by the lack of curiosity most of my patients enter therapy with. Freud was right in many ways when he said people don't want to know. The truth will set you free, but first it will make you suffer.

I love to fly. I love to soar out of the clouds into the wild blue yonder scintillating with the radiance of sunshine. Once at cruising altitude, I love to look down on the big, bulging clouds and the vastness of space. But I always come back to staring at the earth. What a place! In particular, I love to observe the meandering paths of rivers. How unpredictably they move! How unreasonably! They move so leisurely toward their goal, and unlike us, they show no resistance to the obstacles encountered along the way. I wish we could allow ourselves to move like rivers in the world. Again, there was wisdom in the Greeks' choice of butterfly as the guiding metaphor for the psyche. Only in our mind, and in the coercive demands on the psyche, is life ever a straight shot from here to there.

A life of writing is like that river finding its way to the ocean. It moves from its source, bending with the layout of the land, changing directions again and again, searching for the low ground in a relentless journey to the sea. The adventure of exploration and discovery is one of the great thrills of a creative life and a great liberator of the inner world. Developing a relationship of curiosity with yourself is one way to disempower the menacing negating voices within. Allowing the uneven flow of a work of art is similar to accepting the uneven movement of the river of your being. Your characters should be defined but not one-dimensional, knowable and complex, understandable but not predictable. Like you and me. Like everything.

Of course as Lawrence of Arabia said, the plot of our lives is not written. What's next? What's around the corner? Who knows? Is this exciting, nerve-racking, all of the above? I imagine the Sufis were thinking of this when they created the dance of the whirling dervishes. Swirling round and round, faster and faster until the tornado of existence is in full swing. Then the biggest mystery of all makes itself known: the still point at the center. The immovable stillness, the one without a plot, without a beginning or an end. Dancing with and not with the whole wild and woolly stir-fry of life, the unity and diversity, the whirlwind of being and nonbeing. Phew. Are we spinning out of control? If so, is that really such a bad thing? Were we ever truly in control? The plot thickens. What are you? Who are you? Or, as my buddy Larry says, "What makes you think you are anything at all?"

❧

Here's a novel idea: sit down with yourself and ask yourself this simple question: Who am I? Write down the first thing that flashes in your mind. Then ask yourself this question: How do I know that? Keep going; repeat the process and travel deeper. The first question is an invitation. The second, a reminder that you are more. Much more.

Here's another: plot your life from your death backward to the present day. The Hindus say death is an arrow shot at your birth. We don't know where it is on the flight to our hearts. Plot in reverse. Make it an adventure to rival that of Ulysses. Along the way ask yourself again: Who am I? What am I? What changes, and what does not?

25
Dialogue

MY FATHER WAS A VERY RETICENT MAN. THOUGH HE was good at heart, he could be quite stingy with himself. The worst part was, he didn't believe in stories. Actually, it's worse than that—he hated them because they all led back to the one pivotal, terrible story of his mother's death. The poor man could not get out of his story of loss, though he had changed all the props. Sound familiar?

Because there were no stories, there was no conversation other than the story of my laziness and wayward life. The gap that existed between us was wide and full of a terrible absence. I hated that silence. It's a wonder I came to love meditation because the slightest brush with the distance between us made me shrink into depression. I was certain something was wrong with me. As a result it took me years of therapy to learn to talk. I still don't consider myself much of a conversationalist, but I suppose that is one of those faulty stories that grow out of hurtful experience.

What I'm getting at has to do with dialogue. The shadow of my discomfort with my father was so long that I was convinced I was incapable of writing dialogue and therefore a novel was out of the question. End of story. When I turned sixty, I wrote a list of things I was sure I could never do and made a promise to myself to try the impossible. Writing a novel was number two on the list. Number one, playing the piano, fizzled quickly when my left hand refused to cooperate. So I took up a clean notebook, a nice pen, and said, "Okay, here we go," trembling all the way to my desk. Certain, absolutely certain, that I could not write dialogue and that the sadness of unfulfilled longing for my father would take up permanent residence in my heart.

I began the book bargaining with myself. No need for dialogue. Maybe I could circumvent the whole thing. Then one day a funny thing happened in my head. A healthy, skeptical someone climbed out of the backdrop of certainty and said, "Wait a minute! Wait just a dang minute here! You are in dialogue with people all day long—of course you can write dialogue!" And the spell was broken. The trance collapsed around the recognition of what was real. The plot got a lot more interesting. And so I jumped in the water, started swimming, and turned out some decent conversation in *Radiance*. (You probably noticed the word *decent* inserted in there and thought, "I'll bet he still caries a spoonful of shame and insecurity about this." You're right.) Best of all, I found I liked writing dialogue so much that the second novel is two-thirds conversation!

❦

Talk is rather remarkable. It is one of the more satisfying ways we connect with others. At its best, it allows for the wonderful intersubjective experience of shared minds, and the possibility of understanding another as well as being understood. It is the kind of play you can do your entire life. When I learned to speak with others, I was so starving for meaningful conversation that the only kind of exchange I wanted to pursue was serious, heart-to-heart, soul-to-soul heavy dialogue. It had to have big meaning, and it had to be intimate. I pitied the poor folks who just wanted to chat about the weather. Today I enjoy casual conversation with the grocery clerk and strangers on the sidewalk. It seems so comforting to be able to connect with just about anyone, about just about anything and, without saying so, affirm the goodness of the moment and the sacredness of our common humanity.

For sure many conversations are frustrating and fall flat. Some folks are just not there. Others have not discovered the art of listening: while I was mute, they appear deaf. Or not interested. Don't you want to punch them? Or yell, "Shut up!" Of course. I really hate the conversations when I'm trying to make a point and I can see that my talk mate is busy lining up his rebuttal. I feel a particular narcissistic wounding when I say my bit and what comes back is something like "Well, it's more than that..." Let me tell you the real story, buddy. Sorry to be so sensitive.

❧

And the beat goes on, for better and for worse. The music of conversation, whether it is coming from the birds in the tree-tops or from the little flutes disguised as four-year-old children, flies through our common air like the song that has no end. So primary to human experience is dialogue that Rumi took to referring to the psyche as conversation. This is really a fascinating statement because it does seem that psyche is very much structured around language that is both external and socially derived, and internal and personally generated. His poems were great examples of literature as an ongoing exchange between self and other: the one and the many.

Remi belonged to the Sufi tradition that considered conversation to be the highest order of spiritual practice. More important than prayer and meditation. The word for this practice is *Sohbet*. You won't find an equivalent English word. Coleman Barks, our wonderful Rumi translator, refers to it as a "mystical conversation on mystical subjects." Rumi says it best in his "Discourse 53." I quote from *The Essential Rumi*, translated by Barks:

> Human beings are discourse. That flowing moves
> through you whether you say anything or not.
> Everything that happens is filled with pleasure and
> warmth because of the delight of the discourse that's
> always going on.

Coleman Barks sums it up beautifully in the following sentence: "Rumi's poetry mirrors back to us the ocean of woven speech too intricate and dynamic for any grammarian to untangle."

Wow. As they say in the Midwest, "Now ain't that somethin'?" No wonder the gap between my father and me hurt so much. When discourse breaks down, damage is done to the spiritual integrity of our common fabric. You don't know that as a kid—you just have a very troubling, shadowy sense that something is wrong. Really wrong. Being young, it is an easy slide into thinking that something is you. Your essence.

Nothing could be more false, and few things feel more true. For many, this is the original story. The one that continues over time to set the percussive beat to who you believe yourself to be. You might not hear it because it is so familiar. You might not feel you can do anything about it because it feels like it is your core self. In fact, you may have hidden or fled from your core self to protect it from the pounding of this drumbeat. That core may be lost to you, reinforcing the notion that what drones on and on about your unworthiness is the sound of reality.

This becomes the internal narrator in the story of your life. The one you try to undo by way of the Self Project. The story that is told again and again. "When things go wrong, it must be my fault." "When mistakes are made, I am a failure." "When disappointments arise, I am no good." "When good comes around, I don't deserve it." You think I'm exaggerating? I wish I were. These stories are as convincing and dictatorial as a Nazi propaganda machine. They are absolutely authoritarian, and authoritatively absolute. What binds these narrations and makes real people powerless is shame. Shame makes it all stick. Shame makes believers of us. Shame cripples the instinctive impulse in human beings to rise up and protest.

Protest. We think of protest as taking to the streets in support of the noble causes of the abolitionist movement, the labor movement, women's suffrage, civil rights, Vietnam, gay rights: the list is long and the history of protest is an honorable one. We see healthy, instinctive protest in the bodies of babies and children who spit out food and wail in fury whenever the sovereignty of their bodies is usurped by parental authority. Indeed, a healthy protest response is exactly what is undone by the agents of trauma that ignore or overpower the will of the body to stand up to the injustice of an assault on the integrity of the self. This condition leads to either a collapse into despair and passivity or a habitual aversive response to any potential threat.

While protests in the social realm are effective and common, little attention has been given to the utilization of internal, intrapsychic protest to stop and exile destructive self-talk. Instead, gifted people, plagued by these demons of the mind, suffer in bewilderingly helpless and passive ways. For years I woke at 3:00 a.m. besieged by anxiety and dread, contemplating the very worst-case scenarios of the times. About two years ago during a particularly bad wake-up call imagining the loss of everything, like my great-grandfather did nearly a century ago, I did the unthinkable—I said, "STOP." And I said it again. I said it with an unexpected strength and determination, the way you would if you saw a bully tormenting a little boy. And guess what? It did.

I was shocked. I didn't believe it. But I got back to sleep that night, and I repeated the same command the following night. And it worked again. I tried it out with anxious obsessions in the daytime and guess what? Yep. I'm not trying to tell you it is 100 percent effective. Sometimes the flooding happens too fast. Sometimes the fears, real and imagined, are just too salient. But it has helped keep the Xanax on the shelf and my sleep uninterrupted.

Experiment:

Okay now, are you ready? This is the secret teaching. Just kidding, sort of. Next time you are clobbered by the dreaded "High Anxiety"—thank you, Mel—try this out. When you are besieged by big anxiety or self-deprecating thoughts, take this simple approach.

Step one: Say "STOP!" In a firm, no-nonsense voice, say, "STOP. STOP." Say it as you would to a child running out into the street. Firm, no nonsense, solid. Not frantic or angry. A strong, nonviolent protest. Loving but resolute. You are the boss. Breathe deep, slowly.

Step two: Once you have interrupted the circuit of the anxious brain, you need to engage and ground yourself to the world of the present moment. The world of the real. First the three conscious breaths. Then give all your attention to your senses. Start with seeing what surrounds you. Look and identify five things in your immediate environment. Look in detail for colors, shapes, textures, and the like. Look closely. Then listen for four sounds. Listen carefully for nuance. Use your full senses and perceptual field to get out of your head and connect to what is real and close.

Remember, what is in your head driving you batty is not real! Even though it seems so, it is not. It is your anxious brain run wild, not your creative brain. Learn to discern which is which and use this simple method to free yourself from the suffering of these terrible bouts with anxiety and self-reproach.

꽃

The most novel and radical of ideas is to talk back. Be skeptical and critical of the voices that would diminish you. Identify who is talking and make it real. My dad rarely talked to me, and now he won't shut up. Call it out, exaggerate the internal self-talk. Isolate that internal dialogue, hold it up to the mirror, and see it for what it is, an Oz-like figure of distorted power. Give it a name and a face, paint it, sing to it, just don't take it as the gospel truth for one more minute.

Jive with it. "There you are again, you old fool. What are you doing making trouble? Get outta here." Most of all, write the new story of you. Make it sparkle with all the complexity and nuance you can muster. Imagine the little boy or little girl that you were, feeling bad and sure that "something is wrong with me." Put your arm around him. Sing to her. As William Stafford said, "The darkness around us is deep." Bring him into the light of compassion. Carry her onto the lap of kindness. Take in the good that surrounds the dark and hold it close. Wrap them in it. Wrap them in the warmth of a different story. Walk with them. Talk to them. Talk to them in a different voice. Gently, ever so gently.

26
Narration

WHAT'S NOT TO LIKE ABOUT OMNIPOTENCE? WHO
doesn't like playing God now and then? It is a thrill to
shape characters and move events around as you like.
I must confess, the omnipotent narrator is my favorite narrative
style. This clean, uncluttered approach appeals when it seems
everything in life is so messy and confused by the obvious and
hidden agendas of human beings. It is like flying in an airplane
and witnessing from a transcendent perspective. That really
draws me in. Perhaps I've just gotten so weary of the plenti-
tude of "I, me, my," so abundant in culture and the literature of
memoir, that it is refreshing to hear from what I am happy to
accept as the illusion of an objective reality.

Omnipotence appeals on so many psychological levels. The
ego, especially the male variety, is head over heels in love with
any means of prevailing over need and weakness. Not that
women are free from the seduction of the powers of absolute
control. Remember Charlie Brown's friend Lucy with her sign
that reads "The Director of Everything." The way so many
people worship control and talk as though they are mastering
life reveals the anxious urgency with which we strive for control.

My profession is every bit as enamored with the power of
omnipotence. To hear many therapists talk, it would seem that

understanding a human being is as easy as A, B, C and the secrets to life are summarized in a tidy little packet that you can take home and memorize. Nothing attracts the interest of the not-good-enough self like answers and solutions.

⚘

Of course it could as easily be said that the human mind finds the telling of a good story irresistible. You can well imagine the little Greek children and their parents sitting around the campfire listening with rapt attention and mouths open to a particularly good recitation of *The Iliad*. Spellbound. Doesn't it seem as though you and I have a nearly insatiable hunger for narrative? When that narrative is coupled with the mesmerizing voice of a James Earl Jones, it is all the more compelling and we are taken in. Beginning with treasured stories of childhood and continuing into adulthood from the morning paper to the afternoon soap operas, we seek out and devour story after story.

As you know by now, I am a big fan of C. K. Williams, the wonderful American poet. I heartily recommend you read his book of essays *Poetry and Consciousness*, in particular, the last essay in the volume entitled "Admiration of Form, Reflections on Poetry and the Novel." His thinking on the subject of narration has influenced mine in a big way, and I will be quoting extensively from that chapter. Let me start with one intriguing passage right now:

> Our education for the most part consists of the narratives by which our culture wishes to identify itself. We are our stories, or so we believe.

Much of this book has been devoted to understanding the internal narrator that never tires of telling the story of our shortcomings. The good-enough story is seldom told. Our stories are self-conscious—that is, they highlight our insecurities. Isn't it rare to hear within our own mind the story of our courage and integrity? How wonderful it is to sit down every day at the writing desk with only a pad of paper, one's imagination, and the desire to create. The number of people writing and publishing today is extraordinary: why isn't that front-page news? "We are our stories, or so we believe." The power of the narrator is dependent on the inclination of the listener to take in and believe. In one respect, we seem to be a very gullible species.

"Our education for the most part consists of the narratives by which our culture wishes to identify itself." Indeed, we have been told some whoppers. Though we are all too intellectually sophisticated to believe in it today, though we scoff at it and reject the very premise, the story of original sin plays on and on like the reverberating static of the Big Bang. Like a Broadway show that won't quit. You think it isn't active in your story, time and again chanting the gospel of your inadequacy? Think again. Original sin leeched into the collective unconscious a long, long time ago, and it has a very long half-life. We are singing the blues, without the music, of that terrible branding of the soul. And the refrain of our insecurity repeats with the drone-like consistency of the ticktock of a wall clock.

A more contemporary story, but every bit as captivating and influential as that of original sin, is the neoliberal economic creed of unlimited growth. The premise of this system is well defined by William Deresiewicz in his article for *Harpers* in the September 2015 issue. It reads, "Neoliberalism is an ideology that reduces all values to money value. The worth of a thing is the price of the thing. The worth of a person is the wealth of the person." Because we are bombarded from all angles with this ideology, we are somewhat anesthetized to its impact and oblivious to the extent that it has infiltrated and shaped the structure of our narrative. In particular, the personal story of our worth is further corrupted and is now completely dependent on our earning value.

In other words, the dominant culture would have us worship

wealth and success. The preacher in the pulpit is now in every house on the TV screen, on your smartphone, in magazines—it's everywhere, enchanting the public with a song in praise of perpetual progress, and a you-can-have-it-all promise of entitlement. Everything has been turned into a commodity. Every thing. Key word: *thing*. Because the thing, the *it*, has been sanctified. The thou? Who needs it? We've got the Super Bowl, don't we?

These stories seduce. They tantalize and seduce. As Aldous Huxley predicted in *Brave New World*, our gluttony is destroying us. Victims of comfort, we are. Rather than our love of stories being something that enriches and enlightens individuals and bonds a community in mutual understanding, they increasingly serve the capitalist quest for more by distracting us with mind-numbing entertainment. They hypnotize and anesthetize the soul from the atrocities happening outside the front door. Because we can't say no, we are complicit with the story line that promises eternal material success and dooms us to lives of spiritual and psychological poverty.

Too many popular books play into the hands of this insidious and destructive force. Romance novels typically top the bestseller lists. Serious works don't sell very well and are hard to get by an agent who is typically thinking exclusively of profitability. Happily, there are any number of pieces of literary fiction that do make it into the market. They are like the few salmon that survive the long and treacherous journey upstream to lay their eggs.

Most of this we owe to the emergence of small, independent presses. Some of these authors are doing very interesting things with multiple narrators and fluctuating voices. Many, like Lois Leveen's novel about Juliet's nurse, are disrupting the traditional models of narration, reminding us that narration itself is misleading: we are in a sea of stories every bit as varied and simultaneous as the currents of the ocean. Moreover, what we forget, in a culture infatuated with superstars, is that the story of every single person, no matter how common and unnoticed, is important.

❧

I have felt guilty for some time because I can't seem to get enthused about the novels I am told are so great. And then I stumbled upon a paragraph in the Williams essay that validated something that was disturbing me. Listen to this:

> I only rarely feel I'm being educated, or spiritually enlarged by a novel. I've even felt sometimes that the reading of a novel or watching of a film isn't somehow to be trusted. There are moments in fact when I feel I'm actually being discouraged, rather than exalted by prose fiction.

Yes. That's it. Me too, Mr. Williams. Thank you for daring to say it. Much of what I read seems to enhance the trance that the commodity culture would have us live. It seems to thicken the curtain obscuring creative vision and the mirror of consciousness. You could say we are being undone by the relentless crush of narrative.

❧

What to do? At the risk of sounding anarchist or too dramatic, God forbid, I think this calls for a form of nonviolent revolution. A radical questioning. The same kind of pushback as we spoke of against the fundamentalist mind that drives you into the ghetto of self-loathing. One must be skeptical of narrative itself. Skeptical of the lust for gossip, the craving of entertainment, and the propensity for unlimited distractions.

But it is much more than that. The narrative arc itself operates under the premise of such cultural norms as the necessity of conclusion. It more often than not idealizes closure and the reassurance of what we take as our right to resolution. I'd say the narrative promise even stretches to more grandiose, quasi-religious levels when it reaches for, and encourages, the expectation of redemption.

This is a difficult subject and perhaps an unpopular one. Bear with me and consider this long passage from C. K. Williams:

> Might the novel, along with its capacity for edification, also inoculate in us an unconscious belief that human life is a closed narrative, a narrative we are in the process of generating ourselves, and that any direct relations with beauty we manage to become involved with are incidental to the grander narrative shape we imagine encompasses them, as it encompasses everything else?

Better read through that again. If I understand him, Mr. Williams is saying that narrative itself has shaped the structure of our mind and thinking. Even a "grander narrative" is a box canyon assuming control and agency over life and its boundless, unpredictable nature. Our experience is now funneled through the story mill that breeds an illusory annexation of what was once the domain of mystery—beauty and spirit, not to mention color, sound, smell, and a host of other existing delights. These have been gobbled up by the dominant story line. I must confess, there are too many moments when I interrupt my experience by thinking what a good story this will make and plotting out the telling of it on the spot. Dear me, say it ain't so. But it is so. As a people and in the practice of art, we are beholden to the narrative imperative—that is, we are compelled to sing its praises and less so the wonder and mystery of existence.

The capitalist agenda has brilliantly exploited this narrative canyon with a system of meritocracy that holds us captive to economic growth and self-improvement tied to a program of rewards and punishments. This program is supported by the internal narrative, which perpetually takes us to court and judges our performance based on the standards laid down by the materialistic culture and accepted by mainstream America.

If you feel good enough, you don't need all the stuff you are told you do. If not, you'd better have a good retirement plan or you are a failure. If you haven't been published by a major publishing house, you are a loser. If you aren't represented by a big gallery, your painting is worthless. When the dark side of narrative turns to self-reproach and sucks us down into the bog of deficiency, the ruling class has the perfect narrative cure— redemption. Make yourself great. Make yourself a hero. Buy a Lexus. Never give up on the American Dream! These are the narrative conclusions we are up against that we must question and ultimately turn from.

⚘

The problem, as implied in the paragraphs you just read, is that replacing one story with another leaves you vulnerable to the dictates of narrative authority. These dictates are by definition limiting and reduce the vast mystery of your life to a story that pretends to make sense. Equally depleting is the narrative arc that consistently aims for the future and discards the present at the side of the road, having judged it as insufficient.

The last half of *Reflections on Poetry and the Novel* is devoted to the elaboration of an alternative way of being a person. A way that nurtures a poetic mind, one that makes room to receive and be touched by beauty in its many forms. Poetry, and the psychic qualities of the poem, mirrors the poetic response "to more immediately sensuous aspects of consciousness." Oh, don't you love that? Can you feel it? Yum. Love is one of those aspects of consciousness. Not the love that is represented in the typical narrative arc but the love that is a state of being, rooted in the moment and in relation to life, beauty, and the present. Going nowhere. The story that has no end but many beginnings. The story that is always becoming.

❧

I suppose I might sound like a Puritan or like I am hostile to novels and altogether down on narrative. I'm not. Much of my work includes helping people revise their personal narrative into a more complicated and compassionate tale that includes the strengths and flaws of those who wrote the scripts and rules from the preceding generations. I love a well-written read like my friend Suzy Vitello's YA book *The Moment Before*. I love a well-written sentence that seems to come off the page like the headwaters of the Metolius River comes from the earth. And yet, it seems necessary to recognize how the narrative bias has come to occupy our minds, determine our feeling and view of ourselves, and make us vulnerable to manipulation by the advertising and propaganda of those who think only of money and profit.

The good-enough place is not just another story. The existence of inherent goodness within is not just anther fancy twist of narrative suppleness. These can be directly experienced and known independent of the narrative discourse. A difference exists between awareness and narration, between witness consciousness and narrator, and most of all, between the story of a separate entity known as self and a spirit free from binding identities, connected with something grand and unnamable.

This deserves equal measures of questioning and can just as easily fall into a narrative scheme that claims to say what it is and in so doing sucks the joy out of that which cannot be put in a framework. I have been guilty of this many a time. But the fact that countless religions and individuals have done so does not in any way diminish or change the nature of the presence of consciousness that scientists, artists, academics, writers, and people of all colors are coming to recognize and know in a thousand different ways. In a thousand different ways that ultimately dissolve, along with all the accompanying stories, into the vastness of that indefinable presence we can't help but try to write about, talk about, and fashion into pages and pages and pages of wondrous yarns to tell and retell to our children and theirs around the campfire.

27

The Reader

I **F THERE IS A CONTEMPORARY AMERICAN *WAR AND PEACE*** out there, or a *Ulysses* or even a *Sound and the Fury*, we'll likely never know it. The reader doesn't have enough time. The reader is too impatient, or so we're told. Or so the reader is told. We are told any number of things about the reader we never meet. Some are true; some are fabricated to meet marketing criteria. Readers are as varied and hard to classify as writers. Good grief, I had a friend once who read the New York City telephone book cover to cover. I'll admit he was a little quirky, but still the tastes, interests, and desires of readers are multiple and best not summed up and put in a box.

Most people come to reading through listening. This is one reason it is a good idea to read your manuscript out loud. Hopefully as a child you learned the pleasure of being a reader on someone's lap so that reading is forever associated with close connection and the comfort of the human voice. My mother read me books about the Wild Wild West and the We Were There series that was popular at the time. The first books I remember being mine were the Hardy Boys adventures. I devoured those like candy. They were the closest we got to mystery in postwar Ohio. I read some sports books as I got older, but then I stopped reading. Entirely. Why? Simple—I didn't know how to read.

That wouldn't happen until my senior year of high school

when I took senior English with a very creative teacher named Warren Allen Smith. We jokingly called him WAS. But he was not a joke, and his life had little to do with the past tense. Today he is nearly ninety and has written five—yes, five—books since turning eighty! I don't know how he got through the fog I was in, but he did. He brought in an LP stage production of *Hamlet* and went through it line by line translating the odd language and introducing the major themes of the play in a way that lined up with our lives. One day he came in dressed as William Faulkner and, acting half drunk, allowed us to interview him about the South and his writing and drinking practices. We took notes on the drinking! Mr. Smith was and is a genius, and I'll always be grateful to him for what he gave me. Soon I was reading Poe and more Faulkner. Next thing I knew, I was declaring English as my major. A born-again reader.

Before Mr. Smith, I had been well on my way to becoming the type of person Aldous Huxley worried about when he wrote *Brave New World*. His fear was that we would not have to ban or burn books because nobody would want to read them. This isn't exactly the case. Here in Portland, the public library is thriving and visited by more people than the train station. And yet, my kids don't read a new book unless they have to for a school assignment. I hope they get WAS next year. Maybe the death of God will be followed soon by the death of the classics. Imagine no one checking out *Moby-Dick* at the library or *Crime and Punishment* collecting dust on the seldom-visited bookracks.

※

But who, pray tell, is this reader we hear so much about, and how do we reach Ms. Reader? Who are we writing to and for? Ourselves? The critics? Our neighbor? When I wrote my novel, I really didn't have a clue who I was writing for. I just knew I had to. When Jack, my ninety-one-year-old neighbor, dying of prostrate cancer, came to me with tears in his eyes and said he was less afraid of dying after reading my book, I was speechless. I had no idea. That will be remembered as one of the great moments of my life. But it never dawned on me that I was writing to him as my reader. I was just writing from as deep and authentic a place as I knew how.

Nevertheless, all those years of reading had given me a strong unconscious connection to the reader after all. This identification with the individual who holds the book in hand is crucial. That's one reason everyone always lists continuous reading as essential to good writing. Maybe you are the rare individual who, while standing outside on a warm summer night, hears a faint whispering in the air saying, "If you write it, they will read." Most of us aren't that lucky. We write with some knowledge of the population most likely to pick up the book, like my friend Suzy who writes outstanding YA novels. She obviously has an antenna for the spirit and voice of those she writes for, but how is she able to know who will be picking up her book?

A writer must be ruthlessly faithful to the story and at the same time empathic and attuned to the reader. That seems like a pretty tall order, and it is. One way to think of it is that in order to write, you have to be able to *read* people. You have to be able to read people like Mr. Smith taught us to read a story, looking for the varied layers of meaning, the multiple themes, and that which is only alluded to in a person's life. We have to learn to read bodies for what they are expressing, behavior for hidden motivations, and stories for what they leave out. It is, as Naomi Nye has written so beautifully, "the words under the words" that we need to read and find in the scrambled discourse of the world.

When reading people, we look for what is important to them. Not only the known world but also the deep unconscious pull that directs their attention in one way and not another. By this I mean very subtle shifts in consciousness toward that which is most compelling in the moment. Let me tell you an amazing story of what I'm talking about. But hold on to your wallet.

This *New Yorker* story begins in Las Vegas with a man named Apollo Robbins. Cool name, eh? Mr. Robbins is a professional pickpocket. He has not gone to the dark side as you might suspect—instead, he entertains people with his artistry in the casinos of Las Vegas returning a wallet, a cell phone, a piece of jewelry, or even a pair of eyeglasses to one customer after another. If he's feeling mischievous, he might replace a wallet with a chicken leg. But his return policy is always met with the same startled and amused gasp, "What! Holy cow, how in the world did you do that?" He leaves people laughing and shaking their heads. And probably slightly anxious that they are such easy prey.

We meet Mr. Robbins sitting around a table in a coffee shop with a group of magicians. The leader of the pack, a certain Penn Jillette, is deriding the pickpocket trade as inferior to the art of magic and entirely beneath its appeal in the world of show business. He challenges Robbins to demonstrate his skill. Robbins begs off claiming discomfort with the group and the difficulty presented by Jillette's clothing, which is just shorts and a sports shirt. Jillette chides him, "Come on, steal something from me!"

Robbins offers to do a trick instead. He asks Jillette to place his ring on a piece of paper and outline it with his pen. Jillette removes his ring, puts it down on the paper, and takes his pen from his shirt pocket. When he tries to outline the ring, he freezes, looks up, and his face is pale. "Fuck you," he says and slumps in his chair. Robbins smiles and holds up a thin, cylindrical object: the cartridge from Jillette's pen!

Why was I so taken with this story? I had to wonder if I was hiding latent criminal tendencies from myself. Was I intrigued by the possibility of making people look foolish, perhaps to unload my own feelings of shame? Maybe I never grew up and am just a kid at heart in love with a good magic trick. What was so compelling? All of the above?

Perhaps. But reading on, I learned that the remarkable talents of Apollo Robbins have now become the subject of scientific study into the workings of the brain. Psychiatrists and neuroscience experts have recruited Mr. Robbins in their research to explore the nature of consciousness and human attention. Because deft at hand as he may be, his artistry has more to do with understanding human nature than it does with technique. (Writers, take note.)

Obviously, he must have quick hands and a light touch, but Robbins has this to say about his craft: "It's all about the choreographing of people's attention. Attention is like water. It flows. It's liquid. My goal isn't to hurt or bewilder people with a puzzle but to challenge their maps of reality." Now we're on it.

When I was growing up in Ohio, the reality maps were narrow and rigid. But this isn't unique to Ohio. All cultures and institutions have maps of what is and what isn't acknowledged as real within the collective view. The world is flat. The sun orbits around Earth. I suppose the human brain has been constructing reality maps ever since it got big enough to do so, or maybe that is what made it so big and complex. Good stuff as far as adaptation and survival are concerned. This allows the evolutionary genius to play its hand. Not so great for creative and alternative views on what we call the real world.

Most great art is a sledgehammer to conventional maps of reality. Picasso and company are masters at turning our worlds upside down and inside out until our traditional notions fall apart like old bread and the doors of perception open. They show us what we don't see, and how these maps create, limit, and distort our vision. Dying is like that too: dismantling the ultimate reality map, the constructed self.

※

I realize my profession of psychotherapy is a lot like pickpocketing. What do we do? We dip into the unconscious communications of our patients and pull out long-standing and unrecognized beliefs about the self and the world. We reach into the pockets of unwanted emotion and liberate feeling that has been stuffed away. These efforts, which often seem like magic, bring about shifts in reality maps that are tectonic in nature.

And like Mr. Robbins, good therapists return the contents of the unconscious to their patients, enabling the development of new and inclusive personal maps. This process allows for the expansion of awareness beyond maps to take in ever-greater portions of what is. And what that is, we could say, is the unfathomable: that which cannot be mapped, though we cannot help but try. That which cannot be named or cornered by the mind, though it might try. And like Apollo Robbins's happy victims, we can stand in this vast moment undone and in awe of the beauty of this life that again and again does its best to wake us up from our reality to the full radiance of being.

So have a look at the entire article sometime. You'll find it in the January 7, 2013, edition of the *New Yorker*, written by Adam Green. What a great read it is.

But for now take some time to chart out your reality maps. What are some of the ones that govern you most? What culture did you grow up in, and what were its organizing principles? In the Midwest culture, one of the basic commandments was don't brag. Don't talk about yourself. If we did, we were told, "You're too big for your britches." Hardly a compliment. We held ourselves in check, or we were at the least in conflict about feeling good and expansive. Tough to promote your book when that map is always leading you into the corner of the room. Maybe you came from an anti-intellectual world, or one in which telling the truth was disloyal. There are any number of maps that are traps and confine the True Self to the shadows.

And what about your attention—where does it go? Have you noticed the patterns? Try meditating and watching your thoughts move every which way. This can be a telling and embarrassing experiment. Maybe your attention circles back over and over to dreams of success. Maybe you are pulled to sexual stimulation and fantasy. Maybe you're like my son and notice cars at every turn.

Your attention might go to spotting danger or opportunities. You might hate being the center of attention or you might love it. Pay attention to attention itself. This awareness can help you identify the reality maps that govern your perception and motivation.

What books are on your nightstand? That tells us a lot about the direction your attention travels. I just bought three new books: *This Changes Everything, The Story of the Human Body,* and *The Edge of the Sky.* What do you make of that collection? What does that tell you of the nature of my attention?

Where is your reader's attention likely to be headed? How flexible is it? What are you doing, or not, to influence the quality of that attention? What are you including or excluding? Apollo Robbins is able to read his people. He is fluent in the language of unconscious motivation. Are you? What do your people really want?

᙭

Finally, let's talk about you as a reader. What kind of reader are you? What do you like and not like? Do you like simple language or complex sentences? Poetic or mater-of-fact? Most of all, take stock of what type of reader you are in relation to your own work. Where does your attention go? Do you look for faults? Ken Kesey quipped in *Sometimes a Great Notion,* "Look at the donut, not the hole." Which are you looking at? Are you focused on what you are or what you are not?

Here's a novel idea: be kind to yourself. Be a kind reader. I hope you can treat yourself well, with kindness and in recognition of the goodness of your work. Celebrate before you criticize. I know this can be hard. But try. I really hope you can be kind to yourself. Accepting and affirming. You are a writer! You are precious. They say a dog needs four positive words to every negative one. I'd say you and I could use the same kind of treatment. Remember the mantra "good enough." Good enough, good enough, thank God almighty, I'm good enough.

28
Genre

YOU DON'T WANT TO PLAY CHESS WITH ME. NOT BECAUSE I'm good—au contraire—I'm terrible. But I play so slowly that I often frustrate a decent player into making hasty mistakes. This isn't really a strategy of mine; it's a necessity. I just can't think five moves from now. Therefore, you will never read a mystery authored by this guy. Never. Frankly, I really can't even fathom how anyone can write a whodunit. My good buddy John Hohn is pretty damn good at it, and I marvel that he, or anyone, can be so clever and think so far ahead. Seems like I'm always playing catch-up. Maybe in another lifetime.

Which isn't to say that mystery is off limits to someone with a mind like mine. Not at all. Mystery abounds in this world of ours. I like to say that trying to anticipate what's coming around the next corner is like trying to predict your next dream! The same is true for understanding people fully. You can spend a lifetime with one person and still not be able to say that you know that individual completely. The same goes for yourself if you're honest. Can you really say what is going to come out of your mouth next?

The wonder of life is in the play between repetition and the unexpected. What makes for delight is surprise; what makes for anxiety is the unpredictable. Of course one person's delight is another's dread. So it goes, round and round. Where the wheel stops, nobody knows. And then again, it doesn't really stop, does it? We like to think so, or at least that it slows enough for us to catch our breath or get off at the Queens station. But it doesn't, even when what it brings us is the death of a loved one, life is disturbingly indifferent and marches on without so much as pausing to extend its sympathies.

※

On and on it goes spinning out what adds up to an infinite number of happenings. And I'm not even counting the internal calendar of events! How can there ever be a shortage of material? Well, we may never get an answer to that one, but it sure is exciting and heartening how many people are out there trying to give voice to this endless parade of human activity.

Because the numbers approach the infinite, the list of the variety of genres is a lengthy one. We need this broad array of slants on human life to have the slightest chance at capturing any semblance of the mystery, romance, or stranger-than-sci-fi nature of our time on this earth. What an improbably great thing that, for instance, my reading history began with *Mad Magazine* and the Hardy Boys, ventured into the larger-than-life Russians, held hands with Vonnegut for some time, rode on Ken Kesey's broad shoulders during the seventies, flirted with mysteries, did the required reading of *Stranger in a Strange Land*, *Dune*, and *2001: A Space Odyssey*, and finally settled onto the rich literary lap of Toni Morrison.

That list doesn't name all the other stops at roadside attractions, but it gives a sampling of memorable destinations in my reading life. I'm sure yours would sound similar—if not in content, then at least in variety. What remarkable fortune to live in a time of such bountiful expression. It takes my breath away. So many titles and genres. So many authors. It really is dizzying how prolific the creative impulse is manifesting in our time.

One thing I've been trying to bring attention to throughout these pages is the diversity of psychological life, the multiplicity of the self and the audaciousness of generative spirit. The Greeks and Hindus had it right when they gave name to thousands of gods and goddesses in an effort to name the many aspects of the one and only. Unity and diversity are not contradictory opposites but the paradoxical nature of what is. This is the great mystery: How I can be both separate and one with everything? I hope it is clear by now that I hold the same to be true of psyche and spirit. These are different faces of one force moving and dancing its way toward wholeness.

The numbers are large, and as a society that prizes competition, we are so captivated by individual differences that we seem to lose sight all too easily of the commonality among peoples. The genres are separated out at some cost, I believe. One of the costs is the establishment of accepted formulas for what is a romance or young adult novel. As every book contains great mysteries of human nature, so every book is a romance in that the writer must court the reader and romance that reader into the heart of the story. I love what my friend John, the mystery writer, said about writing his last book. He said he had to romance it into existence. So even the writing contains elements of romance, mystery, and the so-called different genres.

Many writers seem to be straining to be different. Straining to be unique, to be noticed. Who can blame them? Still, it is worth recognizing that the Self Project may demand a type of notoriety. When the ego has us by the collar, commonality is a threat. Ordinary is shunned. In fact, things as they are disturb the ego, which is always striving to be better. We want everything to be different than what it is. Nothing is good enough. That review was awful. That agent was insulting. Before you know it, you're fighting everything. Accepting nothing. Fearing that if your work doesn't hit the moon, you'll be invisible and the whole Self Project will be defeated. This is agony.

In fact, you could say that much of the drama of human existence, and the folly of our ways, is found in the efforts to make ourselves feel worthy and the somersaults we attempt while hoping outcomes will make us happy. Often this is the motivation behind the murder in the mystery, the seduction in the romance, the betrayal in the drama, or the daring adventure of science fiction. Humans look to fixing, or changing, the external makeup of their lives when what troubles the soul lies within. Rarely do we turn inside to find satisfaction. Instead, we make and create more stories, like a dog digging holes to find a lost bone. Brene Brown calls this, "Hustling for worthiness."

✹

Were we to pause and ask ourselves what we are really up to, we might be surprised to find that the infinite array of stories and the multiple genres that make up this staggering library are in a very real way one story. The story of longing. The tale of yearning to find love, to find our way home, and to find peace. What seems like a million tales is in essence a single biography of the blind, groping in the dark for the love that does not disappoint.

Whether it is the crime of passion, youthful romance, or lust for knowledge at the heart of all quests, it seems a longing burns. Whether it's Ahab on the back of Moby Dick, Oedipus returning home, or Raskolnikov plotting against the old woman, it seems the longing that is too much to bear becomes perverted into any number of wayward attempts to get what is missing, to complete what is lacking, or to fix what is broken. Enormous amounts of human ingenuity and creativity, driven by anxiety, are directed toward these pursuits. More often than not they end badly or in a baffling type of disappointment when the prize does not satisfy as expected.

Listen to any country-western song and you'll hear and feel the yearning for love and that special someone in its most undisguised voice. Take in a good opera and there it is, that same raw longing in a very different arrangement. But it is that same plea, the same bleeding heart imploring God, life, and the subject of that ache to meet and soothe the longing that pierces the heart. If we the people are afraid of need, it is safe to say we are terrified of longing. Scared silly. Particularly since it is more often than not tied to past heartaches and feelings of rejection. Forget it. Much better to long for success, security, McMansions, fancy cars, fame, and fortune: the list is endless, is it not?

I have found that *terror* is not too strong a word to describe how we may feel toward longing. Because longing is the mother of vulnerability. Longing makes the heart's desire relational. It is an admission that I cannot do it all—I cannot control the world and make myself happy. And this makes us vulnerable. Frightening as it is, this yearning, this wild cry, answers one of the great human questions: Do I belong? Yes, you belong. You belong to humanity and the perennial search for that which will still the heart and mind. That which will open the heart to love and be loved in return. Longing connects you to your neighbor. When you suffer painful disappointments, those feelings connect you to strangers and friends alike. You are not alone. Whether you are living out Shakespeare or Henry James or Virginia Wolfe, you are living out the longings of the human heart as it has evolved these many millennia.

I hope this is of some comfort. There are days it feels like this longing will kill you. Tragically this happened to many of the geniuses of my generation. We lost Janis Joplin, Jimi Hendrix, and Jim Morrison at what was probably the peak of their artistic lives. I have worked with many patients who used drugs, affairs, and excessive work hours to blunt or conceal the longing that was threatening to break through. They risked their lives, their marriages, and their health to avoid an encounter with a yearning that makes us tremble. When the longing did burn through, they felt utterly overwhelmed and barely able to function. It took lots of support and tremendous courage on their part to sit with these feelings.

⚒

One last novel idea: when longing comes surging in like a blistering sirocco off the desert floor, greet it with whatever welcoming acceptance you are able to muster. Nothing is wrong. It will not kill you. If possible, say thank you and live into it, relax into it. Yes, this is counterintuitive; yes, you want to run like hell; yes, you want to look for any distraction available; yes, you feel like your heart is about to explode; yes, you are calling yourself a baby; yes, you feel that way and so do I; and yes, you can surrender, not collapse, to the waves of longing and desire.

Don't pathologize yourself. Breathe slowly and deeply. This is the movement of your deepest self calling for you. This is the moment of opening to your inner being: to that which puts its arms around you and rocks the not-good-enough self to sleep. That quiets and soothes the feeling that you are bad. That sings a sweet song to remind you that nothing is wrong, you are just fine. And, surprise surprise, it is the link to that which infuses body, mind, and soul with the creative fire you so love.

Longing is all tangled up in ambition. Wanting success, wanting to be admired for your beautiful writing. Nothing wrong with that, we all want to be recognized and appreciated. That's fine. The problem is, it doesn't go far enough. It doesn't touch the core where the feelings of shame rule. Even psychotherapy doesn't go the distance. Much as I owe to therapy and much as I advocate that you find a good therapist to sit with you and help process your emotional world, it still doesn't go to the center of the problem. Alarming and scary as the breakthrough of longing can be, it is your invitation, your guide and companion, to making your way home. Home to your big self, home to being and into the arms of the love that is free for all. Home to what the wonderful Spanish poet Antonio Machado referred to in this way:

> What the poet is searching for
> is not the fundamental I
> but the deep you.

I will tell you that I have been searching since I was a young lad, and I am not unique in this pursuit. It is my contention that we live in a land of spiritual poverty and that many, if not most, are restless and hungry. Many are hungry and searching, but lost. When my friends were watching, I went looking in Dostoevsky for answers and reassurance that my mind was working. When no one was watching, I went looking in the refrigerator, blessed friend. Most of my longings were oral in nature: I yearned to kiss the sweet lips of a woman, I yearned to say things that sounded really smart, and I yearned for ice cream, my one true love.

I could swallow nearly anything, and did, and stayed pretty skinny until I turned forty, looked down, and there was my dad's potbelly looking up at me. From that day on, I have wrestled with my cravings, fought them tooth and nail, given in to them, suppressed them, and hated them along with myself and what I took to be unforgivable weakness. At some point in time, I realized they were not weaknesses but perversions—that is, misdirections of a subterranean longing that would not quit.

Be thankful it won't quit. That it is tireless in pursuit of bringing you back home to what we like to call wholeness. Back to presence and deep embodiment. Back to effortless being that we know from experience as our place of origin. As the place we will recognize as the love that has brushed against our cheek many times over the course of our lives. In finding yourself you are found by that ineffable muse we all long for.

But to get there, you have to pass through the dangerous world of shame, emptiness, and longing. All the distractions and substitutes have to disappoint and fail. These are painful days.

But the longing will not be extinguished. It will light up the trail—just as my dear Machado wrote in one of his most illuminating poems "Last Night, As I Was Sleeping":

> Last night, as I was sleeping,
> I dreamt—marvelous error!—
> that a spring was breaking
> out in my heart.
> I said: Along which secret aqueduct,
> Oh water, are you coming to me,
> water of a new life
> that I have never drunk?
>
> Last night, as I was sleeping,
> I dreamt—marvelous error!—
> that I had a beehive
> here inside my heart.
> And the golden bees
> were making white combs
> and sweet honey
> from my old failures.

And isn't that how it is? Longing breaks out of the heart, sometimes flooding us with feelings we don't know what to do with. Where does this force come from? And listen to the tenderness and vulnerability as he asks, "Are you coming to me?"

Your longing is the water of new life. New life that can flood and overwhelm your system. New life that sometimes feels like a beehive inside your heart. Right? It hurts, it stings, it feels like too much, but there is no escape. And all the while, "The golden bees were making white combs and sweet honey from my old failures." Believe it or not, if you can hang with that longing, that bittersweet desire will take the years of shame and turn them to nectar. The dream is yearning and it is real, and it happens right on the spot, right there inside where we may have never looked, much less drunk.

No matter what genre may pull you, no matter if you are writing chilling mysteries, hot romances, intriguing tales for young adults, or mind-blowing science fiction, you are, as Faulkner said, writing for the human heart. That extraordinary place, that place of longing that is so strong it sometimes must take another life to be quieted, that place that is so strong the love for another makes it feel as though it will burst, that place that is so strong it takes adolescent brains and turns them into fireworks of agony and ecstasy, that place that is so strong it is not content with this world but seeks adventure and knowledge beyond our borders. That place that is so strong it makes you pick up paper and pencil and tell the story only you can tell. The story that has been told ten thousand times and never before.

Talk to your longing now. Don't be afraid. Write down all the embarrassing roads it has taken you down. Say you're sorry to anyone you hurt along the way. Say you're sorry to your own self for all the pain you caused yourself. Have a few laughs when you recollect the adventures that yearning has delivered you to. What do you crave? What can you never say no to? Just acknowledge that; feel into it for a moment. Try to release the object of craving to the wind. Just live with the wanting, the raw wanting, for a moment. Feel its temperature. The remarkable power behind it. Let it speak to you. What is it that you really want? What is it that this longing, this serpentine wanting, is asking for? Is it peace? Some peace and quiet? Is it safety, a place to feel protected? Is it to be fully alive, fully present in your life? Do you long for a partner to share that life with? Someone who gets you and whom you get? Is it love? What type of love? A mother's love, romantic or erotic love, or love of nature and its children? Whatever it may be, whatever genre or form, just let it be. Let that holy desire be there as it is. Let it fill your heart.

PART VI

Characters

29
The Villain(s)

RUMI ONCE WROTE SOMETHING LIKE THIS: "PEOPLE CAN'T tell if I'm weeping or laughing. I wonder myself." So do I. This old world is way too cruel a place to love much of the time. Way too heartbreaking to snuggle up to. And yet, how breathtaking it is, how lovely and diverse are the staggering creations of this improbable dance of life. Who can resist its charms? Who does not curse its betrayals? And then, we have humans! I often think it must have been an adolescent God that created us, realized the terrible error of his ways, and fled for another potter's wheel in a galaxy far, far away to craft a more matured version. Humans. No wonder we're laughing and crying, sometimes in the same breath: we are a preposterously foolish and dangerous lot, and somehow ingenious and lovable despite it all.

I still believe there are very few truly evil people. A few exceptions come quickly to mind. And I suspect, if the complete story were known, those individuals would themselves have either lived through experiences too brutal to comprehend, suffered a significant brain injury, or been the unfortunate victim of bad neurological wiring too tangled to overcome. William Stafford said it well when he wrote, "The darkness around us is deep." It is all too easy for us to lose our way.

Call me naïve, call me a bleeding-heart liberal, but I do have sympathy for the devil. Thank you, Stones. If it's hard to tell whether I'm laughing or crying, it doesn't get any easier to tell if someone is good or bad. Some of the best art and literature helps reveal the blurring of these distinctions. Dickens was a pro at this, consider dear Mr. Scrooge and his transformation. Our modern pop culture archetype is Darth Vader. His son, Luke Skywalker, refused to give up on his father's goodness, and his faith was rewarded. I'm sure my teenage sons see me as the villain at times when I yell or lay down the law, and I must admit to a certain amount of confusion in myself as to which I am: good parent or bad.

Perhaps Frankenstein is a good example of a hybrid character. Talk about being misunderstood! It's not much different when a couple enters therapy with me ten years too late. Especially if there has been a betrayal of sorts, the offending partner is introduced as an absolute monster. When I look closely, I invariably see a person with all sorts of very human emotions quivering inside. But the description, often accepted by both parties, is of an unforgivable, terrible person who has forsaken all rights to understanding and compassion. It is as though the bad has completely run any good out of town. These one-dimensional caricatures are long lasting. The outrage that insists on portraits of this nature is understandable, and yet it is also held defensively as a protection against any vulnerability that might allow for repair of the bond between the warring partners. My job is to restore the complexity and humanity of the individual.

❦

Every gripping story needs a villain. The human psyche is no different. For various reasons, it seems we need enemies. After the Soviet Union fell, America was in a vacuum and the aggression normally reserved for the enemy turned on ourselves:

Republicans against Democrats, conservative versus liberal. The contempt with which these parties hold each other is a convincing piece of evidence for the existence of a need for an enemy—that is, a psychological imperative to hate. Political wars and the war on drugs are inadequate substitutes for the mighty evil empire. Not until Al Qaeda took down our phallic monuments to the gods of wealth did we have a suitable enemy to focus our attention on again.

A villain focuses our energies, organizing the aggressive and vindictive shadow elements of our nature into a coherent position that solidifies a sense of self and community. Interpersonally, it allows for the nearly complete displacement of unwanted feelings of shame and badness threatening the equilibrium of people at war with their shadow side. Anger at the enemy is binding in that it brings together groups of people and disparate parts of the self. Following the attack on Pearl Harbor in 1941, a feeling of cohesion and solidarity prevailed on the island that had been missing as different Hawaiian groups unified and organized to protect the country from the Japanese.

Many villains earn their place on the billboard, while others are a clear scapegoat for those who need to renounce personal responsibilities for their own destructive ways. The terrible history of race relations in our country should be ample evidence of this phenomenon. But this is not unique to our country. Nearly all modern societies have an "untouchables" cast built into the hierarchy of the culture: India formalized it, and the industrial nations institutionalized it.

❦

For our purposes, there are two leading candidates for arch villain in the emotional life of a writer: depression and anxiety. These are formidable enemies and about as hard to eradicate as the smell of a noxious gas. How do you get ahold of depression?

And after all, doesn't it have hold of you? What do we do with anxiety when it seems to be in complete control and jerking us around? Is there really any hope of getting free of these conditions that make our lives miserable and interfere with creative work? The answer is, in fluctuating order, yes, maybe, not really. That probably doesn't sound very encouraging to you, and at times I too despair that a more definitive answer is not possible. But let me explain what I mean.

Let's start with depression. And let's begin with a look at medication. Should I, or shouldn't I? What does it do, what does it not do? Rilke refused therapy because he feared the exiting of his demons would mean the loss of his angels. I think he was wrong about that on both counts. Therapy doesn't eliminate demons, and to the extent it does weaken their influence, angels are all the more free to fly. Is it the same dilemma with antidepressants? Do they blunt or eliminate creative juices? Yes, maybe, not really.

First the yes. Medications are used for a reason—they work. Particularly for unfortunate individuals who suffer from major depression or debilitating anxieties, antidepressants and benzodiazepines are effective, and in the case of the benzos, they work quickly. If you have very large spikes in feeling that overwhelm your capacity to keep any semblance of equilibrium or to manage your life, these drugs can help even out the peaks and valleys. Some can help elevate mood if you are lost in a quagmire of depressive or hopeless feelings. Anyone who has been diagnosed with PTSD may want to experiment with a serotonin re-uptake inhibitor, the most commonly prescribed drug. If it is anxiety that is plaguing you, then a benzodiazepine will help subdue the surge of anxiety or panic so you can get some relief.

Some people are worried that taking drugs is a cop-out, or unnatural. What is really unnatural is trauma. It is trauma that disrupts the normal rhythms of the body and nervous system. Daily experience is bewildering and painful and floods the mind with hormones that cause changes in the chemistry of the brain, leaving lasting impressions that shape our identity and emotional balance. By all means, if you are suffering greatly from either or both of these maladies, please consult a trusted doctor or someone who can help find the proper type and dose of medication for you. It doesn't help you or anyone else for you to be overrun and dragged down by these afflictions.

Now for the maybe. Neither the antidepressants nor the anti-anxiety meds are for everybody. Our brains are so complex and the system of neurotransmitters so intricate that the truth is, there is more we don't know than we do. The fact is, it's still a bit of a crapshoot as to which meds will work for you. The good news is, there are many to choose from, so you should be able to identify one that can help. That said, it needs to be noted that they don't work for everyone. There are a couple of problems. Some people react badly and can even feel worse. I have many patients who never seem to adjust. Some feel unreal or as if they aren't all there. While the emotional swings are changed, you may experience a flatlining of your normal sense of aliveness and suffer from a greatly reduced libido. For many people, that is too high a cost and they turn to therapy, exercise, and yoga to address anxiety and depression.

People whose constitutional makeup is on the sensitive side may find that these medications make them feel sick. On the other hand, they may be taking too much and could respond quite well to a low dose, even one well below the typical clinical level. This amounts to a process of trial and error that can be worth the patience it may take to find the right drug at the right dosage. It takes a prescriber with enough experience and a certain sensitivity to people's needs and constitutional makeup to help guide you through the maze. One size does not fit all.

All right, what about the not really part? I don't object to medications for the most part. Often I encourage people to look into finding something that will take the edge off their symptoms so they can do better than just get by. What I do object to is the practice of handing these medications out like candy without a real discernment about whether the problems are situational or truly biochemical. It's not that this is an either-or thing, but it is important that people understand these meds are not a cure and the underlying feelings of unworthiness do not go away even though the moods are improved. If you want a more thorough approach, try using medication to ease the distress you are feeling and combine that with good psychotherapy that will help you deal with past traumas and get to the heart of the feelings that are causing such distress. And don't forget, walking in the great outdoors is the best antidepressant!

❧

The question rarely arises in conventional conversation as to whether it is inevitable that depression and anxiety must take the role of the villain. Is it possible that we could relate to our depressive feelings and anxious states in ways that are not so oppositional? Could it be that these feelings might actually help us along as people and writers? Okay, these are obviously leading questions, but before we cast depression and anxiety once and for all in the role of the modern Dracula, let's take a closer look.

When I first began practicing psychotherapy, it was a great puzzle to me why so many people seemed to need their depression. They held on to it like a life raft in the open sea. Now I'm not saying all depressions are of this type, and I'm not saying that the investment in sustaining depression is a conscious choice, but what I found in my work is that depression is more often than not a preferred state of mind to a deeply feared alternative. That alternative is often related to grief or a very, very painful longing for a lost love or the love one never had. To say this is preferable is to grant too much conscious volition to the movement into depression. Nevertheless, the protective self does slide toward depression as if it were a heavy blanket that buffers feelings believed to be overwhelming and never ending.

This protective strategy develops over time and is so effective, the subject may forget the purpose for which it was created and think of the depression as unrelated to other feelings. In other words, depression is in some respects a solution to the problem of emotional overload. A solution that compounds the depressive tendency by causing a severe disconnect with the core self. Modern medicine and its tendencies toward isolating symptoms from the person collude with the singular disguise that depression presents.

Depression can be thought of as a signal—that is, a helpful clue that something is amiss within. It is in actuality an unintended narrative of sorts whose message is lost if taken only at the level of an acute or chronic disease. For instance, let's return to the Self Project and look at depression from the perspective of the drive to make oneself feel like someone special. Depression is now an obvious outcome of failed expectations and strivings to make oneself feel okay by means of success. When the book doesn't sell, or the reviews are not great, we plummet. We fall into depressions that can feel like the world is ending.

With a different relationship to the inner world, depression can be a friend warning you of the perils of building your house on shifting sands. Major depression, though very layered and complicated, often turns out to be the total collapse of the self under the weight of unbearable loss. However, any attempt to eradicate the symptoms of depression without understanding and supporting the self that has been crushed by life events is doomed.

Anxiety is much the same, only more so because of the nature of human existence and the inevitable presence of anxiety in one form or another. Out on the savannah, anxiety warns you of approaching danger: the lions are coming, better run. In the city, anxiety warns you of other dangers: feelings are approaching, better hide.

At the heart of my thesis has been the feeling of shame. Anxiety is a common reaction to the approaching possibility of exposure that may reveal real or imagined flaws. Better run and hide, shame is on the way. Anxiousness is about the unwanted presence of these emotions. Yikes! Nowhere to run. No escape. But anxiety need not be the bad guy. Anxiety is the flag that says, "Look out!" In that regard, it is possible to view our anxieties as something other than noxious. Tough as it is to be besieged by bouts of anxiety or panic, it is possible to meet them with acceptance and the knowledge that they signal the emergence of important feelings that need attention. It is remarkable how anxiety can dissipate as split-off feelings are reclaimed. I work with an attorney who has terrible bouts of high anxiety. When I remind him to attend to his sadness, the anxiety dissipates almost immediately.

One of those feelings that is so important to the understanding of depression and anxiety is anger. Depression is very often the result of anger turned against the self, and anxiety is a reaction to the emergence of anger. Anger deserves an entire chapter of its own, but suffice to say that anger, or what we might call a healthy protest, is an essential response to traumatic violations of boundaries such as occur when abuses take place. Unfortunately, it is common to think of anger as hurtful and destructive, and to segregate it to the closet. It is typically not safe to express anger in abusive situations; therefore, it is internalized and lodged inside as an agent against the self.

This is the origin of self-blame. Where you and I become public enemy number one. The villain we can't shake. "I'm not smart enough." "I'm not creative enough." "I'm not disciplined enough." This is the "I am not enough" shakedown we all know too well. The one that shadows every moment. The one that jumps out and ambushes us even in a moment of success. Self-blame and self-attack lead to depression and anxiety. The self condemning the self. A lifetime of this treatment wears a person down. No wonder we get depressed and anxious. No wonder we hit roadblocks in our work. No wonder we look for distractions. Maybe I'll just roll over and go back to sleep rather than get up and face my tormentor at the writing table. That guy almost always wins.

❧

What if we could meet these tough feelings with a grain of acceptance or with even a tiny measure of curiosity? When I feel depressed, what is it that I don't want to feel? When I feel anxious, what feelings are nearby wanting to become conscious? Perhaps a feeling that I am utterly alone, or perhaps the insight that I gave up on myself when I was fourteen. What if I could keep from reacting so much and instead make room for what is there and try to be open to what isn't there? What if I normalized some of these feelings and didn't react to them as if they were my enemy? What if I could say yes to the angry feelings simmering within? And imagine if I could hold those who have hurt me accountable. This is not blame or abdication of responsibility—this is the healthy recognition of real injuries.

Anxiety isn't going anywhere. It is fundamental to life and being. The great theologian Paul Tillich wrote *The Courage to Be* and went in depth into the anxieties central to human existence. We can't escape anxiety, but we can face it and learn from it. Tillich identified three primary anxieties: mortality, lack of meaning, and condemnation. You may have guessed I'm particularly focused on the anxiety of condemnation. The point is, you don't have to think something is wrong with you because you suffer from anxiety. You don't have to run in circles trying to fix yourself. You don't have to load up on microbrews to ensure that you won't feel. But you do need courage. The courage to accept and lean in to your feelings. The courage to hold and examine anxiety so that you can understand what it is connected to. The courage to look that villain in the eye and see that it is not as powerful or dangerous as you have thought. In fact, it may be offering help.

Mostly we need the courage to be. How do we find that? How to we ensure that our own inner world is not to become, or stay, the enemy? How do we face death, lack of meaning, and shame without running or collapsing? How do we face emptiness? And can we, or do we lack the courage and strength? I have no doubt that you can, given the right support. The problem isn't you; the problem is the multitude of books and methods of reducing depression and anxiety that make it sound too simple. People inevitably fail at the easier-said-than-done prescriptions and fall into even worse depressive feelings of inadequacy and hopelessness. It's like painting the house before you sand the siding: looks good at first, but soon the paint begins to peel off.

Growth happens through affirmative action. By moving toward what you want, not by trying to rid yourself of what you don't want. By recognizing what is there already, whether it be issues and emotions that need attention or an inner self that is nourishing and full. Those feelings of richness and fullness make the villain melt; comfort depression, bringing you back to life; and soothe anxiety, allowing peacefulness to come forth.

The inner self is actually free from the tyranny of depression and anxiety. This is not your nature. I know this may sound strange. I know when you are under the blankets feeling dark and fearful, that feels like everything, but give yourself a chance to experience what I'm talking about. Sit with yourself and observe these thoughts and feelings. Notice how they are really swimming in a wide ocean of awareness. Turn your attention to that open sea and it will befriend you. Relax into its arms and it will hold you. Bring it everything, depression and anxiety, hopelessness and fear, love and hate: bring all the alleged enemies of the soul, and watch them become waves of being coming and going in the sea of you.

There is a way out of these cycles that goes through the winds and heat. That is about acceptance and not aversion. That relies on engagement and empathy and does not create more enemies and divisions in the psyche. That builds confidence in your abilities to transform, not reject, your experience. To welcome your feelings, not fear them. Yoga works, therapy works, meditation works, exercise works, nutrition works.

God, I haven't even mentioned nutrition! Want to see my anxiety spike? Hand me an espresso! Sensitive types, beware: sugar kills. Sorry, folks.

The point is, you are not hopeless. Be good to yourself. Be careful what you take in, mentally and physically. Trade in depression for sadness, despair for compassion, and anxiety for courage. Trade in the Self Project for the real thing. Do these things and watch your creative force expand.

30
Editors, Agents, and Publishers

I **LIKE TO SING TO MYSELF. ONE LITTLE TUNE I'M FOND OF** seems just right for certain occasions in the writer's life. It goes something like this: "I'm gonna sit right down and write myself a letter, and make believe it came, from you...I'm gonna write words oh so sweet, they're gonna knock me off my feet..."

Oh yeah. I first heard this sweet classic written by Fred Ahlert and Joe Young when Pat Boone sang it on the black-and-white TV sometime in the late fifties. There have been sexier versions produced since then, but no matter the arrangement, the original soothing lyrics and melody can still lift my spirits if I'm feeling down and out from filling up the recycling bin with rejection letters.

Whenever I imagine treading into the lion's den of publishing, I sing this little song to myself. Whenever I open an email from an agent, or a thin little envelope from a publishing house, I hum a few bars from this tune and feel dread give way to sweetness. Ah, much better. I think I'll sit right down, right now, and write myself a letter. Let's see, how about this:

> *Dear Mr. Kenney,*
> *I read your novel and found it truly breathtaking. Our agency would be very pleased to represent you in the search for a suitable publisher.*

Or, better yet:

> *The board of selection editors at Knopf Publishing House would like to congratulate you on the completion of your stellar historical novel. We found it captivating and would be honored to include it with our list of projects for the coming year.*

"...I'm gonna write words oh so sweet, they're gonna knock me off my feet..." Sigh. Put another quarter in the jukebox—I want to hear that song one more time. For the 99 percent, it's kind of brutal out there. Way too many curt rejection slips show up in the mail. If this were a Saturday night dance and you heard no as often, you'd be slipping out the back door or hiding in the corner. How do you keep going? I hold my breath and turn blue even when my wife is reading my work, and she's my biggest fan. The emotional perils of moving from the relative comforts of the writer's desk to the shark-strewn waters of the publishing world are a given. We will be banged up and black and blue sooner than later.

It reminds me of a cartoon I saw in the *New Yorker* not long ago. Two hikers are walking down the trail with beatific smiles on their faces. Perched above them on a boulder are two mountain lions ready to leap on the unsuspecting pair. One lion says to the other, "Wait until they say the thing about how peaceful it is." But this is no joke. This world can tear you up and spit you out, even if you are an accomplished writer. "Oh yeah, I think I'll be a writer. That sounds noble and romantic." Ouch.

❧

My first encounter with an editor's scalpel came in a seventh-grade English class with the notorious Mrs. Simmons. She was all business and used the dreaded red-ink pen to mark her papers! We were reading, or supposed to be reading, *David Copperfield*.

You must be joking! From the Hardy Boys to Dickens in one jump? I remember laboring over my paper as best I could, having read what I could and understood little to nothing of the story. When the less-than-gracious Mrs. Simmons handed back our papers, it wasn't the D that shocked me. I was expecting worse and actually felt a flash of gratitude when I saw that she had not flunked me like I probably deserved. What I remember to this day was the shock and shame I felt when I saw all that red ink decorating my paper like she'd popped a blood vessel trying to make sense of my gibberish. Something in me froze on the spot and made a barely unconscious promise to stay clear of that kind of bloodbath forever.

Actually, since then my experience with editors has been fine. I still stiffen like I'm going to the dentist, but I ask my editors to use a green pen and, with the help of spell-check and Word grammar corrections, I'm not too much in the red—I mean green. Damn, there are a lot of commas in life! My last editor was a peach, and I learned a bunch from studying her corrections. But I've known writers who were brought to tears by the publisher's hired gun and the number of copyedits to their manuscripts. Must have been the great-granddaughter of Mrs. Simmons. Some nearly gave up on their books. Others felt battered. As my friend Ross once said, writing the book is 10 percent of the work—now it's time to run the gauntlet!

There are those days when the editor's gauntlet is nothing compared to that inner voice that is not content with editing but extends its authority to all-out censorship. No kidding. What is self-editing if not repression? Be honest with yourself. How much do you edit, rehearse, and censor your words? I know authors who stay up all night rehearsing and editing what they have to say. Some put a gag order on their vocal cords and threaten severe penalties should they say the wrong thing. Really, self-editing is the worst. Bite your tongue.

Once my mother washed my mouth out with soap. People did that in Ohio in 1955. She had threatened many times, but I never thought she would really do it. Guess what I internalized from that blessed occasion? Needless to say, anxiety arises for some people when they are about to say what they really think. Such a crime. Is that you? How do you edit your thoughts? What type of expression do you strike from the record? Do you edit your thoughts so much that they don't resemble what was originally in your head? Maybe you take the opposite track and have fired all editors. You say whatever you damn well please, no matter the consequences. No matter who or how much it hurts, after all, you're just being honest. Are you any better off? Pay attention—what is it you do not dare say? What is it you do not dare feel? How are you limiting the depth that the story can develop? Are you editing your characters before they can stretch and find out who they are?

❧

Self-editing is an essential part of social relationships, and it is an important feature of being considerate to others. The questions are always as follows: How far does it go, and do you have a choice about when and with whom to speak your mind? Can you write as directly as you need to? Many writers have one foot in the camp of being straightforward and the other in the camp of being too careful. The results can be confusing. The reader isn't quite sure what's going on. A good editor will pick that up and push an author to take a stand. Good self-support allows for an expressive voice that allows our real thoughts and feelings to be known and communicated.

❧

Agents are another breed altogether. I have found them to be a nasty bunch. Mind you, I am not as experienced as many of you, but in my limited time seeking out representation, I found most to be rude and full of themselves. Lately they have been giving me the silent treatment big-time. Okay, they are busy—who isn't?—but it wouldn't take much to send a respectful form letter to authors who deserve a better shake. Obviously I prefer to sit down and write myself my own letter. A little make-believe never hurt.

But agents are just a reminder of a deeper psychological issue, the development of personal agency. Personal agency is aggression in its original meaning—that is, the ability to move toward something of meaning or interest. Since *aggression* has become a bit of a dirty word, we refer to this as *assertion*. It doesn't matter what we call it, but it does matter if you have access to the capacity to act in ways that promote the goals and interests of your True Self. Personal agency is the power of the deep self, not the Self Project. It is the ability to facilitate the movement and growth of the talents you possess and to take risks in the world on behalf of that talent. In short, it is what you do to be seen, to be taken seriously, and to accomplish what you set out to do.

Ah, to be seen...

Some people have a knack for making things happen. They don't hesitate. They don't overthink the situation at hand. They know what they want and move toward it with unwavering resolve. This is personal agency. Many artists struggle with this aspect of their lives. Advocating for themselves does not come naturally, and it is necessary to hire coaches to help them write a good elevator speech, prepare for a radio interview, and do assorted other necessary tasks along the way to being successful. Aggression in my household was tolerated if it was aligned with the status quo, the False Self. Moving toward a life in the arts was considered economic suicide and a betrayal of the Protestant culture of hyper-normality. Don't stand out. Don't want too much. These were unspoken commandments of the times.

Lack of agency can be related to anxiety and the risk of exposure. But it is also one of the muscles of the self that develops in a facilitating environment. Ask yourself how strong your sense of personal agency is. What are your personal boundaries when it comes to reaching out? Maybe these ideas never even come into your mind. I have one patient who really does not experience herself as a subject with desires. She does not have the impulse to act on her own behalf. We have worked hard to get to the place where she can feel and say, "I want..." If this is hard for you, practice little ways to take responsibility for wanting. Ask for small favors. Let yourself feel the desire for little things, a full breath, fresh air, a glass of water. Practice making small declarations—"I want to go to dinner at Jake's." Take a few risks at defining who you are to those around you. Say no at least twice a week. If these seem too rudimentary, then expand on them.

Schedule something out of the norm at least once every two weeks. Look to a friend or mentor for inspiration and modeling. Read a biography of someone you admire. When I feel stalled or fearful, I try to remember what Georgia O'Keeffe said: "I've been afraid every day of my life, and it never stopped me from doing anything." Now there's agency! Be encouraged—you don't have to be fearless, just free from the shackles of fear.

Personal agency isn't limited to what you want. It certainly is not synonymous with the Self Project. In fact, a deeper understanding reveals the relationship of agency to the capacity for concern and the ability to give. I'm talking about knowing when the situation calls for you to put yourself aside for the good of another. Being able to do so is a hallmark of agency and a strong sense of self. It is the root of empathy and compassion for the feelings of others. Without it, listening feels like disappearing. Giving feels like self-sacrifice. Personal agency develops within the space between I and we. Between what I want and what life wants. In other words, it takes a lot of personal centeredness to let go. To serve your art and not expect it to serve you. To listen and be guided by your characters and not feel you have to control every detail. It's a lot like love when you think of it.

When I began outlining this book, I thought it would be fitting to make publishers the villains of this story. After all, their approval ratings are lower than the president's! They hide out in those dark, monolithic towers in Manhattan and wield absolute control over the fate of the written word. Why not paint them the bad guys? Isn't this institutional censorship?

It is easy to demonize those faceless executives at Penguin Random House, but when you think about it, the book publishers of the world have done enormous good over the years for the development of a literate and educated society. They too seem victims of a profit-driven system gone berserk, and indeed their days may be numbered.

But there is a lot more to it than that, and what is so heartening to me is the huge outgrowth of mid- to small-size presses coming to life all over the land. The power of the creative spirit and the people's thirst for free expression cannot be denied. The power of the powerless is beautiful to behold. I never thought I would see the Soviet Union come down in my lifetime, but I did. I never thought I would see Nelson Mandela freed and apartheid defeated, but I did. Human beings yearn to be free and eventually find a way. It may be ugly, bloody, and imperfect, but it happens.

Writers and artists are no different. You can't be kept down or out of the collective consciousness. "Power to the People!" We chanted that in the streets in 1968, and the force behind that voice continues to reverberate through the many branches of society and especially in the publishing world. Self-publishing has taken off in breathtaking numbers. What a remarkable phenomenon! I heard one source report that 30 percent of ebooks are now self-published. And that number is growing.

Last year a kind and respected literary agent came to Portland and spoke to a large crowd about the publishing maze. She has twenty-five years of successful experience as an agent, and she told the packed audience that self-publishing was in most cases the way to go. She said if you are lucky enough to find an agent, and if that agent is lucky enough to find a publisher, you may regret it in the end because your book will take years to get through production and you may not recognize it when it does. Well, that was enough for me to hear. I ended my nine-month search for an agent that night and signed up with CreateSpace.

The CEO of my Self Project wasn't very happy with me, but I had a truly wonderful experience from there on out. He was right: I didn't sell a lot of books, and the movie version of *Radiance* didn't get picked up by Hollywood (I had the soundtrack all ready for them), but the satisfaction was huge, and next time I'll be far more prepared to support the book in the marketing frenzy. I know it's easy for me to say this because I'm not struggling to make a living off my writing, but how many people do? Be real—not many.

Back to publishing. We live in the best of times and the worst of times. But for a moment just step back and marvel at the explosion of creative endeavors happening throughout our country. Too bad we don't see much about that on the evening news. You could say, "Yeah, but a lot of that is trash." Well, maybe so, but it doesn't really matter much to me. It's the pulsing of the desire within so many people of different backgrounds and talent levels that gives me hope.

If you have been published, great, congratulations, may you be again. If not, don't despair, please. Dream and dream big, fail and fail better, but don't build everything around that one aspiration. Enjoy the moment. If you touch one person with your work, the world will never be the same. Get outside yourself and rejoice that you are part of something so big, we cannot fully grasp its dimensions, not to mention where it is leading us. Publishing houses will come and go, but the spirit that inspired Homer and Sophocles, Hemingway and Fitzgerald, Virginia Wolfe and Toni Morrison runs through your veins. Yes, yours. A best seller is of minor importance compared to the tremendous privilege of that visitation. Bow to it. Give thanks every morning. Honor your ancestors. What great fortune it is to be a writer.

31
The Protagonist

"I AM THE GREATEST!" I WAS FIFTEEN WHEN CASSIUS Clay stood over the fallen body of Sonny Liston shouting these words and shaking his fist at Liston and a shameful era that was going down with him. "I am the greatest!" In a matter of days, he would be Mohammad Ali, the greatest and most beautiful heavyweight champion of all time, and for the next twenty years, Ali would shake his fist at the entire white, racist establishment of America. He was bold and brash, and he broke all the rules of conventional society when he opposed the war, and when he spoke. And how he spoke! His words were like his fists and feet: floating like butterflies and stinging like bees. He was something else, and this fifteen-year-old kid from Ohio sat with his mouth gaping, in awe of Ali's courage, his intelligence, and the presence with which he commanded not only the boxing ring but the world stage as well.

I still get goose bumps thinking of him in front of the microphones, those great big bulging eyes and that huge mouth out of which poured poetry, and blasphemy, "I'm a BAD man." He was a villain to many but a hero to a generation about to take down another seemingly invincible opponent, the undisputed heavyweight champion of the world: American materialism and the Vietnam War. Martin Luther King Jr. was the spiritual and intellectual leader of the civil rights movement. Ali was the guy you wanted to be like. King was brilliant and eloquent. Ali was crude and irreverent. We loved him. Dr. King led the march on Birmingham; Ali led the march on local custom. Even white kids like me could relate to Ali and the rebellion he led against the norms of middle-class oppression. He was our champion.

⚘

When we think of protagonists in our culture, people like Ali come to mind. Individuals who had such command of themselves that they could influence broad segments of culture and make those around them bigger and better than they might have been otherwise. Rosa Parks was such an individual, as was John F. Kennedy. We look to these people for leadership in our struggles for freedom, justice, and a response to human suffering. They become our models for living a life of integrity.

Of course these people become larger than life in the public eye. In most cases they are idealized, and elaborate mythologies grow up around them. We don't hear until years later about the crisis in faith that Mother Teresa suffered. Now we know that Lincoln suffered terrible bouts of depression and doubt. The American way requires our heroes to be grandiose, and for all flaws and weaknesses to be airbrushed out of the public image. The humanity of these people is sacrificed because of what must be a deep anxiety in our psyche that believes any human frailty diminishes the stature of the protagonist.

Consider what we know about JFK. In today's political climate, his behavior would give cause to drive him out of office and back to Cape Cod for an early retirement. One of our great writers, Louisa May Alcott, addressed this head-on in *Little Women.* In the film version the protagonist's boyfriend confronts the characterizations in her first novel by saying to her they are not real. He goes further, enlightening her with the reality that "we are all flawed, hopelessly flawed."

Of course the Self Project does not want to hear this. Flaws from the point of view of the project coordinator are not normal imperfections that go with the territory of being human—they are a cause for shame and humiliation and are considered something that should be banished, not accepted and integrated. The wounded self sets up the project of becoming an ideal image of a human being, a godlike figure, and in doing so is doomed to perpetual cycles of inflation and deflation. A seesaw of feelings of superiority and inferiority that leaves emotional self-regard utterly dependent on the results of any given situation. What could be a more insecure spot to build your house?

Oh dear, flaws. What to do with those blemishes on one's personality? There doesn't seem to be enough makeup or camouflage to hide them. They come out like rodents at the most inopportune times. Yikes! We seem to walk a narrow pathway navigating our need to be seen and the fear of exposure. We sometimes crave a glowing mirror to sing our praises: "Mirror, mirror on the wall, who is the fairest of them all?" Don't you know the anxious yearning behind that question? And as much as we may long for that kind of recognition, we shrink in fear of being invisible, peripheral, or God forbid, irrelevant. No! Anything but that!

I can remember being so desperate for mirroring that, walking down the street, I couldn't take my eyes off my reflection in the shop windows. Pretty sad, right? Constantly checking to see if I was all right. Constantly checking to see if I was there. Constantly checking to see if the skinny, ninety-eight-pound weakling was showing. It got so bad that I was utterly dependent on praise from others, and a discouraging word could cut me to the core. In fact, I seemed to have no ability to hang on to my own core identity, and the perceptions of others took over as easily as the Nazis marching into Paris. I thank the day I walked into my therapist's office for the first time.

There are those among us who fear disappearing, and there are those who insist on being seen. You may have both tendencies. And yet, we know that every story has its minor characters, its supporting actors and actresses. Isn't it strange how threatening that can be? How fearful one can be of being ordinary? Regular isn't good enough. We have to be special and extraordinary, or the fear of being a nobody swamps the mind. What distances people will travel to be noticed. Everything depends on it. I have seen so many people sink into despair when they are ignored or passed over by reviewers or publishers. The demand to be bigger than life, to fulfill grandiose ambitions, disfigures any and all real but modest successes along the way. The Pulitzer Committee should be calling any day! You may not relate to this. You may shrink and disappear behind the scenes, into the periphery. Panicked at the possibility of being noticed. I get that. But I bet deep in a secret chamber of your heart a burning fantasy exists to be the one on stage. The headliner. If you were guaranteed immunity from shame, I bet you just might run to the front of the line for your fifteen minutes of fame!

❧

I remember the first time I realized that courage and fear were not mutually exclusive. Sometime earlier I had read the autobiography of Bill Russell, the Hall of Fame center for the Boston Celtics, arguably the most successful athlete of all time. I was shocked to realize the great man threw up before every game! How could this be? What a mind bender it was to learn that he experienced self-doubt and anxiety every night. What an even greater surprise to learn that feelings are not flaws! No way. I had been walking this earth for a long time thinking these crazy feelings were living proof that something was very wrong with me. In fact, our flaws can often be reduced down to the behaviors we evoke so as to avoid shame and the stable of other impossibly threatening emotions.

How did we get this way? How did we come to believe the protagonist must be superhuman, that anything less is proof you are a loser? Look around. What do you see on TV, on magazine covers, on advertisements at every turn? You see the capitalist agenda pressuring and seducing the American psyche into believing that happiness must be earned or purchased. You see the soul being turned toward commodity lust by an extremely effective campaign manipulating our longing for love and acceptance. No wonder we are always grading ourselves. How am I doing? Am I okay? Under the spell of this system, the mind turns to obsessive comparisons, relentless competition, and the illusion that life can be harnessed and controlled for the purpose of acquiring more and more goodies and achievements.

And of all the grand illusions bombarding our senses, perhaps the most insidious and eroding of the True Self is the promise that you and I can have it all, that we can have the leading role in the drama of our life and bend it to our will. The protagonist is triumphant. Not even erectile dysfunction can keep him down! We have a pill for it. If you are unable to fulfill this grand design, then you have failed and something must be wrong with you. I have worked with neurologists and lawyers, artists and writers, computer programmers and teachers, gay and straight people, men and women, and I promise you we are all subject to this tyrannical trance.

The thing is, on the artist's path the protagonist is not heroic. She does not triumph over all obstacles. He is not a magician. We fail, and fail again, maybe better, maybe not. The central character of your story and your life is not there to ascend the podium of success but to serve the story. The real protagonist is there to serve the creative spark. To put himself aside and follow the lead of an inspiration that is not fully his and is only his as a privileged offering from a benefactor we can never fully know or touch.

When Mohammad Ali shouted, "I am the greatest," he was,

in actuality, shouting, "You are the greatest!" He shouted with indignation and a power seldom heard before. He shouted and was heard above the roar of the white, capitalist machine, "I am the greatest!" And we shouted with him. We stood up with him and shook our fists and refused to shrink before the army of war and consumption. Women assumed their true stature. Men stood for something besides their own glory. You are not small. You are the greatest. And so am I. And so is my neighbor.

And why? Because something moves us, as it moves the rosebud to open, as it moved the slaves to sing the blues, as it moved Rosa Parks to take her seat, as it moved Ali to say no to the United States Army, as it moves you to take a pencil in your hand and write a few simple words down on paper, as it moves others to read those words, as it has for millennia moved and inspired your ancestors to express what it is like to be alive. What more could humans want?

Who is the leading character? There is only one. One disguised as many. One heart beating. One life, pulsing through all of this. All of this. All these books, these poems, these paintings, these plays, these sculptures, these everyday words, reaching out, all of these, like birdsong, singing with the spreading light, here I am, I am! I am! Where are you? And what are you? Where? What? Who?

Yes, what are you? What is this protagonist, this writer, this artist, these identities, these songs to ourselves? This marbled someone who is as constantly in flux as tropical weather systems, as steady as the sky above; who is a mystery and a novelty, extraordinary and nothing special, master and servant, free and bound, proud and humble, strong and weak, a collection of opposites and the glue that gives them coherence. All of it, the entire stir-fry, sizzling in the wok, in the hands of this magnificent force we call creation.

And here we be, standing in its current, fording its width, stumbling on river rock, toppled by whitewater, shivering from the cold, invigorated by its energies, in love with it, hating it, overcome by it, feeling it take us where it likes, feeling the creative necessity in our blood, feeling the yearning to plunge in, feeling the pull to stay upright, crying out in pleasure and pain, but unwilling, unable, unlikely to drag ourselves to dry land. Hoping we don't drown, hoping the ride never ends, forgetting ourselves, remembering who we are, becoming one with the surging, becoming two with the water. Not thinking, "Am I this or that?" "Am I okay or not?" "Am I good enough?" Sometimes not thinking, eclipsed by being taken over by, consumed by, devoured by, love. By love, by a presence we cannot touch, by a presence we cannot locate or lose. By being that shines on, and on, and on. By radiance and beauty, that is not ours, not ours, not anyone's, and everyone's. And everyone's.

Epilogue: Words without End

NASRUDIN IS SITTING WITH A GROUP OF FRIENDS DIS-
cussing the merits of exercise. He says to them, "My
mother has been walking five miles every day since she
turned sixty. She's eighty now, and we have no idea where she
is." Twenty years ago I woke up to the creative spirit calling my
name. It rode into my being on the back of an anxiety attack, of
all things. You never know. Something in me was listening and
picked up a pen. I wrote a poem that morning in praise of fear.
The next morning I wrote another poem, and the next morning
another, and if you had asked me in any of those quiet hours
where I was going, I would have honestly said, "I have no idea."
Nor could I have ever, ever imagined, like Nasrudin's mother,
where I might end up twenty years later.

This reminds me of one of my favorite poems. It was written
by Kenneth Rexroth, and it is the first poem I committed to
memory when I began to write. The title is "Waking," and the
repeated verse is as follows:

> I wake to sleep, and take my waking slow
> I learn by going where I have to go

The Zen people say you can find satori in an instant, but
enlightenment takes thirty years. I think I'll need thirty lifetimes,
give or take. But who cares? As long as I'm listening and "going

where I have to go," it's a pretty rich ride. I hope we can let life, and the art we love, take us by the hand where we need to go. Maybe then we can let our characters take us where they need to go and you and I can learn to serve the longing of the moment.

This morning was like every other morning. I woke, felt anxious, rolled out of bed, watched the anxiety dissipate, drank a glass of water, meditated, said good morning to the dog, took out the computer, pad of paper, and pen, and began to write. I may finish this first draft sometime tonight. And then, like Nasrudin, I will have no idea where I am going. Should I rewrite the novel on the shelf? Should I begin a new one? Should I write more essays, maybe go back to poetry? I know, I'll take a break and just read for a while. Maybe sit around depressed. Yeah, a few days or weeks of postpartum blues sounds in order. And perhaps a serving of "Will I ever write again?" Will I ever again wake up to the creative impulse firing in my belly, or will the muse abandon me, without notice or farewell, as easily as it arrived and found me twenty years ago?

Don't know. But if I had to make a wager, I'd say yes, I will live to write more of something, and the unlikely, unbidden visitations of inspiration will return and ask that I play along. That's fine with me. I'm hoping it is a story with no end. I'm hoping it is the way it feels, words without end, amen. I'd like to find myself one day on my deathbed reaching for a pad and pen to jot down one last line of verse, or a timely sentence. Maybe haiku would be appropriate. Don't want to keep the guy with the sickle waiting too long, do we?

"Enough." Say it out loud. Say it slowly. Slower, so you can hear the old English come through: *genog*. Hear the German come through: *genug*. Listen for the sound of satisfaction, the note of being pleased resonating in the deep cello music of this blessed word, *enough*. Try to feel it deep in your chest, the deep pleasure of enough—the need is fulfilled, the wanting answered. Bring that feeling to yourself, all the wrinkles and warts, the beautiful blossoms of you. What if you really are enough? Good enough. Good and plenty. What then?

Time to go. But I don't want to go! But you must. As Baby Suggs said, "The trouble with the white man is he don't know when to stop." Time to put it down. After all these words, I hope what you take away will fit in the palm of your hand. Practice kindness in all directions, and remember, you are precious. No matter what comes your way, you are good enough. Write on, and be encouraged. Namaste.

CPSIA information can be obtained
at www.ICGtesting.com
Printed in the USA
BVHW030751050319
541165BV00006B/79/P